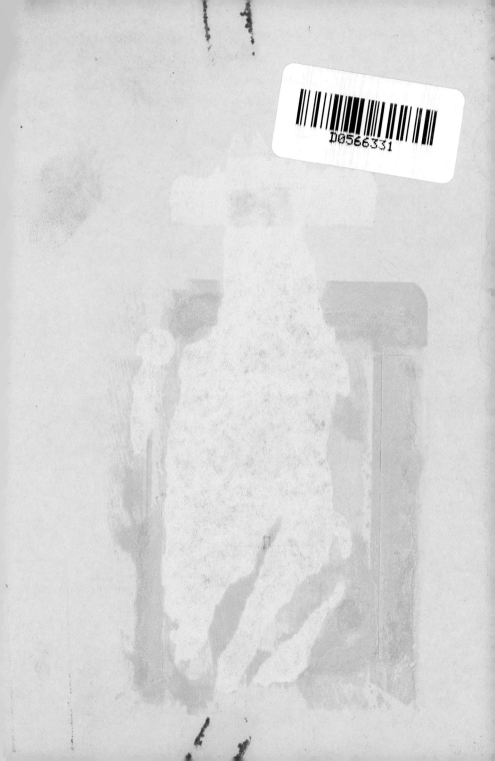

TWENTIETH CENTURY VIEWS

The aim of this series is to present the best in contemporary critical opinion on major authors, providing a twentieth century perspective on their changing status in an era of profound revaluation.

Maynard Mack, *Series Editor*
Yale University

KAFKA

KAFKA

A COLLECTION OF CRITICAL ESSAYS

Edited by
Ronald Gray

A SPECTRUM BOOK

Prentice-Hall, Inc., *Englewood Cliffs, N. J.*

Current printing (last digit):

13   12   11

"Up in the Gallery," "On the Tram," and "A Message from the Emperor" from *The Penal Colony*, by Franz Kafka. Copyright 1948 by Schocken Books Inc., New York; translated by Willa and Edwin Muir. Reprinted by permission of Schocken Books Inc. and The Hogarth Press, Ltd.

"Homecoming," from *Description of a Struggle*, by Franz Kafka. Copyright 1958 by Schocken Books Inc., New York; translated by Tania and James Stern. Reprinted by permission of Schocken Books Inc. and The Hogarth Press, Ltd.

© 1962 BY PRENTICE-HALL, INC., *Englewood Cliffs, N.J.*

LIBRARY OF CONGRESS CATALOG CARD NO.: 62-18127

Printed in the United States of America

51446-C

Table of Contents

Introduction

Kafka is primarily a writer of novels and short stories. Any fame or notoriety he has as a religious thinker or critic of religion is secondary, although it is quite true that he also wrote a number of aphorisms on religious themes. So far as the bulk of his work is concerned, it stands or falls on literary grounds, and no amount of original thought in any field could in itself make of him a great novelist. In making this selection, therefore, I have placed in the foreground such essays as are directly related to his skill and talents as a narrator and observer, and as a maker of language.

One result of this, I notice, has been a certain amount of agreement between many of the contributors. Reading about Kafka, one is usually struck by the chaotic variety of interpretations, in which each reader makes his own associations, and each seems equally arbitrary. This need not indicate a fault in Kafka's writings; many interpretations can be found for *Hamlet* or *Faust,* or almost any work with a measure of symbolism. It may indicate, on the other hand, a reluctance in readers to receive a novel or a story purely on its own terms, and a tendency to ignore the "writerly" qualities and concentrate, instead, on abstract modes of thought. When an underlying message, or some other hidden form of meaning is sought at the expense of a confrontation with the nuances of situations, word by word, confusion seems to result. When this divisive method—digging out and separating content from form—is replaced by a reading that takes account of both simultaneously, there is more unanimity.

Certain qualities of Kafka's writing emerge from these accounts time and again, all of them interrelated. Max Brod, in the enthusiastic passage which was one of the first acts whereby he championed his friend, spoke of "matter-of-factness." Edwin Muir, whose fine translations first made Kafka widely known in the English-speaking world, finds him "exquisitely just." "Absolute precision," "complete honesty and candidness," "scrupulous care," "an almost scientific lucidity"—phrases gathered from several essayists of widely differing personalities—are the terms with which others seek to record a similar impression. Kafka, says one, has his eye always on the object, and, while this causes an attention to minutest detail and endless intricacy and subtlety (for any object is infinitely complex), the impression of clarity and purity from moment to moment remains. The

1

style is found "plain and natural." The most obvious quality in *The Trial*, says Camus, is naturalness, while Winkler notes the almost complete absence of explicit figures of speech, devices which Kafka himself deliberately rejected as a distraction from the plain business of setting things down.

Coupled with this is Kafka's preference for the concrete image, which, as Caroline Gordon points out with apt quotation, is the work of a scrupulous novelist. If you want a moonlight night, Chekhov advised, write that on the dam of the mill a fragment of broken bottle flashed like a small bright star. As though following Chekhov's advice, Kafka never gives the moonlight, always the incident or detail that brings home its presence. His deletions are often significant in that they eschew even the slightest metaphor. Thus in a fragment later excluded from *The Castle*, Kafka speaks of K. confronting the authorities "immovable in his earthly weight." The suggestion of straightforward allegory is unmistakable here, and a direct clue to the nature of the Castle authorities is given. Yet had it been allowed to stand, the elusive mystery of the Castle would have been broken, and instead of the concrete detail, significant and evocative but still unexplained, there would have been the bald statement which the writer of genius avoids. In the fact of the deletion we can see Kafka's mind veering into abstraction and halting itself as at a misdemeanor.

The Metamorphosis illustrates this care in avoiding the cliché throughout a whole story. As Austin Warren says, "There is here no possibility of allegorical sterilization." Much as one might like to explain away the transformation of Gregor Samsa into an insect calling it an allegory of the sense of degradation such as St. Augustine employed when he wrote that his soul had become a spider, the story will not allow it. Gregor is not dreaming; his fantastic plight becomes convincing reality, and all efforts at reducing it to terms we can admit in the everyday world merely diminish its force. So it is with nearly all Kafka's "symbols." Whether it is a castle or a law court or an instrument of torture and execution, to substitute the name of God, or heaven, or the sufferings of the artist or the saint is to do violence to the fully embodied sense. By contrast, the angels and devils outside the Oklahoma Nature Theatre, at the end of *America*, stand out as painful contrivances, lacking real impact.

Because of this "unity of meaning," as Friedrich Beissner calls it, the various levels of significance found in Kafka's novels are often beside the point. *The Trial* has been taken as a satire on bureaucracy, and so it is. To deny that, and claim for it only a metaphysical meaning, is absurd. The courts are just what they are, and suggest just so much as they do suggest. The important thing is to realize, as Winkler observes, that the whole experience recorded in these works, whether spiritual, mental, emotional, or physical, is absolutely continuous, that there are no distinctions between the religious, social, and individual levels. Or, in the compressed phrase of Nietzsche's quoted by Camus, "Great problems are on the street." One can paraphrase this, extend its close-packed suggestiveness, by saying as one essayist does say, that for Kafka "it is in and through the natural that the supernatural operates." Kafka himself said something rather like that himself when he denied smuggling the miraculous into ordinary events—"ordinary events are a miracle in themselves." But once again the essential unity of meaning is lost, and one is left with two halves that won't make a whole, at least not in terms of a novelist's or a poet's direct communication.

Kafka's humor is less often mentioned, and of course it is not present in all his works, although even the most gruesome often have a touch of it. People find affinities with Mack Sennett comedies, Disney cartoons, music-hall clowns, and Charlie Chaplin, and one recalls Max Brod's account of Kafka's friends bursting into laughter as he read *The Trial* aloud. No one has presented this "grave and casuistical" humor more tactfully or with more evident appreciation than Edwin Muir, who found the root of it in the realization of the complete incompatibility of the ways of Providence and the ways of man. Yet in the very assertion of this incompatibility, which many agree to be the fundamental perception of Kafka's work, there appears to be a contradiction of the "unity of meaning" to which Beissner refers. On the one hand, there is this identity of all layers of meaning, the concrete detail with its "constant sense of apocalyptic significance"; on the other there is this reiterated assertion of utter remoteness, of the impossibility of communicating—there is Kafka's injunction to his friend to burn his manuscripts and never to republish anything that had already appeared in print. There is the achievement we see, and the utter rejection of it. Perhaps this is the genuine paradox, that the moment of defeat, as Muir has it, is the moment of victory, and that the moderately stated tragedy is the most immoderate in its effect, to paraphrase Camus. Nevertheless, it is not unjust to ask whether only such extremes as Kafka embodies in his life and in his work are truly liberating. Joseph K. dies "like a dog"; K. never knows of his liberation, however much he may change in the course of the novel; the officer of the penal colony dies untransfigured, with the iron spike piercing his forehead; Gregor Samsa is swept away with the rubbish, Georg Bendemann drops from the bridge into the river. Is this not a reflection of what Erich Heller calls the identification of life with Evil, a Gnostic loathing of physical reality which will rest content with nothing short of total self-annihilation? To lose one's life to save it, that is a paradox at least verbally familiar to us. But if there is meant to be any "victory in defeat" in these stories, the defeat seems to consist in a quite unallegorical extinction. Gregor Samsa is swept away and that is that; there can be no "sterilization" of that fact. Are we not rightly impelled, in the face of it, to make such a protest as Edmund Wilson's, denying that such "meaching compliance" can possibly be the mark of either a great artist or a moral guide? The ways of Providence may be different from the ways of men, but if they are "so different that we may as well give up hope of ever identifying the one with the other," suicide or indifference are the only alternatives. Erich Heller rightly recalls to us the perverse pleasure which Kafka felt at the "turning of a knife" in his heart. And surely the thoughts of Joseph K. near the end of *The Trial* are revoltingly unaccept-able, when he realizes that his executioners expect him to finish the job for them and seems to suppose that only such compliance will satisfy the supreme authority: "He could not completely rise to the occasion, he could not relieve the officials of all their tasks; the responsibility for this last failure of his lay with him who had not left him the remnant of strength necessary for the deed." What else could be implied by this, but that the giver of life and strength requires self-destruction from men, and cruelly withholds the power to achieve it? K. does not fail to kill himself because he prefers to live; he merely resents the vindictiveness of an authority which demands suicide and yet renders it impossible. A more gruesomely untragic ending can hardly be imagined.

The issue already begins to border on extraliterary questions, which will have to be faced in due course. First, however, the further questions of structure and integration, beyond those of language and presentation, deserve some notice. In thinking of the moral aspects of Kafka's works we are already beginning to see them not in the light of their detail, but as wholes, and wholes are what Kafka could never achieve except in the short story, the vignette or prose-poem, or the aphorism. None of his novels are complete, and while *The Trial* has an ending, it is one which comes abruptly, without preparation. (The fact that the execution fol-lows immediately on the cathedral scene must not obscure the fact that, as the fragments show, further development between the two scenes was intended.) Poe's precept, as quoted by Caroline Gordon, that the "very initial sentence" should tend to bring out a preconceived effect, is cer-tainly not adhered to in *America,* where the sudden appearance, after a gap, of the Oklahoma Nature Theatre is out of key with the earlier part of the novel, and where the progression from chapter to chapter seems aimless. *The Trial* is really a series of loosely connected or unconnected incidents: Fräulein Bürstner is never heard of again after the first chapter until she is dimly glimpsed in the last; the warders who were to accom-pany K. everywhere are soon forgotten; the uncle, the advocate, the com-mercial traveller Block, the painter Titorelli emerge and fade, the prison chaplain supersedes them, and not once does K. or the author reflect on any connection or contrast between them. In addition, if Herman Uyttersprot's investigation of the time sequence in this novel has done nothing else (I doubt whether it is as revealing as he thinks) it has shown how difficult it is on internal evidence even to arrange the chapters in order with any certainty. Should the cathedral scene come before chapter seven or later? Why does K. in fact submit to the authority of the court? How was it that until Charles Neider drew attention to the fact, nobody noticed that chapter four should have been chapter two? * *The Castle,* it is true, is a different matter. As Camus notes, there is here a "rigorous development," but if my view of this novel is accurate, its whole spirit is very different from that of *The Trial.* Confronted with the latter, one can only ask with Austin Warren how there can be a logic of composition when one's theme is the irruption of the irrational. The untragic ending is so because tragedy needs to be, for one thing, inevitable, and inevitability implies logic, cause and effect, progression. The decline of Joseph K., though it progresses, is haphazard, sporadic, and arbitrary, and in this last quality it resembles the court which brings it about. The theme of an utterly disconnected justice, incomprehensible to man, is bodied out in the way the novel is built. But if there is really no tragedy, if there is at most pathos or horror, there can be none of the liberation that goes with tragedy.

Kafka's failure to complete any of his major works is in the view of Eliseo Vivas a legitimate basis for the most devastating criticism that may be levelled against Kafka's version of reality, and with this I would agree, save for reservations about *The Castle.* The short stories, on the other hand, are complete wholes, despite the fact that many more un-completed fragments are to be found in Kafka's diaries. *The Metamorphosis,* indeed, as Johannes Pfeiffer shows, has a quite classical form, a division into three parts, each moving to a climax, a consistent development for each of several characters who are kept in mind from start to finish, and a superb control of the movement and rhythms of emotion throughout. This seems at first sight hard to reconcile with what was said of *The Trial*: why the formal excellence in one case and not in the other? But then, of course, the mood of each story is, despite some similarities, quite different. Gregor Samsa dies wretchedly, as Joseph K. does; he is cut off just as decisively from all contact with human society. But unlike Joseph K., he is not arrogantly determined to assert his innocence of unknown charges, or self-destructively bent on confessing his deserved condemnation, still in ignorance of what the charges may be.

---

* The transference of most of Kafka's MSS in 1961 to the Bodleian Library at Oxford will not solve this problem, for they do not include the MS of *The Trial.* All that may be hoped for at present is a re-editing of the other works. This, however, will apparently not so alter their wording as to justify in itself any new interpretations.

Gregor is rather concerned to be reconciled with a situation which in its grisliness can only be compared with Kafka's own. This insect form is his, as Kafka's neurotic disposition was his, and it is apparently so final and ineluctable that all talk of release from it must sound trivial. Yet Gregor dies thinking of his family with "love and affection"; he is persuaded that he must "disappear," but his head sinks down at the end "without his willing it." And once he has gone, the story ends with a moving picture of the family restored to life and health, a picture touched with a smiling irony, it is true, but not unrelated to Miranda's perception of the brave, new world. If anywhere in Kafka's work, it is here that what Martin Buber calls "Emunah" is seen, that Jewish faith in the togetherness of Israel which sees salvation less as an individual matter than as something inherent in the race.*

Kafka was not a systematic philosopher or man of religion, he was an artist, a writer, and there is no one body of doctrine to which all his work can be referred. Given the situation in which he found himself, a situation which could not simply be altered by a determination to think and feel otherwise than he did, he was extremely prone to see vindictiveness, hatred, malicious spite even at the heart of things. His predicament was—I think the diaries show this—that he felt called on to accept this disposition as a dispensation of Providence, so that even the most torturing of perceptions was not a matter for denial or refusal, but a matter for acceptance. He abandoned himself to it, with a trust that even the worst would be taken up and transformed:

> There are surprises in evil. Suddenly it will turn round and say "You have misunderstood me"—and perhaps it really is so. Evil transforms itself into your lips, lets your own teeth gnaw against it, and with these new lips —none that you ever had before sat so snugly along your gums—to your own astonishment you pronounce the words of goodness.†

The worst could be said, since there was a great fire prepared, in which all would be consumed and purified. Nothing could affect the Paradise which continued to exist whether men were aware of it, or rejected it, or not, a frame of mind which Buber echoes when he writes "If the whole world should tear the garment of His honor into rags nothing would be done to Him." With such a belief, Kafka could run into every kind of heresy and even blasphemy; he could engage in the scepticism greater than Pascal's which he proposed for himself, while still maintaining a

---

* Cp. "The Indestructible is one; every individual man *is* it, and at the same time it is common to all, which is why mankind is so incomparably and inseparably united." 'Reflections on Sin, Suffering, etc.," No. 70/71.)

† Cp. *Wedding Preparations*, p. 76.

core of belief. Equally well, there were times when other perceptions prevailed, and a mood of charitable compassion ruled. The signs of Gnosticism and Manichaeism which critics find, some to condemn them, others to approve, are not to be denied, any more than are the signs of orthodox Jewish or Christian thought. They are present, and when Kafka uses them in his private utterances, he presumably means them seriously. In his stories, however, he may well be using them impersonally, projecting them onto his characters in order to see what becomes of them. The great mistake is to identify Kafka with K. or Joseph K.: for all their similarities they are no more than "possible worlds," potential developments from his initial situations at given moments. And it is just as mistaken to assume any identity of beliefs between one story and another. *The Metamorphosis* is not *The Trial*, nor is *The Trial* identical with *The Castle*. Each is *sui generis;* each needs to be approached with as full a receptivity to its whole nature, and as full an awareness of one's own being, as can be managed.

What, then, is to be said about the moral objections that have been raised? They are not negligible, despite the assertions often heard, that literature is remote from such considerations. If Joseph K. arouses horror, it is right that this should be said, if only because the author may have expected it. Without moral concern in the reader, novels may well have no discernible pattern. But should we go so far as T. S. Eliot did when he wrote that "the greatness of literature cannot be determined solely by literary standards; though we must remember that whether it is literature or not can be determined only by literary standards"? Hitherto, I have been largely concerned to state the grounds on which Kafka's work has been held to be genuine literature, "Dichtung," and I do not think they can be denied. When we come to the consideration of how much his work means to us, however, are we perhaps obliged to sort out wheat from chaff in accordance with some nonliterary criterion? Do we need to ascertain first where our religious allegiances lie, and do we suffer from spiritual starvation so severely that, as Erich Heller says, "even a rotten fruit of the spirit may taste like bread from Heaven," or can we trust in the evidence of our own discriminating sense of realities, unaided by revelation or instruction? Issues of great magnitude are raised here and can hardly be satisfactorily solved, all the less since in an account like this the editor has the last word. Yet this is a crux of criticism, especially where Kafka is concerned, and it ought not to be neglected.

My own answer would begin by saying that literary criticism, while it has to aim at completeness, is rather what Dr. Leavis calls a "common pursuit." It is a pursuit of right standards and wholeness of receptivity, but it is also a common one, in which the perceptions of one reader may modify those of another, so that it is constantly being redirected. (An anthology such as is offered here can thus have a special value.) At best, then, it is an approximation, an asymptote. Nonliterary criteria, on the other hand, can be blinding to experience: it is useful to have a yardstick for measuring, but difficult to use it on curves or distant objects, and yardsticks have been known to be off standard. Nevertheless, if there is to be any measuring at all, some standards there must be, and the literary critic of any persuasion will have some, whether by conviction or assimilated tradition or pious acceptance. A careful reader, whether his assertion comes from an unconscious, undoctrinal source or from deliberate adherence to a moral or religious creed, may thus shock others into recognition of a truth. But in literature at least—religion may well be different here—nothing in the reception matters unless it is felt on the pulses.

With Kafka's stories and novels, then, the readings of the critics who see them mainly from some moral or religious standpoint are valuable, for all that they are not directed to what is in this case the fundamental issue. There are, unfortunately, far more of them in Kakfa criticism than of the other kind, and it has not seemed right to preserve those proportions here. (Dr. Reiss's survey will provide many useful pointers.) I believe, however—and I hope this does not sound too grudging—that all the contributions presented here will modify the reader's views in one way or another. It also seems to me that a complete receptivity would ultimately serve not to damage orthodoxies but in some ways to make their meanings more apparent and persuasive. In discussing *The Trial,* it began to emerge a little, I thought, that the disastrous beliefs in which the novel was conceived had also been disastrous for its literary form, whereas the excellence of *The Metamorphosis* was related to its differing orientation. It may be, but I can only be tentative here, that the pursuit of a fuller appreciation of purely literary matters will end by coinciding with a fuller appreciation in other spheres.

Finally, however, these contributions must surely force on our attention the contrast between appreciation and doing. We live in a time when the study of literature has largely replaced the practice of religion for many people. Plays, and novels, and rather fewer poems are read where earlier generations read sermons or devotional works, and this has the advantage that the experiences can come alive for readers in a way that was not usual before. Kafka's *The Castle* invites to a sharing of his experience in a way that Bunyan's allegory or St. Teresa's *Interior Castle* never do: with the two Christian works, it is often only much later that one makes the recognition—*that* was the Slough of Despond, or Apollyon. Moreover, this sharing of experience, interior realization of it, has been a growing feature of literature since the Renaissance. The writer expresses, the reader registers, both as fully as they are able to do, yet ultimately there has been no more than this communication of the situation. Goethe makes his Tasso say

> Und wenn der Mensch in seiner Qual verstummt,
> Gab mir ein Gott, zu sagen, wie ich leide.

While all mankind grows silent in its torment, the poet is endowed by a god with the power to speak his suffering. So Rilke also finds solace in the thought that things are there to be said, said with such intensity as they never dreamed of. Schopenhauer contemplates the world as it is seen through the masterpieces of art. More flatly, but with a kindred meaning, Bouvard and Pécuchet sit down, in the sequel that Flaubert never accomplished, to write out in full the history of their futilities. I do not for a moment mean to suggest that it is only futilities that can be recorded in art. Yet when a writer, as intensely concerned with religious issues as Kafka was, attempts a resolution solely in terms of art, it seems he must be dogged by failure. "What was meant to become the lifting of a curse through art," Erich Heller says, "became the artistically perfect realization of it." There was only the saying to be done, and the saying could only bring home the situation. The concrete detail is there in Kafka's work, precisely worked out, candid and matter-of-fact, and often hinting at more than itself as the glint on the broken bottle hints at moonlight. To use Eliseo Vivas' words, Kafka is faithful to the limitations of his empiricism—and there is just the same sense of limitless expanse beyond as in the carefully circumscribed thought of Wittgenstein. Yet Vivas also does right to remind us that this empiricism, this holding to experience, is a mark of the "aesthetic" stage, and, I would add, both in the work of Kafka and in the history of Western civilization since the Renaissance. The fact that literary studies play so large a part in our schools and universities means that we are concerned with the good, the true and the beautiful, but also that we are concerned as appreciators. "But it all comes to this," says Kierkegaard, "that the highest is not to understand the highest, but to act upon it, and be it noted, with all stress upon it." Understanding and appreciation are not the most vital things, necessary as they are. For, to quote Kierkegaard again, "the majority of men . . . live and die under the impression that life is simply a matter of understanding more and more, and that if it were granted to them to live longer, that life would continue to be one long continuous growth in understanding. How many of them ever experience the maturity of discovering that there comes a critical moment where everything is reversed, after which the point becomes to understand more and more that there is something which cannot be understood." Some of Kafka's work can lead towards that critical moment.

But it cannot, nor can any literary work, of itself "act upon the highest." That is possible only for men and women, with grace.

Yet while the reading of literature has in some ways come to resemble a contemplative's quest for wholeness of perception, so that warnings about its limitations are as relevant as parallel warnings were in medieval times,* there is a value in the undertaking. Exploring our condition, dangerous though it can be, is as necessary now as it ever was, and Kafka is the least prejudiced of any explorers. Since he scarcely knows at all what he can expect to find, his discoveries have a trust-worthiness not easily achieved by less candid writers. His successes matter. It is true, however, that all Kafka's work is written in the shadow of a fear that verges on insanity, so closely in fact that for some the fear and the insanity are almost indistinguishable. Seeing this, and seeing how representative Kafka is for a generation that includes writers even as far apart as Beckett and Salinger, Georg Lukács has argued that the choice before American and European writers lies in the words "Towards fear (*Angst*) or away from it?" "*Angst*," in the view of the Communist critic (whose essay I have had to exclude on account of its length†), is the product of capitalist society, the reflection not of a transcendental contact but of the fears of the writer at the approach of Hitlerism or atomic war, and within capitalism it can scarcely be escaped. Thus for Lukács the content of Kafka's work is "the world of present-day capitalism as Hell, and the helplessness of all human power against the power of this under-world." ‡ Inescapable as Kafka's world was for him, it was conditioned by his environment, and in another form of society it might have been completely transformed. (Brecht may have had a similar attitude in presenting the spiritual anguish of the "good woman of Setzuan" as a torment that could at length be avoided.) In Communist society, on the other hand, the power of the "underworld" has vanished, or is vanishing, and with it "*Angst*" itself. Thus, Lukács would argue, the Western writer not yet committed to Communism is well advised to acquire an open-eyed awareness of "the sphere which my effectiveness can fill," where each presentation of reality is a step in the progression in the life of mankind—a progression which, Lukács undoubtedly must have felt, will end in the genuinely communistic society. There can be no hurrying of this process: writers can only be true, as Kafka was, to the perceptions they have of the world they live in. Yet it is only by turning

---

* E.g., "To the knowing power [of man] God is evermore incomprehensible, but to the . . . loving power he is, in every man diversely, all comprehensible to the full," quoted in D. Knowles, *The English Mystical Tradition*, London 1961, p. 79.

† "Franz Kafka oder Thomas Mann" in *Wider den missverstandenen Realismus*, Hamburg 1958.

‡ *op. cit.*, p. 87.

away from sterile fears of an unknown Nothing, and away from the compliance with existing society which goes with them, towards a critical portrayal of the present capitalist reality that a way out from the impasse of "Western avantgardism" can be found.

There is some truth in these contentions, and the various relationships to Fascism of, say, Yeats, Gottfried Benn, Pound, and Unamuno at least account for Lukács' misgivings. The tendency of some of the most individualistic writers to court or acquiesce in or even to welcome what he would call the final, totalitarian stage of capitalistic development is relevant to his charges. Yet he made his diagnosis and proposed his cure a little more than a year after the death of Stalin, at a time when he could say with rather more justice than formerly that with the recession of the cold war, and the prospects of peaceful coexistence, the material causes of *"Angst"* were disappearing as much for the "bourgeois" writer as for the Communist. Seven years later, his grounds for optimism look short-lived. There are evidently as powerful influences towards fear within Communist society as outside it, and it seems that the fundamental dread, whether its causes are material or not, is less easily disposed of than Lukács wanted to believe. He was right to point out its sterility when it is taken as an end in itself or as part of a nihilistic acquiescence such as Benn's; when it is overleaped, however, or given at most a stylized recognition as it is in the work of Thomas Mann which Lukács prefers, the outcome is also sterile. In so far, then, as the issue between "Western" and Communist writers can be limited to the question of *"Angst,"* as Lukács seeks to limit it, the most urgent need is to let the fear bear fruit, fear being traditionally not the end, but at any rate the beginning of wisdom. The wider significance of Kafka's work, as we look at it from this particular part of the twentieth century, depends very largely on what it made of this beginning.

To Franz Kafka

If we, the proximate damned, presumptive blest,
Were called one day to some high consultation
With the authentic ones, the worst and best
Picked from all time, how mean would be our station.
Oh we could never bear the standing shame,
Equivocal ignominy of non-election;
We who will hardly answer to our name,
And on the road direct ignore direction.

But you, dear Franz, sad champion of the drab
And half, would watch the tell-tale shames drift in
(As if they were troves of treasure) not aloof,
But with a famishing passion quick to grab
Meaning, and read on all the leaves of sin
Eternity's secret script, the saving proof.

EDWIN MUIR.

Kafka the Artist

by *Friedrich Beissner*

Many readers are not aware that Kafka, though he died a generation ago, was younger than both Thomas Mann and Hermann Hesse, if only by a few years. And as to the question whether he is younger than his contemporaries in reputation, the answer is that he is some decades their junior; his reputation is indeed not yet made, however fashionable his name may be today.

His reputation is not yet made: this truly Kafkaesque misfortune, like that which visits the characters in his stories time and again, still operates posthumously. When he died on June 3, 1924, not quite forty-one years of age, only five or six slim volumes and a few contributions to periodicals had appeared in print. The publication of one of his "scribbles," as he called his work, always caused him disquiet. This personal evidence of his human weakness, or so he thought, was printed because his friends had taken it upon themselves to make literature out of it, and because he had not the strength to destroy these witnesses to his loneliness.[1] This is in accord with his last request, written down on two separate occasions, that any writings found among his possessions after his death should, without exception, be burned unread. It is to the lasting credit of Max Brod that he did not carry out his friend's wish.[2] The first editions of the three great novels—*Lost without Trace (America)*,[3] *The Trial,* and *The Castle*—had at first only a small popular success, like the selection of shorter prose pieces published in 1931. And when at last the first four volumes of the *Collected Works* appeared, in Berlin in 1935, they could be sold only in Jewish bookshops, and to a definitely circumscribed

"Kafka the Artist," by Frederick Beissner. Original title, *Kafka der Dichter.* (© 1958 by W. Kohlhammer Verlag.) Reprinted by permission of the publishers. This contribution was first delivered as a lecture in 1957.

[1] Gustav Janouch, *Conversations with Kafka* (London, 1953), p. 32.

[2] See Max Brod's epilogue to the first edition of *The Trial* (Berlin: *Verlag die Schmiede,* 1925), reprinted in later German editions. Objections can be raised, however, to Brod's treatment of the text as he found it; see Friedrich Beissner, *Der Erzähler Franz Kafka* (Stuttgart, 1952; 2nd edition, 1958), pp. 44-48 (1st edition).

[3] [Kafka referred to the novel known as *America* as *"Der Verschollene."*]

group of customers. The two remaining volumes came out two years later in Prague. Thus the great majority of the German-speaking world was denied access to this collected edition.

It was not until 1946 that Kafka's works were reprinted in German, this time in New York. By that time they had had a great effect abroad, and especially in translation. But in Germany, just after the war, they were still not easily obtainable. What did arrive, in the form of contributions to periodicals and newspaper articles in translation, were profound interpretations together with extravagant praise. There seemed to be a genuine need to catch up on what had been missed, and so the average German reader found himself in the strange position of having heard a large number of opinions about Kafka while knowing nothing— or next to nothing—of his work. If it is objected that this situation is not at all unusual, seeing that many would-be literati are intent only on picking up the current phrases about a new literary phenomenon in the easiest way possible so as to join in the chit-chat without wasting time and energy on a detailed reading of their own, I will offer no contradiction. Where Kafka is concerned, however, the discrepancy between a view of one's own and parrot-talk derived from gleaning the opinions of others is particularly glaring. One would after all suppose that at any rate the translators of foreign interpretations of Kafka would know his work, and that they would give the titles of Kafka's writings, and quotations made from them by critics, in the original German. It was not entirely impossible to obtain copies of his works. But anyone who examines such retranslated quotations will make (according to his temperament) some highly annoying or some highly amusing discoveries. To take but one example, the first sentences of the short piece of prose, *A Crossbreed* (*Eine Kreuzung*), are given in a translation of a French pamphlet, published in Vienna in 1948, a form quite different from that in Kafka. The theme of this strange fantasy is a "cross" in the zoological sense, an imagined cross between a kitten and a lamb; the translator, evidently misunderstanding the French, gives the title as "Cross-talk" (*"Eine Unterhaltung"*).[4]

Such falsification and negligence with regard to a writer's work may perhaps annoy no one but the academic student of literature. More important than either of these is the by no means commonplace confusion caused by those precipitate heralds of a creative work, each of whom proclaimed a different Kafka, the philosopher of religion announcing one, the depth-psychologist another, the existentialist or the enthusiast for picturesque surrealism yet another. Moreover, quite a few interpreters

---

[4] Robert Rochefort, *Franz Kafka*, translated by Josef Žiwutschka. "Symposion" Series, No. 26 (Vienna, 1948), p. 22.

from abroad knew the writings only in translation. But even those interpreters for whom German was not, or need not have been, a foreign language, showed their insensitivity to the creative writer's word by translating it into the conceptual language of some fashionable philosophy. It was against such "translators" as these that Heinz Politzer, who assisted and collaborated in the first complete edition of Kafka's works, raised a warning voice, not excepting from his accusations even Max Brod, the editor.[5]

A further hindrance to a proper reception of Kafka as a literary artist in Germany—that is, in the largest area where his language is spoken and understood—was perhaps the circumstance that in the situation just outlined, with all its confused expectations, *The Trial* was the first volume of the *Collected Works* to become at last generally available. In 1950 it lay as a Christmas present on many a table, and most of its expectant readers were wearing unsuitable spectacles. Bafflement seemed general. Hadn't we been told that this novel was a glorious satire on the corrupt officialdom of the Austro-Hungarian monarchy? But granted that a satirist exaggerates, and has to exaggerate for clarity's sake, this surely went beyond all bounds, this caricature must inevitably miss the mark. And then, said others, weren't we told to expect a great allegory of one of the two manifestations of the divinity as taught by the Cabala, namely "Judgment," and weren't we to find in *The Castle,* according to trustworthy reports, a complementary picture, in the same kind of cipher, of the other manifestation of the divinity, namely "Grace"? But this didn't add up: far too many details and quite a few more important characteristics simply would not fit into the allegory. Perhaps we should try some other way, some other symbolical explanation? And so on.

I don't mean to say by any means that some work belonging to an earlier period of artistic development—the American novel *Lost Without Trace* perhaps—would have been more suitable for the first encounter with the writer himself. With this enigmatic artist there is in fact no development, and not because his allotted span of life was so short. Schiller, for instance, did not live much longer, and yet it is quite easy to distinguish in his career quite precisely marked developmental phases. Kafka was himself from the outset, and never altered. Comparing himself with an uncle, he writes in his diary (22 January 1922) of both men "living the most unvarying lives, with no trace of any development, young to the end of our days ('well-preserved' is a better expression)." The almost boyish appearance of his own slender figure, his pale face, his forehead, covered over with thick hair, and his dark, wide open eyes,

[5] Heinz Politzer, *"Problematik und Probleme der Kafka-Forschung"* (*Monatshefte für deutschen Unterricht, deutsche Sprache und Literatur;* Madison, Wis., 1950), pp. 273-280.

all go with this. There are some amusing anecdotes about misunderstandings arising from false estimates of his age. The pleasantest of them all was not made known until Autumn, 1952. Kafka tells it himself in a letter to Frau Milena Jesenská[6]—how he, Franz Kafka, Doctor of Laws, almost forty years old, one of the chief officials at a large government insurance office in Prague, was taking a last stroll round the pool at the swimming school on Slawisch Island before getting dressed, when a well-meaning swimming master came along, looking round as though seeking somebody, and noticing Kafka, obviously picked him out and asked him whether he would like to take a short walk—there was a gentleman, an important building contractor, who wanted to be rowed over to the Juden Island.

> Well, one shouldn't exaggerate the whole thing, [Kafka writes] the swimming master detected me, and decided to offer the poor boy (me) the pleasure of a free boat-ride. However, in deference to the *important* builder, he had to choose a boy who looked sufficiently reliable not only in strength and in skill but also one who, having accomplished the job, wouldn't use the boat for clandestine pleasure rides but would return it at once. All this he thought he had found in me.

Kafka—and this trait is characteristic of his human nature—treated the thing as a joke, did as he was asked, let the important building contractor treat him affably as a good boy, astonished the instructor by his good behavior in coming back by the shortest route, and on the evening of this "chief day of glory," as he called it, was "swollen with pride."

But to come to the question, what work would have been more suitable than *The Trial* for a first introduction to Kafka the artist? I think it would have been better if the German reading public had had the opportunity of getting to know the shorter prose pieces. These are by no means fragments. On the contrary, for all their brevity and simplicity, they are astonishingly rich in content, and with these the reader would not have been impeded in advance by confused expectations. He could have read them and taken them as they stood, and would more easily have found a bridge from them to a proper understanding of the novels. He would then, perhaps, have noticed that in both cases, in the shorter prose pieces as well as in the stories and novels, something is missing which most modern novelists imagine to be an indispensable element in a story: there is no unartistic reflection. The unprejudiced reader would have noticed also that there are in Kafka no contemptuous irony, no anachronistic romanticism, and no flourishes of "playful" artistry. But

---

[6] Franz Kafka, *Letters to Milena*, edited by Willi Haas, translated by Tania and James Stern (London, 1953), p. 169ff.

these of course are all negative definitions. What is left for a creative writer who scorns the evasions adopted, in their increasing helplessness, by modern novelists? He is left with his loneliness. He still has himself in his loneliness, himself as subject and object of his portrayal. And that is Kafka's achievement, raising him high above all those who follow in his steps today, merely acting a little madly in an abstrusely macabre atmosphere—Kafka's achievement: the miraculous "unity of meaning" whereby the narrator becomes one with the character of his fiction, even when he speaks of him in the third person, and whereby the reader is himself transformed into that character. There is only the purity of the narrated course of events, seen from within, not from some "serene point of vantage" which no longer exists. And, seen from within, the narrated events—often distorted by a weary eye—nevertheless always have unity of meaning, never giving way to an ignoble curiosity as to content, or stupidly fabricating an artificial "tension" as novels of entertainment do. Outside the narrated event, then, there is no room for the narrator, let alone for didactic reflections. Reading Charles Louis Philippe's novel, *Marie Donadieu* (1905), and unable to get on with it, Kafka was pain-fully annoyed.

> When Raphael seduces Donadieu, [he wrote] it's very important for her, but what business has the author in the student's room, and even less so the fourth person, the reader, until the little room turns into a lecture hall of the medical or psychological faculty? (Milena, p. 234).

You will observe that this is not the fleeting expression of some momentary mood: by contrast, it shows how clearly he sees the necessity for his own severe attitude to his art, an attitude which by no means involves an impoverishment—however paradoxical that may sound at first. The unity of the themes—or more correctly, of the theme—is in pure correlationship with the unity of meaning in the portrayal. It is often said that great writers have in fact only one theme, a "permanent note" running through all the manifold realizations and variations of the theme. Kafka's recurrent theme, *the unsuccessful arrival or the failure to reach the goal*, results from the basic experience of inescapable loneli-ness.

A young friend once asked him whether he was lonely, and, at a nod of assent, whether he was as lonely as Kaspar Hauser. "Kafka laughed: 'Much worse than Kaspar Hauser. I am as lonely as—as Franz Kafka.'" (Janouch, p. 43)

He felt deeply the uncertainty of all relationships, and felt at the same time that this was not merely a defect and a misfortune of his own. He wrote to Milena (p. 100),

. . . this Fear [*Angst*] is after all not my private Fear—although it is in fact all that, and terrible—but it is as much the Fear of all faith since the beginning of time.

And when his human experience seems to cancel this loneliness, the fear, the fundamental fear, becomes all the greater, and seeks to argue away the kindlier appearance of things. In another letter to Milena (p. 194) he writes:

The either/or is too great. Either you are mine, in which case it's good, or I lose you and then it's not just bad, but simply nothing—in that case there wouldn't be any jealousy, no suffering, no anxiety, nothing. And there's certainly something blasphemous about building so much on a human being, which is why Fear [*Angst*] creeps round the foundations, but it's not so much the fear about you as the fear about daring to build like this at all. And this is why, in self-defense (but it has probably always been so) so much that's divine mingles with what's human in your clear face.[7]

Let us take that in just as it stands, in all its tormenting seriousness: *And there's certainly something blasphemous about building so much on a human being, which is why fear creeps round the foundations, but it's not so much the fear about you as the fear about daring to build like this at all.* And then he explains—this needs weighing carefully—he explains to the woman he loves, and to himself: *And this is why, in self-defense . . . so much that's divine mingles with what's human in your dear face.* But I have just omitted the parenthesis which seems to me the most important thing about these sentences. He says in this parenthesis (but only in parenthesis) of the divine in this dear human face: *but it has probably always been so.* Let us underline these words and keep them in mind as we turn now to the works themselves.

· · · ·

To make plain the creative character of Kafka's work, I shall not speak about any of the three novels. In the short time available I could only speak past the man in broad—very broad—outlines, and it would depend entirely on your being well disposed whether you believed me or not. Instead, being convinced that every one of the shorter prose pieces is a completely valid representative of the larger works, fully developing Kafka's basic theme even in the narrowest confines, I should like to present you with a page from one of them, and show by a close textual interpretation the peculiar quality of the "unity of meaning" in the portrayal, and of the permanent theme, the unsuccessful arrival.

[7] [The editor has departed slightly from the standard translation of this passage.]

HOMECOMING

I have returned, I have passed under the arch and am looking round. It's my father's old yard. The puddle in the middle. Old, useless tools, jumbled together, block the way to the attic stairs. The cat lurks on the banister. A torn piece of cloth, once wound round a stick in a game, flutters in the breeze. I have arrived. Who is going to receive me? Who is waiting behind the kitchen door? Smoke is rising from the chimney, coffee is being made for supper. Do you feel you belong, do you feel at home? I don't know, I feel most uncertain. My father's house it is, but each object stands cold beside the next, as though preoccupied with its own affairs, which I have partly forgotten, partly never known. What use can I be to them, what do I mean to them, even though I am the son of my father, the old farmer? And I don't dare knock at the kitchen door, I only listen from a distance, I only listen from a distance, standing up, in such a way that I cannot be taken by surprise as an eavesdropper. And since I am listening from a distance, I hear nothing but a faint striking of the clock passing over from childhood days, but perhaps I only think I hear it. Whatever else is going on in the kitchen is the secret of those sitting there, a secret they are keeping from me. The longer one hesitates before the door, the more estranged one becomes. What would happen if someone were to open the door now and ask me a question? Would not I myself then behave like one who wants to keep his secret?

An unsuccessful arrival—the theme is directly and literally embodied here. He is a stranger, this man who has returned home, "the son of my father, the old farmer." And though he does say "I have returned," and notes again, "I have arrived," he does not know, and he is uncertain whether he feels at home. This is simply asserted. The lonely strangeness is simply a fact. It is not commented on, let alone lamented. And the growing fear, which is doubtless also a fact, is not even expressly named. There is reference to the others sitting in the kitchen waiting for supper. But they are and remain "the others," and no link with them can be established. It is even emphasized that the cautiously observed detachment, the distance, makes communication impossible, and that the faint striking of the clock which makes itself heard is perhaps only a hallucination—the sound, says the stranger, is "passing over from childhood days, but perhaps I only think I hear it." So he remains alone and lonely—and above all, the narrow farmyard is not turned by some didactic reflection into a psychological or philosophical or theological lecture room. The writer leaves the man standing in the yard, he does not lead him out again, nor does he let him release himself by an upward glance, a move-

ment of the soul into some other dimension. There is no longer any
other dimension for Kafka.

A poet of an earlier century, who despite all temptation retained his
faith, wrote of the same situation: of the returning wanderer who cannot find his parents and friends again. He, however, was able to address
the old watchman of the house, and at length—in a mighty stream of
words which do not merely express a certainty but rather in themselves
achieve it and consolidate it—was able to assure himself of a lasting
link and restore to it what merely seemed to be lost:

> Und so bin ich allein. Du aber, über den Wolken.
>> Vater des Vaterlands! mächtiger Aether! und du
> Erd' und Licht! ihr einigen drei, die walten und lieben,
>> Ewige Götter! mit euch brechen die Bande mir nie.
> Ausgegangen von euch, mit euch auch bin ich gewandert,
>> Euch, ihr Freudigen, euch bring' ich erfahrner zurück.
> Darum reiche mir nun, bis oben an von des Rheines
>> Warmen Bergen mit Wein reiche den Becher gefüllt!
> Dass ich den Göttern zuerst und das Angedenken der Helden
>> Trinke, der Schiffer, und dann eures, ihr Trautesten! auch
> Eltern und Freund'! und der Mühn und aller Leiden vergesse
>> Heut' und morgen und schnell unter den Heimischen sei.[8]

[And thus I am alone. But you, above the clouds,/ Father of the Fatherland, mighty
Aether, and you,/ Earth and Light, you three in one that govern and love,/ eternal
Gods! my bonds with you shall never break./ From you proceeding, with you too I
have wandered;/ you, you joyful ones, you do I bring home, taught by experience./
And therefore offer me now, filled to the brim/ with wine from the Rhine's warm
hills, offer me now the goblet full,/ that I may drink first to the Gods and the memory
of those heroes,/ the seamen, and then to the memory of you, my dear and intimate
ones,/ and to parents and friends, and forget the labors and all the suffering,/ that
I may be today and tomorrow and soon among those who are on native soil.]

For Hölderlin such song was still possible. In Kafka's sober prose such
comfort, such a positive conclusion seems ruled out. Should we—may
we—blame the writer for that? Has he, by his own fault, omitted something? There may be people who will reproach him for "not having
tried" to—what is it such people say?—to "overcome" the crushing experiences of an age that is breaking in pieces. As though there were no
more to that than a little good will. But do such people know what art
is, or what the conscience of an artist is? The only creative literature they
recognize as genuinely valuable is that which arises from what they
judge to be a praiseworthy attitude or ideology, and which encourages
the reader in the misery of his humdrum existence in as uncomplicated a

---

[8] Hölderlin, *"Der Wanderer,"* second version, lines 97-108.

manner as possible. But suppose a writer has grown so lonely, has foreseen the destiny of his age in an increasing sense of loneliness so painfully
and so fearfully that he is incapable of so lighthearted a lie? "Lying is
terrible," says Kafka, "a worse spiritual torture doesn't exist" (Milena,
p. 221). This writer is so lonely in the ruins of the world that the only
place he knows of where a whole, hale, world exists is within himself.

In his diary (6 August 1914) he finds the formula for the thing that
still gives him the possibility of a link with literature—or more correctly, with writing, as he modestly puts it. He calls it the ability to
portray his dreamlike inner life. And in conversation he once remarked
that his stories were a kind of closing of the eyes. (Janouch, p. 34.) [9]

. . . .

It is from this point of view that the stories should be interpreted.
What use, for instance, are all the superimposed psychoanalytical explanations, which are now as cheap as blackberries, for a real understanding of a story like "The Judgment," when they fail to observe how
Kafka's very introversion gives rise to that "unity of meaning" in the
portrayal? The externally visible action can be sketched in a few
sentences: Georg Bendemann, a young businessman, imagines he has
reached the goal of his efforts. In the last two years, his widowed father
having withdrawn more and more, he has had a great deal of success
in business, and a month ago he became engaged "to a Fräulein Frieda
Brandenfeld, a girl from a well-to-do family." The fiancée is thus literally
mentioned in the introductory part, which, it is true, speaks of Georg
in the third person. But this story is clearly imbued with the retrospective
thoughts of Georg himself, who "on a Sunday morning in the very
height of spring" has just finished a letter to a friend who has been
living abroad for some time past, and is sitting contemplatively at the
window. "What could one write to such a man who had obviously run
off the rails, a man one could be sorry for but could not help?" The
letters have become more and more impersonal. He has absent-mindedly
told his friend "three times, in three fairly widely separated letters" of
the "engagement of an unimportant man to an equally unimportant
girl," but has said nothing until now of his own engagement. Only at
the end of the letter just finished has he told him of this, and with almost

---

[9] Kafka did not fail to observe the danger of *hubris* lurking in such introversion.
See *Wedding Preparations in the Country*, London 1954, p. 382. "We are digging the
pit of Babel"—to be spoken with the emphasis on *we* and *pit*. Compare also "Reflections on Sin" etc., No. 18 (*Wedding Preparations*, p. 40): "If it had been possible to
build the Tower of Babel without climbing up it, it would have been permitted" and
also "The City Coat of Arms" (*Description of a Struggle and The Great Wall of China;*
London, 1960, p. 99ff.).

the same phrase in mind as before he presents his own fiancée: "I have got engaged to a Fräulein Frieda Brandenfeld, a girl from a well-to-do family." And going on he finds what he must think to be a few warm, friendly words ending in an invitation to the wedding—although only in the form of a question, it is true. The first part of the story then ends with two sentences, thus:

> With this letter in his hand, Georg had been sitting for a long time at the writing table, his face turned towards the window. He had barely acknowledged, with an absent smile, a greeting waved to him from the street by a passing acquaintance.

There follows an account of Georg crossing over to his father's room to show him the letter. From here on everything becomes phantasmal. The room, "even on this sunny morning," is dark. The windows are shut, despite the heat. The father is reading a very old newspaper, the very name of which is quite unknown to the son. In a grotesque argument, which is clearly given from Georg's standpoint (twice he means to do or say something but forgets it, and there are other references to his unspoken observations and decisions), the father maintains first, in the course of some strange reproaches, that the friend in Petersburg does not exist. Georg speaks soothingly to his father and gets him into bed, imagining he has covered him up well, but:

> "No!" cried his father . . . , threw the blankets off with a strength that sent them all flying in a moment and sprang erect in bed. Only one hand lightly touched the ceiling to steady him. "You wanted to cover me up, I know, my young sprig, but I'm far from being covered up yet. And even if this is the last strength I have, it's enough for you, too much for you. Of course I know your friend. He would have been a son after my own heart. That's why you've been playing him false all these years. Why else? Do you think I haven't been sorry for him?"

And in a passionate accusation he even calls himself the friend's "representative here on the spot," says he has written to him long ago about it all, including the engagement "Your friend is going to pieces in Russia, even three years ago he was yellow enough to be thrown away"—and at last, at the top of his voice:

> "So now you know what else there is in the world besides yourself, till now you've only known about yourself! An innocent child, yes, that you were truly, but still more truly have you been a devilish human being. And therefore take note; I sentence you now to death by drowning."

Georg rushes out to the river, vaults over the railing of the bridge, and so executes the sentence.

This last section is part of the external action once again. The grotesque and phantasmal main part of the story, however, is the portrayal of a "dreamlike inner life," which by its uncanny intensification and compression makes us see that the apparently attained goal is in reality unreached. The Kafkan unity of meaning in the narration does not allow the narrator to manipulate his characters like a puppeteer or to explain the external facts and the external course of events to the reader through some knowledge he possesses by virtue of his detachment—rather, he has completely transformed himself into the lonely Georg, even when he talks about him in the third person. And Georg is, from an external point of view, the only character in a story that is—to all intents and purposes—a monologue.

This conception is confirmed, I think, by Kafka's own interpretation, written in his diary (11 February 1913) on the occasion of a proofreading of "The Judgment":

> The friend is the link between father and son, he is their strongest common bond. *Sitting alone at his window*, Georg rummages voluptuously in this consciousness of what they have in common, *believes he has his father within him*, and would be at peace with everything if it were not for a fleeting, sad thoughtfulness. In the course of the story the father . . . uses the common bond of the friend to set himself up as Georg's antagonist.

Kafka was thus able to sense the meaning of the last sentence in the story, as he explained it to his friend Max Brod in conversation, only if the preceding part was interpreted as an uncanny inward compression.[10] Coming after the death of Georg, after the soliloquizing which brings about the decision entirely within his own mind, this single sentence is hurled with tremendous impetus in another direction: outwards. In this one sentence, Georg—in whose lonely spirit the whole story has been told, first in the fairly realistic introduction, and then above all in the grotesque main part—in this one sentence Georg is no longer there: "At this moment an unending stream of people was just going over the bridge."

. . . .

[10] When Kafka, speaking to a man who was his intimate friend, compared the dynamic force of this final sentence with a physiological action, he can scarcely have suspected that the latter would publish his remark in so painfully misunderstandable a fashion. See Max Brod, *Franz Kafka, a Biography* (New York 1947), p. 129.

It is in some such way as this that Kafka needs to be read—with a delicate and exact regard for his ability to portray his dreamlike inner life—the ability which, by his own confession, made it possible for him to write creatively. The reader will then see also, from this unitary point of view, the impressive coherence of the great novels, in which characters other than the main one also appear. But if the reader of *The Castle* takes the account of the landlady of the Bridge Inn doing this or that as implying that the land surveyor K. sees or learns that she does it, or the account of Olga saying this or that as implying that the land surveyor K. hears her say it, he will have gained a good deal in artistic under-standing. Nothing happens without K; nothing happens that has not some relationship to him, and nothing happens in his absence. Everything that happens, happens to him. And everything is told as clearly and as unclearly, as distortedly and as precisely, as he himself perceives it in his disappointment, his vexation, and his weariness. The "writer" does not stand beside him, explaining, teaching, and reflecting.

The lonely man discovers, from his fundamental experience that there is no longer any link between him and the ruins of a world that has fallen to pieces, the saving factor on his radically unromantic path to the inward self. Kafka fashions the whole and hale inward world without that high-flown appeal to his fellow mortals or to certain beloved women which his Prague compatriot Rilke, by virtue of and even in the teeth of the same experience, so mellifluously sounded forth. Kafka fashions his experience and presents it. He sets things down, apparently without any particular aim.

But why then does he fashion experience at all? Why does he put words together, when he seems not to be addressing anyone? Is it not a self-deception—and a completely disproportionate one in view of the situa-tion—that this deeply pessimistic writer, completely turned in upon his dreamlike inner life and banished to his insular self, should think it possible, according to his diary (25 September 1917), for him to "raise the world into the pure, the true, and the immutable"?

No, it is not self-deception; for the giving of literary form to a state of extreme need really does "raise the world into the pure, true and immutable," whereas expressed encouragements would merely sound labored. The philosopher only defines extreme need and makes us con-scious of it. And he occasionally illustrates his definition by reference to the work of a poet, which he then places within his categories, although only in accordance with the scheme in which he encloses his material.[11]

---

[11] In my lecture I intentionally did not mention names which would readily suggest themselves, including Kierkegaard's, out of a perhaps exaggerated fear that my audi-ence would at once take the writer's words in their nonpoetic sense—the "translatable" sense—and would grasp, instead of the full seriousness of the words themselves, the

Since his readers often, or even generally, take this for an interpretation of the poet, he destroys the work as a work of art, since for very many people who do not know and have not learned that art is "great above all content" [12] he makes it impossible for the work of art to exercise and display its specific effectiveness. I am not thinking now of "form," but of the simple and yet mysterious experience which is had by everyone with any sense for poetic values, that a word in a poem as it stands in relation to the other words in the line, or one in a prose sentence by a creative writer, means something different and says more than those identically sounding and therefore identically significant words heard by an insensitive ear in colloquial everyday speech.[13]

Let me remind you now of the parenthesis I singled out earlier from a sentence in one of Kafka's letters, which seemed to suggest that beyond all the self-torturing disillusionment there is nevertheless not a last vestige of illusion, but a real faith in something divine which thereby becomes all the more credible—so much that's divine (*so viel Göttliches*). And, let me ask, was not this contained also in the words of "Homecoming"? Unspoken, it is true, and not even added in parenthesis, but was it not present nevertheless, and clearly to be felt? And was not our paraphrase incomplete, to say the least, for all that it seemed so precise, and incomplete by virtue of its very efforts to bring home the hopeless sense of loneliness?

This may appear to some a strange and improbable thing. But it exists, and poets have always known that it does. The further I go back in the history of literature to illustrate it to you, the more convincing you will find it. Let us take, then, a poem in which so far as the surface is concerned, and as regards that much of the so-called "content" which can be translated into the language of philosophy or theology or even of everyday speech, a deeply pessimistic disillusionment is expressed—a poem in whose actual words not the faintest gleam of hope is suggested, and yet one which somehow uplifts the reader and moves him with its succoring power. I choose a poem by Matthias Claudius,[14] which in its

---

"translation" that would make them shallow and easily placeable. But the criticisms of Kafka, with their numerous standpoints, have already drawn attention to a large number of such relationships with nonpoetic spheres, and these references will no doubt remain valid insofar as they do not cancel each other out.

[12] Rilke, in the *"Bremer Festspielszene"* (1902): *"Die Kunst ist über jeden Inhalt gross./ Er gilt nicht mehr, sobald sie ihn ergreift/ und ihn verwandelt."* ("Art is great above all content. Content is no longer valid, once art has seized on and transformed it.")

[13] Rilke speaks of this transformation in his letter to the Countess Sizzo of 17 March 1922 (*Die Briefe an Gräfin Sizzo*, im Insel Verlag 1950, p. 19f.).

[14] [Claudius lived from 1740 to 1815; he is the author of the hymn translated as "We plough the fields and scatter . . ."]

brevity and manifest simplicity seems to me to show what I mean without extensive analyses. No one will suspect this pious poet of having gone even momentarily astray in his Christian belief. And yet—we read in the poem entitled "Man":

> Empfangen und genähret
> Vom Weibe wunderbar
> Kömmt er und sieht und höret,
> Und nimmt des Trugs nicht wahr;
> Gelüstet und begehret,
> Und bringt sein Thränlein dar;
> Verachtet und verehret,
> Hat Freude und Gefahr;
> Glaubt, zweifelt, wähnt und lehret,
> Hält Nichts und Alles wahr;
> Erbauet und zerstöret
> Und quält sich immerdar;
> Schläft, wachet, wächst und zehret,
> Trägt braun und graues Haar
> Und alles dieses währet,
> Wenn's hoch kömmt, achtzig Jahr.
> Denn legt er sich zu seinen Vätern nieder,
> Und er kömmt nimmer wieder.[15]

If we try not to hear the melody by which these words are sustained, they say with sober insistence that all that men hope for, desire, believe, and build is pointless and vain. In fact, as the lines go on, the negative expressions predominate. The hopeful note which, at the beginning at least, has a whole line to itself, is finally refuted, one might almost say blow by blow, and the negative weighs down the scales:

> Believes, *doubts,* thinks he knows, and teaches,
> *Thinks nothing and all things true;*
> Builds and *destroys*
> *And torments himself all the while.*

[15] [Conceived and nourished/ by a woman, wonderfully,/ he comes and sees and hears/ and never notices the deception;/ lusts and desires,/ contributes his small tear;/ despises and esteems,/ knows joy and danger;/ believes, doubts, thinks he knows, and teaches,/ thinks nothing and all things true;/ builds and destroys/ and torments himself all the while;/ sleeps, wakes, grows and feeds,/ has brown hair and gray,/ and all this lasts/ at the most eighty years./Then he lays himself down among his fathers,/ and he never comes again.]

Then the sad wisdom of the 90th Psalm is echoed in the words, without that widespread, kindly misunderstanding which calls toil and labor delightful. The final couplet, clearly marked off by the rhyme, is hard, and without hope:

> He lays him where his fathers lay before,
> And comes home nevermore.

No mention here of Christian confidence overcoming death and distress and the misery of finite life—as far as the direct expression is concerned. But what happened to us in listening to this poem? It is hard to put into words, let alone to prove that all must feel the same. At all events the effect of this poem with its disillusioning "content" is by no means oppressive. The listener is gently moved, agreeing sadly—yes, that's how it is—and yet feeling also a succoring comfort. It is there without any explicit demonstration or any explicit refutation of what has literally been said.

Klopstock called this phenomenon "the wordless"—the wordless quality which moves within a good poem, he said, like the gods in Homer's battles, seen only by a few. By this expression Klopstock did not mean the silences, the pauses in a poem. Since it was only recently that, in a *History of Form in German Literature*,[16] Klopstock's theory has been misunderstood on this point—the " 'silences and stillnesses,' " the author emphasized, are "thought of as an essential element of speech" —we must call to mind the context in which the sentence concerned appears. In his important fragment of dialogue "On Representation," printed in 1779, Klopstock has two friends speak to one another as follows:[17]

"The poet can express latently those feelings for which language has no words, or rather (I say this in relation to the riches of our language) only the secondary developments of such feelings, by means of the strength and the positioning of similar feelings which he expresses completely."

"Or perhaps only hint at them."

"True enough, if the similar feelings are not strong enough, and are not in the right place, if neither the one nor the other is of such a kind as to spread the fire in the soul."

"It seems to me that the meter also can help here and there to express something latent."

"Indeed, the wordless quality moves within a good poem like the gods in Homer's battles, seen only by a few."

[16] Paul Böckmann, *Formgeschichte der deutschen Dichtung*, 1. Band, Hamburg [1949], p. 582.

[17] Klopstock, *Sämmtliche Werke*, 10. Band, Leipzig 1855, p. 199f.

True, particular mention is made here of the meter, as being able to create such a marvellous effect, but yet not of the meter alone. The astonishing thing about Kafka is that he can achieve as much in a decidedly unornamented language. There is no ornament whatsoever in his prose, and yet we should not fail to hear the soft, almost involuntary accentuations in "Homecoming," which do after all reveal an emotional participation—as for instance when the returning traveller suddenly speaks to himself, and his aching loneliness seems momentarily annulled: *"Ist dir heimlich, fühlst du dich zu Hause?"* ("Do you feel you belong, do you feel at home?"). Three times in these few words of German does the personal pronoun occur and then come those pulsating repetitions: *". . . nur von der Ferne horche ich, nur von der Ferne horche ich stehend, nicht so, dass ich als Horcher überrascht werden könnte. Und weil ich von der ferne horche, erhorche ich nichts."* [18] ("I only listen from a distance, I only listen from a distance, standing up, in such a way that I cannot be taken for an eavesdropper. And since I am listening from a distance, I hear nothing.") While the lonely sense of unrelatedness is noted, the powerful longing for relationship is expressed also, and perhaps too the belief in a possibility just like that in the parenthesis interrupting the sentences in Kafka's letter.

Let us finally make a test on one other short piece, so that "Homecoming" may be not the only work we have considered as a rounded whole in (to use Hölderlin's words)[19] its "course and spirit in shape." "A Message from the Emperor" is a whole. Kafka published these sentences himself, as part of the collection *A Country Doctor* (1919), and they are full and rounded even though they later proved to be part of a larger context entitled *The Great Wall of China.* The literal content is simply that the message will never reach you, and that the one who sent it died long ago. But in the course and the spirit of these sentences there runs contrapuntally the certainty that the messenger is on his way to you. His friends saw an imperial messenger in Kafka himself.[20]

The Emperor—so the story goes—has sent a message to you, the lone individual, the meanest of his subjects, the shadow that has fled before the Imperial sun until it is microscopic in the remotest distance, just to you has the Emperor sent a message from his deathbed. He made the messenger kneel by his bed and whispered the message into his ear; he felt it to be so important that he made the man repeat it into his own ear. With a nod of

---

[18] [The insistent beat of the syllable 'horch-' is not represented in the translation.]
[19] Hölderlin, Bruchstück 67, 10.
[20] Franz werfel to Dr. Robert Klopstock (2 December 1934): "When I first saw Kafka a quarter of a century ago I knew at once that he was 'a messenger from the King. " (*Der Monat* 1, 1949, Heft 8/9, p. 65)

the head he confirmed that the repetition was accurate. And then, before the whole retinue gathered to witness his death—all the walls blocking the view had been broken down and on the wide high curve of the open stairway stood the notables of the Empire in a circle—before them all he empowered the messenger to go. The messenger set off at once; a robust, an indefatigable man; thrusting out now one arm, now the other, he forces his way through the crowd; where he finds obstacles he points to the sign of the sun on his breast; he gets through easily, too, as no one else could. Yet the throng is so numerous; there is no end to their dwelling-places. If he only had a free field before him, how he would run, and soon enough you would hear the glorious tattoo of his fists on your door. But instead of that, how vain are his efforts; he is still forcing his way through the chambers of the innermost palace; he will never get to the end of them; and even if he did, he would be no better off; he would have to fight his way down the stairs; and even if he did that, he would be no better off; he would still have to get through the courtyards; and after the courtyards, the second outer palace enclosing the first; and more stairways and more courtyards; and still another palace; and so on for thousands of years; and did he finally dash through the outermost gate—but that will never, never happen—he would still have the capital city before him, the center of the world, overflowing with the dregs of humanity. No one can force a way through that, least of all with a message from a dead man. But you sit by your window and dream it all true, when evening falls.

Franz Kafka

by Edwin Muir

The reputation which Franz Kafka has won since his death in 1924 is a peculiar and in some ways unique one. To a few people he is a great writer, but one can never tell to what school of taste they may belong. Since the appearance of the English version of *The Castle* a few years ago he has been praised in the highest terms by writers as diverse in their ideas of what constitutes literary excellence as Mr. Aldous Huxley, Mr. Herbert Read, Miss Rebecca West, and Mr. Hugh Walpole; and when his most recent book, *The Great Wall of China*, was published in Germany, Thomas Mann, Hermann Hesse, André Gide and several other well-known literary men united to pay homage to him as one of the greatest writers of modern times. It is fairly safe to say that anyone who admires him would agree with that verdict; for if one acknowledges his virtues at all one has no choice but to put them in the first rank. On the other hand, there are many who simply can see no merit in him; and it is inconceivable that there should exist any large body of readers who consider him a writer of respectable talent, which is the way to fame.

The reason for his unique reputation, and unique lack of reputation, is, I think, quite understandable, and lies in the fantastic strangeness of his imagination. A reader beginning *The Castle* may easily feel that he does not know what he is reading about, and not because of any obscurity in the language—for Kafka's style is scrupulously clear—but because such extraordinary things happen and such curious conversations are carried on. In reality Kafka is a great story-teller and a great master of dialogue; but that can matter little to any one who cannot understand either the characters or the happenings or the conversations in his books. His obscurity is not caused by any desire to puzzle or impress his readers (no other modern writer is more candid or seeks less to exploit his gifts); it is caused simply by the peculiar originality of his genius, which is one for thinking in concrete images. He is a profound religious thinker,

"Franz Kafka," by Edwin Muir from *Life and Letters*, London, June 1934. © 1934 by Mrs. Willa Muir. Reprinted by permission of Willa Muir.

but the product of his thought is not a system but a world of imagination. As his thought, however, is subtle and comprehensive, his imaginations demand from the reader an effort somewhat like that required to follow a close line of abstract reasoning. To think in this particular way was clearly natural to him; many of his best aphorisms are really short parables. Consequently his semiallegorical stories are really the most simple and unaffected expression that could have been found for his genius; not in the least a form of mystification, though to many people they must read somewhat like that. Given Kafka's special kind of imagination and complete honesty in following it, something like this was inevitable, and there is no help for it.

Kafka himself, indeed, did his best to injure his reputation beforehand. His three greatest stories, *The Castle, The Trial* and *America,* might have been lost to us altogether if it had not been for the courage of Dr. Max Brod. Before he died Kafka left instructions that they should be burned along with all his other papers. Dr. Brod has publicly explained his reasons for setting aside his friend's request, and they are entirely to his honor. Had these three books never appeared Kafka would still have been known as an exquisite minor artist in the fable, the parable and the short story: these books alone support his claim to be considered a great writer. I shall have space in this essay to consider only one of them, *The Castle,* which has the advantage of being available in English; and even it I shall have to treat somewhat perfunctorily; for Kafka's stories are so packed with meaning that what they really demand is not a general criticism so much as a running commentary. Anyone who wishes to have a good portrait of Kafka as a man will find it in the figure of Richard Garta in Dr. Brod's novel, *The Kingdom of Love,* which the author tells me is based entirely on biographical data. No life of Kafka has yet appeared; and little is known of him except that he was born in Prague of well-to-do Jewish parents, studied law in the university there, worked later in an insurance office, had an unfortunate love affair, fell ill of consumption, spent many years in sanatoriums and Bohemian mountain villages trying to recover, and finally went to live in Berlin, where the effects of the Allied blockade helped to carry him off in 1924 at the age of forty-two. The writers he seems to have studied most closely were Pascal, Flaubert and Kierkegaard, the Danish writer, the last of whom deeply influenced him.

II

Between 1917 and 1919, a few years before his death, Kafka jotted down over a hundred aphorisms. He evidently attached more importance to them than to his other work, for he went to the unusual pains of copying them out on separate slips of paper and numbering them. They are striking compressions of the chief problems that troubled him during his life, and are not only remarkable in themselves but throw a great deal of light on *The Castle* and *The Trial*. Probably the best approach to the world of these books is therefore to be found in the aphorisms, and I shall begin by quoting a few.

On the problem of conduct which occupied Kafka in all his work:

> The true way goes over a rope which is not stretched at any great height but just above the ground. It seems more designed to make people stumble than to be walked upon.

On salvation, which is the main theme of *The Castle*:

> There are countless places of refuge, there is only one place of salvation; but the possibilities of salvation, again, are as numerous as all the places of refuge.

On the universal effects of the Fall of Man:

> Some people assume that in addition to the great original betrayal a small particular betrayal has been contrived in every case exclusively for them, that, in other words, when a love drama is being performed on the stage the leading actress has not only a pretended smile for the lover, but also a special crafty smile for one particular spectator at the back of the gallery. That is going too far.

On the law of this world:

> The hunting dogs are playing in the courtyard, but the hare will not escape them, no matter how fast it may be flying already through the woods.

On its incommensurability with divine law:

> Only here is suffering suffering. Not in the sense that those who suffer here are ennobled somewhere else because of their suffering, but in the sense that what is called suffering in this world is, without any alteration except that it is freed from its opposite, bliss in another.

On the confusion caused by our divination of this:

> He is thirsty, and cut off from a spring by a mere clump of trees. But he is divided against himself: one part overlooks the whole, sees that he is

standing here and that the spring is just beside him; but another part
notices nothing, has at most a divination that the first part sees all. But as
he notices nothing he cannot drink.

On the impossibility of transcending this state:

You are the problem. No scholar to be found far and wide.

These questions and others connected with them are what Kafka is
concerned with in all his voluminous imaginative work—or rather, they
are the roots out of which it grew. They are not philosophical, but religious questions. They do not aim at an intellectual criticism of religious
conceptions, in which religion is accepted merely as one among several
worlds of discourse; but rather take the main categories of religion as
self-evident truths, and concern themselves with what, after full acceptance, remains inexplicable or unresolved within religion. To a rationalist
impervious to their force they would probably provide as fine a set of
arguments showing the absurdity of believing in religion at all as could
be found. Indeed Kafka himself was conscious of their absurdity; it was
the root of a great deal of his grave, casuistical humor. But the absurdity
was to him a real and actual absurdity; not a figment of the mind which
could be done away with by thinking differently, but an absurdity incarnated in all the circumstances, great and small, of human life. Religion
was, in other words, the whole world to him—or rather, he saw the
total sum of possible experience in terms of religion. His imagination
moves continuously within that world and does not acknowledge that
there is anything, no matter how trivial or undignified, which it does not
embrace. Accordingly, it is in its unique way a complete world, a true
though unexpected reflection of the world we know. And when Kafka
deals in it with the antinomies of religion, he is throwing light at the
same time on the deepest riddles of human life.

We must give a contingent assent to Kafka's religion, therefore, before we can understand the world of his imagination. It is a world
absolutely definite in main outline, but endlessly subtle and intricate in
its working out. At its center, and in its most remote manifestations,
lies the dogma of the incommensurability of divine and human law
which Kafka adopted from Kierkegaard. Man is incapable of apprehend-
ing the divine law, and it is possible for the divine law even to appear
immoral in his eyes: Kierkegaard founded his argument on the sacrifice
demanded by God from Abraham, which according to human standards
was arbitrary and unjust. On the other hand, it is man's duty to direct
his life in accordance with this law whose workings he cannot understand, even if all aid from Heaven should be denied him; and that is

the other side of Kafka's belief, and the dramatic foundation of his greatest work, *The Castle*. The hero sets out to mold his life completely, to the most pedantic detail, in the pattern of the divine will. He can get no acknowledgment from Heaven, he is tricked and repulsed, according to his own lights, again and again: he is not granted even his small preliminary request: an earthly vocation by which he can live honestly. Nevertheless he fights on, getting further and further from his goal; and at last when, quite exhausted by the struggle, he lies on his deathbed, word comes down from the Castle that though he has no legal right to live in the Village, the community of the faithful, he is to be permitted to live and to work there henceforth in consideration of certain auxiliary circumstances. It is a highly ironical conclusion, yet it is also a statement of faith: the hero's struggle is justified at last—not by any earthly standard, it is true, for he is finished with the world—but by the fact that he has achieved a moment of pure reconciliation with the divine will. It is in the strict sense a final victory, yet one of which, as a human being, he can make no use, for it gives him nothing but the recognition of the Castle which all his life he has been vainly trying to win. Thus even his death does not abrogate the law of the incommensurability of divine with human law, for his victory is, humanly considered, the most complete and final defeat of all.

III

The root of Kafka's peculiar humor lies in this incompatibility between the ways of Providence and the ways of man. It is a comedy of cross-purposes on a grand scale, and ranges from the most farcical to the most delicate effects. It is in the very texture of his work and can only be illustrated by showing how he manages the action of his stories. At the beginning of *The Castle*, K., the hero, is challenged by an official on his arrival at the Village, and says on the spur of the moment that he is a land-surveyor sent for by the Castle authorities. Appealed to, the Castle authorities reply that they never heard of him before, but a moment later they ring up again to say: "There's been a mistake: K. is the land-surveyor." Next morning K. sets out for the Castle, which he can see quite clearly perched on a hill and hopes to reach by an easy walk. But he finds that he never gets any nearer to it:

. . . for the street he was in, the main street of the Village, did not lead up to the Castle hill, it only made towards it and then, as if deliberately, turned aside, and although it did not lead away from the Castle it got no nearer to it either.

This kind of thing keeps happening to him over and over again. He had told a Castle official whom he met in the Village that his assistants were following on and would presently arrive. On his return from his unsuccessful walk he finds two young men, exactly alike, awaiting him, and they introduce themselves as his assistants. They are really from the Castle and their names are Arthur and Jeremiah. As K. cannot tell one from the other he decides to call them both Arthur. He commands them to ring up the Castle; immediately they both rush to the telephone, keep snatching the receiver from each other, and shout into the mouthpiece at the same time, until he has to drive them away. Next he decides to speak to the Castle himself, and having grown wary by this time, tries to pass himself off as his original assistant, Joseph. The Castle is quite complaisant and replies: "Very well; you are the old assistant Joseph." On the top of this, Barnabas, a messenger from the Castle, arrives with a letter in which K. is told that he has been engaged for the Count's service and that the authorities wish him well. As Barnabas leaves, K. rushes after him and takes his arm, hoping to get into the Castle with him unobserved in the darkness, for it is by now midnight. But Barnabas merely goes back to his own shabby home in the Village, where he lives with his parents and his two sisters. And so K. goes on, finding complaisance everywhere and making no progress at all. His first serious rebuff comes from the Village Superintendent, who is to assign him his duties. He discovers that there was some question of a land-surveyor many years before, but that there has never been any conceivable use for a land-surveyor at any time and that there is none now. In compensation he is offered the post of janitor in the Village school. A little while later, when he is suffering from a still more crushing rebuff, Barnabas brings him another letter. It runs:

> "*To the Land-Surveyor at the Bridge Inn.* The surveying work which you have carried out thus far has been appreciated by me. The work of the assistants too deserves praise. You know how to keep them at their jobs. Do not slacken in your efforts! Carry your work on to a fortunate conclusion. Any interruption would displease me. For the rest, be easy in your mind; the question of salary will presently be decided. I shall not forget you."

Not till much later in the story does K. discover that the letter from the Count purporting to engage him was an old one probably not intended for him at all, and that Barnabas is not an authorized messenger. As time goes on K.'s relations with the Castle become more and more involved, the communications he receives from it more and more questionable, and he discovers that "the reflections they give rise to are endless."

This comedy of misinterpretation, at once farcical and intellectually subtle, is, then, peculiarly characteristic of Kafka; but he also has another kind which is related to it and probably flows from it: the comedy evoked by the imperfection of all human arrangements. The janitor's job that K. was offered in compensation for his intended post is a good example. There are many curious things about it. First of all the school has no need of a janitor, and secondly it has no accommodation for one, possessing only two classrooms. Accordingly K. has to live in one of them along with his fiancée and the two assistants, and move into the other whenever the curriculum requires. He arrives very late the first night. It is the middle of winter, the stove is almost out, for the teacher has carried away the key of the woodshed. K. decides to break open the shed with a hatchet. Immediately the assistants begin to carry in huge piles of wood, and keep flinging them into the stove so quickly that the room becomes unbearably hot and everybody has to undress and lie down in his shirt. In the morning they are all awakened by the arrival of the lady teacher and the school-children.

> With Frieda's help—the assistants were of no use, lying on the floor they stared in amazement at the lady teacher and the children—K. dragged across the parallel bars and the vaulting horse, threw the blankets over them, and so constructed a little room in which one could at least get on one's clothes protected from the children's gaze . . . The assistants, who had obviously never thought of putting on their clothes, had stuck their heads through a fold of the blankets near the floor, to the great delight of the children.

(The last touch is the very quintessence of Kafka.) The humor here is the kind that rises from the contemplation of pedantically conscientious inefficiency; every action is perfectly reasonable yet, except to the actors, senselessly absurd. It is really a hackneyed music-hall type of humor, the sort we laugh at when we see a comedian frenziedly trying to do two jobs at the same time, rushing from one to the other across the whole breadth of the stage, and punctually falling each time over the same obstacle in the middle. Kafka uses it deliberately as an image of imperfection of human action. K.'s life as a janitor in a school that does not need and has no accommodation for a janitor is for him a symbol of existence. Man lives at cross-purposes and attempts impossible tasks in ludicrous situations. One of the aphorisms runs:

> His weariness is that of the gladiator after the combat; his work was the whitewashing of a corner in a state official's office.

Had Kafka described the scene, one feels that he would have put the corner beyond reach, made the brush too short, and perched the pail of whitewash where it was bound to overturn at the slightest movement. He would then have gone on to prove circumstantially that there was no other place where the pail could have been set, that if the brush had been longer it could not have been used at all, and for all this he would have such solid reasons that he would completely convince us. For, although it persistently reminds one of the knockabout comedian and the circus, his humor is also founded on the most grave and sound reasoning.

The form which Kafka's imagination takes most often is, then, that of comedy; but the originality of this comedy lies in its union with the deepest seriousness. K.'s predicaments are not only absurd; they are also desperate. The letter from the Castle telling him not to slacken in his efforts and carry on his work to a fortunate conclusion really represents a crushing defeat. The passage which follows is a good example of the way in which Kafka can combine broad comic effects with a sense of disaster.

K. only looked up from the letter when the assistants, who read far more slowly than he, gave three loud cheers at the good news and waved their lanterns. "Be quiet," he said, and to Barnabas: "There's been a misunderstanding." Barnabas did not seem to comprehend. "There's been a misunderstanding," K. repeated, and the weariness he had felt in the afternoon came over him again, the road to the schoolhouse seemed very long, and behind Barnabas he could see his whole family, and the assistants were still jostling him so closely that he had to drive them away with his elbows. . . . He could quite well have found his own way home, and better alone, indeed, than in this company. And to make matters worse one of them had wound a scarf round his neck whose free ends flapped in the wind and had several times been flung against K.'s face; it is true, the other assistant had always disengaged the scarf at once with his long, pointed, perpetually mobile fingers, but that had not made things any better. Both of them seemed to consider it an actual pleasure to be out, and the wind and the wildness of the night threw them into raptures. "Get out!" shouted K., "seeing you've come to meet me, why haven't you brought my stick? What have I now to drive you home with?" They crouched behind Barnabas, but they were not too frightened to set their lanterns on their protector's shoulders, right and left; however, he shook them off at once. "Barnabas," said K., and he felt a weight on his heart when he saw that Barnabas obviously did not understand him, that though his tunic shone beautifully while all was going well, when things became serious no help was to be found in him, but only dumb opposition, opposition against which one could not fight, for Barnabas himself was helpless, he could only smile, and that was of just as little help as the stars up there against this tempest down below. "Look what Klamm has written!" said K., holding the letter before his face. "He has been wrongly informed. I haven't done any surveying at all, and you see yourself how much the assistants are worth. And obviously too I can't interrupt work which I've never begun; I can't even excite the gentleman's displeasure, so how can I have earned his appreciation? As for being easy in my mind, I can never be that." "I'll see to it," said Barnabas, who all the time had been gazing past the letter, which he could not have read in any case, for he was holding it too close to his face. "Oh," said K., "you promise me that you'll see to it, but can I really believe you? I'm in need of a trustworthy messenger, now more than ever."

While this conversation was going on the assistants had

kept on slowly raising their heads by turns behind Barnabas's shoulders as from a trap-door, and hastily disappearing again with a soft whistle in imitation of the whistling of the wind, as if they were terrified of K.; they enjoyed themselves like this for a long time.

It is a situation made up of a number of great and small touches, serious and comic, but all, down to the last purely music-hall one, exquisitely just, and deepening by their apparent irrelevance our sense of the gravity of the defeat K. has sustained. The scene is viewed from every side, and seized simultaneously by all the faculties of the writer's mind operating in conjunction at a uniform intensity. It is objective in the only sense one can apply the word to a work of imagination: in the balance achieved by an intense employment of all the requisite powers of the writer. As pure imaginative creations K.'s scenes have this packed fullness which gives them simultaneously several meanings, one concealed beneath the other, until in a trivial or commonplace situation we find an image of some universal or mythical event such as the Fall of Man. It is in this way that Kafka's allegory works. He has been blamed for confusing two worlds; for introducing real people, living in real houses, walking through real streets, working in offices, going about earthly vocations, and then by a sudden twist making all their actions symbolical and bringing them into actual contact with emblematical figures. The answer is that this was obviously the thing he was trying to do. He was not interested in pure allegory; it could not have expressed his conception of life or his idea of man's actual moral problem. His hero does not have to walk a beaten though admittedly difficult road like Christian in *The Pilgrim's Progress,* overcoming certain set dangers, refusing certain traditional temptations, and after each victory drawing nearer to his goal. Kafka did not deny that this road existed; but he found it almost impossible to recognize. The way K. has to take is the right way on this earth, which, in the words of the aphorism I have already quoted, is stretched "just above the ground" and "seems more designed to make people stumble than to be walked upon." There are many signposts along it, but the difficulty is that they never mean what they say. One may actually be going in the wrong direction. One's ostensible victories may turn out to be defeats, while an occasional aberration may have very fortunate results: here once more we find the incommensurability of divine and human law. The strength of *The Pilgrim's Progress* lies in its directness and simplicity; it shows Christian resolutely treading out the scheme of salvation in a purely allegorical landscape.

Kafka quite clearly accepted a plan of salvation which was not so very unlike Bunyan's. But what essentially concerned him was how man could walk the way of salvation in this present confused and deceptive life, where "there are countless places of refuge" but "only one place of salvation," and where accordingly "the possibilities of salvation . . . are as numerous as the places of refuge." It is not that he did not believe in the fundamental certainties of religion, divine justice, divine grace, damnation, and salvation, for they are the very framework of the world of his imagination. The problem of which all his stories are the direct imaginative statement is how man, stationed in one dimension, can direct his life in accordance with a law belonging to another, a law whose workings he can never interpret truly, though they are always manifest to him.

IV

The mixture of realism and allegory which is Kafka's peculiar invention is accordingly perhaps the most economical and effective means that could have been found for expressing his vision of life. It is also a unique weapon of inquiry into the workings of Providence. Bunyan's allegory, though full of psychological truth, has this weakness: that it is incidentally a kind of demonstration; it provides a model for imitation by the evangelical Christian. Kafka's allegory, on the other hand, is an investigation into an endlessly intricate world, an investigation that is urgent and dramatic, for on its outcome may depend the hero's salvation. He does not question the justice of that world, for he held that, compared with divine law—even when it appears most unjust in our eyes—all human effort, no matter how noble, was in the wrong. But though he did not question it, he penetrated into its infinite mazes as no other modern writer has done. *The Castle* is a picture on a scale never attempted since the seventeenth century of the relation to God of the soul seeking salvation. Kafka enters into all the intricacies of that relation with a psychological penetration and thoroughness as great as Proust devoted to the relations between human beings. To the stages in it, moreover, he gives plastic form; they are incarnated in figures, scenes, situations, all of which have the most convincing reality. His thought in itself is endlessly subtle, but perfectly solid at the same time; for he never lost, while pursuing it into its most remote recesses, his center of reference, which was the reality of religious truth. Thus, at the heart of his work is a great, simple, yet endless thought, and all his writings are a working of it out by the light of human understanding. The attempt took him into stranger places than have been touched by any other modern novelist or psychologist, and there are scenes in his two greatest books which, though evoked with complete objectivity, are almost impossible to understand, and seem to belong to an unknown world of experience. Yet we never doubt their reality. A German critic has said finely that Kafka has a power of deducing the more real from the real, of starting from some concrete situation and sinking his thought into something which gives the impression of being still more concrete. It is this extraordinary substantiality, this sense of the almost oppressive solidity of every object, which gives his stories their strange and sometimes frightening atmosphere. His world is a sort of underground world where we feel that the force of gravity and the weight and mass of every object are far greater than in the ordinary world of the upper air. It is a world in which life itself becomes denser, and where accordingly it is almost natural for immaterial forces to assume palpable shapes. It is an image of what the actual world might be if it were subjected to some process of condensation by means of which the invisible agencies that environ man, hopes and fears, devils and angels, are forced to contract and solidify, peopling a scene which before man thought he had to himself. This probably explains the peculiarly charged and overcrowded atmosphere that fills *The Castle* and *The Trial,* giving the sensation that the hero has scarcely room to move or even to breathe. It is a nightmare atmosphere irradiated by gleams of the purest humor.

Perhaps, then, the most extraordinary thing in *The Castle* is the solidity of the metaphysical world it builds up. Throughout, the imagination follows the thought with such closeness that it is hard to say where the one ends and the other begins. Every detail is exactly worked out, yet has the shock of a discovery. The style is as plain and natural as Swift's, but it has an endless variety of inflection, and is capable of expressing with enchanting ease the subtlest shades of meaning. It can convey an overwhelming sense of approaching disaster by two simple sentences such as: "K. stepped out into the windswept street and peered into the darkness. Wild, wild weather." It can be exquisitely simple:

She drew her hand away from K., sat erect opposite him and wept without hiding her face; she held up her tear-covered face to him as if she were not weeping for herself and so had nothing to hide, but as if she were weeping for K.'s treachery and so the pain of seeing her tears was his due.

Kafka's style, simple and beautiful, was, like his peculiar kind of allegory, only the best means to the end he had in mind. His two great stories are marvellous constructions of thought and imagination working in unison, and they were made possible by his ability to say with absolute precision whatever he had to say. He was a great imaginative thinker, but a perfect artist.

The Novels

by R. O. C. Winkler

The unfamiliarity of Kafka's method as a novelist offers the literary critic an opportunity for discussing quite a wide range of subject-matter with some show of relevance. The sound critic of impeccable orthodoxy can run through his mental card-index where, somewhere among Tragedy, the Lyric, and the Epic, he will find a neglected but still serviceable dossier on the Allegory (cf. Bunyan). Those more fully equipped with modern conveniences can pass many a pleasant hour tracking to earth Kafka's castration complex or super-ego fixation. Or if everything else fails, it is always possible to analyze one of Shakespeare's plays in detail just to how what a good literary critic you are even though you can't understand Kafka.

The most obvious of the temptations that offer themselves is a discussion of Kafka's philosophy. The Kierkegaardian system of belief that was responsible for much of the form and content of Kafka's novels is sufficiently remote from contemporary English habits of thought for an account of it to give an appearance of throwing light on the novelist's apparent obscurities. And it does seem as though the Danish philosopher's conception of a religious way of life transcending human codes and sanctions was peculiarly profitable in stimulating Kafka's approach to his material. For whether or not we care to admit from a doctrinal point of view the possibility of a teleological suspension of the ethical, there can be no doubt that something of this kind is assumed whenever one asserts the universality of a work of art. The explicit moral concern of any given artist (and most have something of the sort) may be his source of strength, but what will make his work of lasting significance will be his insight into the sensible and mental reactions of the human being to everyday experience and into the problems that arise therefrom. Whether or not, therefore, Kafka was proselytizing on Kierkegaard's behalf isn't relevant to literary-critical evaluation. Our concern is with his success in recreating from a sympathetic and consistent standpoint the complexity

"The Novels," by R. O. C. Winkler. From *Scrutiny* (vol. 7, no. 3) © 1938 by R. O. C. Winkler. Reprinted by permission of the author.

of the individual problem in its wider and profounder implications. I
think it can be shown that he does this with an insight as penetrating as
that of any other novelist of our time.

The Castle was Kafka's last and greatest achievement in the novel form,
and any estimate of his significance as a novelist is bound to start from a
consideration of this apotheosis of his method. Here the trends of interest
that appear rather diversely in the earlier novels are fused to give an
account of the whole range of human experience in what seemed to
Kafka its most significant implications. The ultimate concern is religious.
In Kafka's view there is a way of life for any individual that is the right
one, and which is divinely sanctioned. So much is perhaps admitted by
most of our moral novelists; but to Kafka this fact itself constitutes a
problem of tremendous difficulty, because he believes the dichotomy between the divine and the human, the religious and the ethical, to be
absolute. Thus, though it is imperative for us to attempt to follow the
true way, it is impossible for us to succeed in doing so. This is the fundamental dilemma that Kafka believes to lie at the basis of all human
effort. He gives some insight into its nature in *Investigations of a Dog,*
where the dog-world corresponds roughly to human society and we as
humans bear something of the same relationship to the hero as the Castle
officials bear to Kafka in *The Castle.* The solution of the Dog's problems
is perfectly plain to us, yet we can see that the Dog is constitutionally
incapable of ever realizing the solution.

This fundamental problem, however, doesn't present itself to the
human mind in naked simplicity. It isn't the Puritan problem of justify-
ing one's behavior in the eyes of God alone. The dilemma is conceived of
as becoming known to us only at the ethical level; that is, it emerges as
the general problem of the individual's relation to society, and any
attempt at a solution must involve an attempt to come to terms with,
and find a place in, the social organism. We are told, and it is probably
true, that Kafka felt this problem with peculiar acuteness in virtue of his
racial isolation as a Jew and his general isolation as a consumptive; but
it is important to realize that this only made more keenly felt a difficulty
that is implicit in any attempt as social organization, and one that has
manifested itself particularly in recent years as a result of the centrifugal
tendencies of modern civilization. In *"He," Notes from the Year 1920,*
Kafka writes:

> He was once part of a monumental group. Round some elevated figure
> or other in the center were ranged in carefully thought-out order sym-
> bolical images of the military caste, the arts, the sciences, the handicrafts.
> He was one of those many figures. Now the group is long since dispersed,
> or at least He has left it and makes his way through life alone. He no

longer has even his old vocation, indeed He has forgotten what he once represented. Probably it is this very forgetting that gives rise to a certain melancholy, uncertainty, unrest, a certain longing for vanished ages, darkening the present. And yet this longing is an essential element in human effort, perhaps indeed human effort itself.

One has only to run one's mind over the more significant literature of Kafka's generation, from *St. Mawr* and *The Waste Land* to *Ulysses* and *Manhattan Transfer* to realize how prominent a part this view of modern European civilization has played in determining the artist's attitude to his material. Preoccupation with this problem—the problem presented by the corruption, not of the individual as such, but of the interhuman relationships that give him significance as a member of civilized society —recurs throughout Kafka's work, and is realized most effectively in his short story, *The Hunger-Artist.* Its more positive aspects are persistent throughout *The Castle,* where the hero's whole efforts are directed immediately towards an attempt to establish himself in a home and a job, and to become a member of the village community—to come to terms, in fact, with society.

Kafka's particularization of the teleological problem doesn't stop at the social level, however. Just as the attempt to follow the religious way of life is seen as a social problem, so the social problem is in its turn seen as one that appears in terms of individual human relationships. The complexity of relationship that exists between the individual and the undiscoverable way of life emerges as the complexity of the relationships between the hero and the other characters in Kafka's novels. In this his method isn't essentially different from that of most other novelists; the difference lies in that, in his treatment of interhuman relationships, Kafka's concern is always for their more general implications, their significance for the social, and ultimately for the religious, problem, and the framework and properties of the novels are constructed with this consideration in mind. But just for this reason he is scrupulously careful in presenting even the minutest detail relating to any given situation, so that the complexity never becomes confusion, and the nature and extent of the subtlety and delicacy of the network of relationships are always exactly determined at any given point. His language maintains an almost scientific lucidity, and there is an almost complete absence of explicit figures of speech in his prose. His eye is always on the object, noting carefully details like change of tone in a person's voice, whether a person is sitting or standing, and even what he is wearing—all such points are noted with a view to objectifying the exact relationship between two people. Explicit comment is rarely offered by the author; the implications of every detail are allowed to speak for themselves in creating the atmospheric tension that arises as soon as two people enter one another's sphere of consciousness, and the detailed precision with which the shifts and changes in that tension are traced invests them with a constant sense of apocalyptic significance; so that sudden shifts into the physical are quite in keeping with the whole effect:

> For a moment K. thought that all of them, Schwarzer, the peasants, the landlord and the landlady, were going to fall on him in a body, and to escape at least the first shock of their assault he crawled right underneath the blanket. [*The Castle,* Definitive Edition, p. 15.]

The effect of this passage is to crystallize the whole emotional atmosphere when it is discovered that K. has no right in the village and has lied about it in the bargain, and the explicit physical action of crawling underneath the blanket, though obviously useless as a protective measure, serves to epitomize K.'s emotional reaction to this atmosphere.

The basis of Kafka's method thus lies in the creation of a complex and continually changing dramatic situation subsisting mainly in the relation between the hero and the other characters. Where the prose is not concerned with defining some element in an interhuman relationship, either external or introspective, but with describing the hero's situation purely objectively, it frequently becomes itself dramatic in movement:

> *So ging er wieder vorwärts, aber es war ein langer Weg. Die Strasse nämlich, diese Hauptstrasse des Dorfes, führte nicht zum Schlossberg, sie führte nur nahe heran, dann aber, wie absichtlich, bog sie ab, und wenn sie sich auch vom Schloss nicht entfernte, so kam sie ihm doch auch nicht näher. (Das Schloss,* New York, 1946, p. 21.)

> So he resumed his walk, but the way proved long. For the street he was in, the main street of the village, did not lead up to the Castle hill, it only made towards it and then, as if deliberately, turned aside, and though it did not lead away from the Castle it got no nearer to it either.

The effect of the prose here is to produce the sense of physical effort appropriate to the situation. The short phrases and the jerky movement of the sentence suggest the feeling of frustrated effort that K. experienced, striving to get nearer the Castle, but repeatedly being prevented. The end of the sentence gives us a closer view of the process: the movement forward—"*sie führte nur nahe heran,*" the pause—"*dann aber,*" the moment of suspense—hanging on the tortuous syllables of "wie absichtlich," then the sudden recoil, like a spring snapping back into place—"*bog sie ab,*" then the ensuing sense of disappointment and disillusion, embodied in the flat phrasing "*so kam sie ihm doch auch nicht näher.*" One is reminded of the similar passage in Donne's third Satyre in more ways than one.

It is necessary to insist on this fusion of the mental with the physical in Kafka's work for two reasons. In the first place, it is the basis of his allegorical method. The whole of his hero's experience—whether spiritual, mental, emotional, or physical—is regarded as absolutely continuous, and the distinctions that for the sake of exposition I have drawn between the religious, the social, and the individual levels simply do not exist in the actual writing. The objectification of emotional experience into physical that I have noted emerges in the large as the concrete visualization of the individual's sense of the wider issues of existence in terms of the institutions and officials that characterize his novels and stories. Secondly, it is this preoccupation with the concrete and the physical that forces itself first on the reader's attention, and the remoter implications of the hopeless struggle are realized only over a wide area; the stress, that is, is on the struggle and not on the hopelessness, and the preoccupation with this struggle in the most immediate sense engages the reader's emotional energies, directs and disciplines them, and offers him a positive interest amid what would in abstraction be described as a philosophy of pessimism.

Cogent criticism of Kafka's work is bound to direct the reader's attention to *The Castle,* and it is more important that he should have before him in approaching *America* such general considerations as I have outlined above rather than a "placing" of the novel under review that would leave him with no conception of Kafka's importance as a novelist. Nor is this approach of no immediate relevance, because those standards by which *The Castle* is appraised must also be referred to in finding the two earlier novels of less importance. In *The Trial*—which in point of time comes between *America* and *The Castle*—the religious considerations which are the implicit ultimate in the later novel predominate, and it is the dichotomy between the actual true way and our conception of the true way that is insisted on, with the result that the unity and continuity of method isn't here present. In *America* this preoccupation with teleological considerations doesn't intrude at the expense of more immediate interests, not because, as in *The Castle,* it has been completely assimilated to those interests, but simply because religious considerations haven't yet become so pressing to the author. Although the novel has the same purposive air of endless pilgrimage about it, the purposiveness is not insisted upon, and the light-hearted symbolization of spiritual salvation in the incomplete last chapter is entirely in keeping with the implicit general assumption that "it will all come right in the end"—an assumption that allows the whole question to be a less constant concern. The disruptive effect of *The Trial* is thus avoided, as the general organization at the more immediate levels—what I have for convenience called the social and personal levels—is complete. With this source of emotional pressure much diminished, the whole texture of the novel is much looser and the effects less concentrated, though the method is the same.

The hero, Karl, is expelled from his habitual environment for a venial sexual offense, and makes his acquaintance with a new order of things, first on the liner in which he leaves Europe, and then in America itself. In the liner we find that same highly organized, incomprehensible hierarchy of officials that appears in the later novels, and they serve much the same function of objectifying the individual's sense of human society, both locally and generally, as a complex organization the nature of whose bonds he can scarcely comprehend. Kafka gives his account in terms of an encounter between Karl and the captain and officers of the ship, and he uses to the full his powers of expressing the interaction of human personality in order to achieve his effect. American civilization later plays a similar function in the hero's life, and Kafka makes clear that full participation in community life is something to which there is no golden road. As in *The Castle,* his attempts to achieve this meet with the more *real* success the less ambitious they become. Hobnobbing with social organization at its most sophisticated proves a complete failure: as soon as its assistance is required in quite a trivial matter in the process of living, it lets him down completely. Then Karl becomes one of the time-serving bellhops of the social organism with which we are all familiar (Kafka, of course, makes him a real bellhop in a big hotel), and seems to have achieved some real success in establishing himself in a satisfactory way of life; but when the crucial moment comes, his second position proves of little more value than the first. So he sinks lower and lower in society, coming closer and closer to grips with the realities of the problem that arises from being a member of a complex civilization, until finally ("finally" in a purely relative sense; since the novel is not only incomplete but endless, there can be no finality) he is submitted to all sorts of indignities at the hands of the mistress of a ruffianly tramp, and at last approaches some degree of the awareness of his problem which is the asymptote to success of solution. The technique is less accomplished than that of *The Castle* because of the sense of unrealized possibilities that indicates the author's incomplete grasp of his material; yet the achievement is comparable, and in a final estimate it would probably have to be ranked as Kafka's second greatest work; because a final estimate of Kafka's work would have to take account of limitations which didn't seem relevant to a short review.

Such an estimate would, of course, rest upon the German texts. But

English readers have been most unusually lucky in having translators who have been at such pains to render their original not only accurately, but with sympathetic attention to details of style and expression. It seems to me that in the future Mr. and Mrs. Muir's translation will stand as a model for any others who undertake the thankless job of rendering a German novelist into English.

The Metamorphosis

by Johannes Pfeiffer

Kafka's story *The Metamorphosis* is a parabolic story in the sense that what is narrated affords glimpses of a background of meaning which gives immeasurable depth to all that takes place. But since we are concerned here with a work of creative literature, this does not imply that the point of departure is some abstract thought which is subsequently illustrated by a manifest event and could be extracted from that event; rather, the significance is encountered from the outset in the medium of a pictorial reality which flashes on our brooding imagination with the force of something seen in a vision.

//To begin with the composition: the story is arranged in three sections of roughly equal length. Between the first and the second section there is an interval of a day, between the second and the third a longer and indefinite period. Each of these three sections culminates in a catastrophe which increases in intensity each time. The first, brought about by the arrival of the chief clerk, ends with the father using his stick and newspaper to drive the monster his son has become back into his room; the second, set in motion by the clearing out of the furniture, ends with the brutal bombardment of the son with apples; the third, occasioned by the sister's violin-playing, ends with the voluntary withdrawal. The first catastrophe leads to a "heavy, swooning sleep"; the second, to a swoon and a dangerous injury; the third, to death.//

This balanced composition has a certain correspondence in the exactness with which the room is imagined and in a kind of "magic realism," whereby objects are presented with such a compact wealth of detail and such sober pithiness that they are constantly turned into something unreal or more than real. The metamorphosis is accomplished with relentless consistency in the mode of presentation itself, the bodily nature of the monster being grasped from within, while the outside world is built

"The Metamorphosis," by Johannes Pfeiffer constitutes the third portion of his research on "Dichterische Wirklichkeit und weltanschauliche Wahrheit, erlautert an Novellen von Hans Grimm, Thomas Mann und Franz Kafka," in his book, *Die D chterische Wirklichkeit. Versuche uber Wesen und Wahrheit der Dichtung* (Richard Meiner Verlag 1962). Reprinted by permission of Vandenhoeck & Ruprecht.

up entirely from that embodiment. Slowly Gregor's room emerges into view: the table with the textile samples laid out on it, and the picture above; the window looking on to the narrow street, at first enveloped in the morning mist in such a way that later, when it has become brighter, the street is seen to be terminated by "a section of the endlessly long, dark gray building opposite—it was a hospital—abruptly punctuated by its row of regular windows," the alarm-clock on the chest-of-drawers, the door near the head of the bed, the two side-doors to left and right. Later, when there is a ring at the door of the flat, and the maid goes "with a firm tread" to open it, a first vague picture of the rooms adjoining is given. Then the carpet lying in Gregor's room; the heard presence of the neighboring rooms; the arm-chair with which Gregor shuffles himself to the door. After the door is opened, a glimpse of the next room: the table laid for breakfast, Gregor's photograph on the wall opposite; a glimpse, through the door leading to the outside room, of the open door to the flat, and beyond this the landing "and the beginning of the stairs going down." Later, the banisters which the chief clerk clasps, and the indirectly presented staircase, when the chief clerk jumps down several stairs at once and his yell resounds up and down every flight; the window thrust open on the other side by the mother, the draught between the street and the staircase, the curtains flying up, the newspapers flapping on the table; finally the door which is too narrow to crawl back through, and whose other leaf the father does not think to open. All this has an oppressively suggestive spatial reality, never being portrayed once and for all as a finished picture, but emerging piece by piece as the events proceed—and moreover, emerging only as it is seen from the point of view of the man in his metamorphosed shape.

"As Gregor Samsa awoke one morning from uneasy dreams, he found himself in his bed." With this sentence the story begins as though it were a matter of a normal awakening; and when in the development of the same sentence the decisive turn follows, this also is given with sober matter-of-factness: "transformed into a gigantic insect." The unassumingness with which the weird fact is mentioned is later emphasized, in the words:

> Gregor tried to suppose to himself that something like what had happened to him today might some day happen to the chief clerk; one really could not deny that it was possible.

At the beginning of the second paragraph, however, a clear definition preserves the characteristics of completely everyday reality. " 'What has happened to me?' he thought. It was no dream."

But an essential feature of the inward process is first of all the persistent attempts of the suffering man to act as though it were all a mere question of indisposition, from which he has to return to his customary activities. Cut off by this mysterious transformation from all community with other men, he yet does not truly realize his new position in all its gravity; his thoughts continue to run on in the same groove for the time being:

> He remembered that often enough in bed he had felt small aches and pains, probably caused by awkward postures, which had proved purely imaginary once he had got up, and he looked forward eagerly to seeing this morning's delusions gradually fade away. That the change in his voice was nothing but the precursor of a severe chill, a standing ailment of commercial travellers, he had not the least possible doubt.

But this extenuating attempt at self-pacification is combated by an in-stinctive clear-sightedness which makes him see his true position in all its inescapable actuality. He, whom the others no longer understand, al-though he himself can still understand them well enough, is forced to see himself left more and more to his own devices, and irresistibly growing more and more into his new rôle. While the others look after him at the beginning and try to keep in touch with him, in the course of time their alienation—and therewith their indifference—becomes greater and greater. Whereas at the beginning his sister chooses his food with love and care, later she merely:

> . . . pushed into his room with her foot any food that was available, and in the evening cleared it out again with one sweep of the broom, heedless of whether it had been tasted, or—as most frequently happened —left untouched.

Whereas in the beginning the room is thoroughly cleaned, later the clean-ing can scarcely be done fast enough, so that the dirt gradually gets out of control. And finally the room is merely used as a lumber-room where anything that is an obstruction in the other rooms is shoved in or thrown away.

After the scene with the lodgers, Gregor is referred to only as the "monster," to be got rid of in one way or another. The pronoun "it" replaces "he" and "him." What the charwoman says and does after Gregor's death is fundamentally what they all think, except that in her robust way she says it with neither shame nor inhibitions. She is promptly dismissed for this, of course, since the family feels its own secret impulses laid bare by her conduct, just as earlier its bad conscience turned into a forced attitude of pride in confronting the lodgers. When at the end, the story opens up for the first time into the outside world, and Gregor's relations take a ride into the country, we see symbolically how life turns away from the burdensome interruption and returns with relief to its vulgar self-affirmation: "And it was like a confirmation of their new dreams and excellent intentions that at the end of their journey their daughter sprang to her feet first and stretched her young body"—a conclusion of merciless, not to say cynical, coldness which seems to leave us in a region completely undefined and undefinable.

Leaving out of consideration the last five pages [of the story], all events are seen with a quite dictatorial one-sidedness through the eyes of Gregor —the main character who dominates everything.[1] Any attempt to disregard this fact, so vital for the meaning of the whole story, and to transfer the center of gravity to the family, disturbed and distracted by Gregor's transformation, amounts to arbitrary distortion. As far as the remaining figures are concerned, however, they are grouped round Gregor in such a way that they can be arranged in degrees of increasing distortion. While the mother is the only one whose sympathy remains reliable, for all her helpless weakness, even the sister has a certain ambivalence in that she performs her task—attending her transformed brother—not without some childlike pride and childlike defiance, and in that her genuine desire to help and her genuine sense of responsibility become more and more of a pose which satisfies her secret wish for recognition or even her will to dominate. The father, for his part, reveals himself even more clearly in that, on the one hand, he really begins to come back to life from the moment he has to take a share in maintaining the family himself, and in doing so seeks to give himself a swollen authority, while on the other hand he increasingly shows how much he suffers from his son's failure— apart from the fact that the pressure of the situation unmasks traits of frightening brutality. The secondary figures also show an arrangement according to the degree of distortion: while the chief clerk, for all the grotesque sharpness of delineation, is half realistically portrayed as the type of place-hunter who has to be flattered, the servant who later replaces the dismissed housemaid is simplified with the clarity of a woodcut as "a gigantic bony charwoman with white hair flying round her head," and later as "this old widow, whose strong bony frame had enabled her to survive the worst a long life could offer." The three lodgers appear as real caricatures: "these serious gentlemen," every one of them with a

---

[1] Friedrich Beissner, in two perceptive lectures ("*Der Erzähler Franz Kafka,*" Stuttgart 1952, and "*Kafka der Dichter,*" Stuttgart 1958), has brought out particularly clearly what he calls the "uniqueness of meaning" of Kafka's narrative style, defining it more precisely as the one-sided as well as "unitive" point of view of a narrator who has transformed himself into the main character and apparently never has more knowledge than the similarly transformed reader.

full beard, puppet-like in their behavior whether they are eating, or smoking, or complaining, or—finally—when they are leaving the flat.

Since the strict reticence and close-lipped equanimity of the narrative method refrains from giving any explicit hint, there is no allusive reference whatever to a hidden background that might give meaning to the course of events presented. If we attempt to inquire cautiously after this background meaning in all its transrational complexity of levels, we may be afforded a hint by the passage in which it is said, with reference to Gregor's attraction towards his sister's violin-playing: "Was he an animal, when music had such an effect upon him? He felt as if the way were opening before him to the unknown nourishment he craved." That music is a sign of the unknown and unknowable to which the longing for liberation and salvation is directed—this accords with Wilhelm Emrich's well-documented perception that in Kafka's work the true and essential always appears as sound and singing, melody and voice.[2] And if we take also into consideration the following diary-note by Kafka, we have a lightning glimpse into the hidden background of his story: "Beyond a certain point there is no return. This point has to be reached."

Let us reflect on this. The metamorphosed Gregor Samsa, having dropped out of the system of coordinates of normal existence, having been irrevocably removed from everything that constitutes life, exhausts himself in constantly renewed efforts to retain a connection with this existence until he gradually resigns himself and finally perishes. Since he regards the metamorphosis, as—so to speak—a mere occupational injury, a misfortune, the possibility implied in his yearning for some unknown sustenance remains uncomprehended—the possibility, that is, of breaking through the constraint of living, of escaping the imprisonment in existence which is our lot, of recognizing the original guilt of this involvement in existence and of thereby becoming free, free to return into essential, true, absolute Being. As always in Kafka the way out remains blocked; it is only from a great distance, and only by devious paths that there falls a ray of grace—a grace dimly perceived as a possibility—upon the hueless blind alley of this seemingly bewitched, this unredeemed world. In other terms, the riddle of the man cut off from society shimmers indeterminably, like the reflections on shot silk, between damnation and grace. Through the simile of an extreme situation man realizes the

---

[2] I refer here to Emrich's essay, "Franz Kafka," in the collection of essays *Deutsche Literatur in 20. Jahrhundert*, edited by Hermann Friedmann and Otto Mann (Heidelberg, 1954). The point elucidated by Emrich here with complete cogency, as the basic event in Kafka's novels and stories, is the way in which man is challenged by a radical self-estrangement to perform something like an absolute self-justification. Emrich's comprehensive monograph, *Franz Kafka* (Bonn, 1958), also contains a section on "The Insect in the Story *The Metamorphosis*."

depth of his indissoluble loneliness, a loneliness which has its basis in
the fact that he does not belong to this security-minded illusion of life,
with its superficial aims and its unreal distractions, nor to this threadbare
activity, but to the mystery of a final vocation which points past all
provisional standards towards the "other world"—towards the uncon-
ditionally infinite. The basic tension implied in all this was adumbrated
by Kafka in two complementary and contradictory utterances: "Life is
a continual distraction which does not even allow us to reflect on that
from which we are distracted"; and, on the other hand:

> One of the first signs of the beginnings of understanding is the wish to
> die. This life seems unbearable, another unattainable. One is no longer
> ashamed of wanting to die; one asks to be moved from the old cell, which
> one hates, to a new one, which one will only in time come to hate. In this
> there is also a residue of belief that during the move the master will chance
> to come along the corridor, look at the prisoner and say: "This man is
> not to be locked up again. He is to come to me." [3]

To make a summary review, Kafka's story /The Metamorphosis con-
jures up a vision of a man cut off from society/radically estranged from
it, in such a way that the distantly sensed door into the open remains
blocked, while the presentation in its astringent consistency, dispensing
with all forms of instructive signposts, nevertheless indirectly gives us a
feeling of the hidden background which gives meaning to the whole.
This would remove at once one objection that still has constantly to
be reckoned with, namely the objection that such a work is completely
"negative" and "pessimistic." For what do "negative" and "pessimistic"
mean, when it is a question of a work of art and the valid shaping of an
original insight into essentials? That very fact implies something like a
spiritual conquest of the world, something that is surely thoroughly
positive. And what is the use of such "all-too-human" standpoints, completely tied to our shortsighted sensual need for meaning, or desires in
life, when it is a question of what will give to our existence truth and
reality, and thereby content and direction?

That is more or less what one might say about Kafka's story so long
as it is viewed entirely from within itself, in pursuance of an autonomous
understanding of the world—in other words, so long as it is interpreted

---

[3] Erich Heller, in "The World of Franz Kafka" [see p. 99ff], has attempted to show
—in opposition to Max Brod's religious-allegorical interpretation, and with a precise-
ness that perhaps also goes too far in its intellectually rigid method of deciphering
—that Kafka's relation to the world can best be defined as Gnostic-Manichean, in the
sense that the Absolute here, as a pure origin of Being, is just as powerless in its
transcendent remoteness as it is inaccessible, whereas the earthly creation is basically
dreary and corrupt.

on grounds that are or ought to be common to us all. For a mature, critical man, anything like honest objectivity is, after all, bound up with a lively consciousness of the relative self-determination and autonomy of the media by which we see the world. Any way of looking at things that makes direct demands and expectations from a work of art—in the name, say, of Christian faith—tends to make the faith into a totalitarian ideology and, imperceptibly yet irresistibly, to infect the work of art with a regard for the mere subject-matter in itself that has little to do with literature. But though we must, especially today, be on our guard in this respect, the self-determination and autonomy we certainly have to recognize is nevertheless only relative, which is to say that for anyone who has been gripped by the Christian message it is subordinate to a claim that at once sets a seal on and limits to all claims made within this world. In this sense, then, we are not only justified, but compelled to put the concluding question: what are we to say to a work of creative art such as Kafka's if we are convinced of the kernel of truth in the Gospel, with all the effort and discipline that involves in every department of our lives? We must surely always give at least our assent wherever a human situation, credibly presented in a consistent and necessary shape, reveals the deep cleft which runs through all our activities in this fallen world, and which makes it so untrue and so unreal. Further, anyone who thinks in the spirit of the Cross will come to see truth and reality also—and above all—at that frontier where, through the desperation and desolation of a life that has stumbled into an impasse, there is a sight of the hidden light for which we all stretch out our hands and which we can never reach of our own strength.

On the other hand, it is true, we must also ask whether the way in which Kafka narrates, the way in which he carries everything to extremes, does not contain after all a factor which can scarcely be adequately grasped through the visionary significance of the whole. We must ask whether we have not here a form of artistry which is no longer stimulated by a need for truth, anxious for salvation, but is interested only in the success of an experiment in portrayal and therewith constantly comes to serve the needs of a hidden desire for torment. Such a subsequent reservation must disturb the self-completeness of the interpretation, yet to suppress it would be insincere.

Kafka the Writer

by Ronald Gray

I remember looking with interest once at a newspaper article under the headline, "Kafka in Iraq," not knowing that he had ever been there or that his works were read in that country. The intention of the sub-editor who put the headline in, I discovered, was to give a hint of gruesome nightmares and chaos which the recent revolution had brought about. The name was enough. And in fact the name can suggest by its sound alone something grim and oppressive. Kafka himself pointed out, ruefully, that it comes from the Czech word *Kavka,* a black daw, a bird of ill-omen. There is a sort of menace about it, a foreboding of evil which his works do a great deal to justify.

He is not, however, a writer of horror stories pure and simple. Only a small proportion of his writings portray hideous scenes after the fashion of Edgar Allan Poe, with whom he has some affinity. (A comparison of *The Penal Colony* with *The Pit and the Pendulum* would show Kafka's sober confrontation with the meaning of suffering in stark contrast to the hysterical horror-mongering of Poe's tale.) More often, he conveys a sense of insidious, indefatigable evil sapping silently all the time at the roots of human existence. *The Trial* is the story of a war of attrition conducted by a secret court against a man's demand for justice. *The Castle* relates the attempt of a man to reach some knowledge of truth about himself, an attempt which seems to be frustrated at every turn by those who by all accounts are the very guardians of truth. Neither novel has much in the way of physical horror; nothing, in fact, except the flogging-scene, and the execution of the hero in the last pages of *The Trial.* The oppressive sense that comes from both of them is more a matter of the mind.

Josef K. searches continually for some clue to the guilt of which the secret court accuses him: he is executed, still in ignorance. His namesake K. (the initial only is used, though it must recall Kafka) never learns from the equally secretive Castle—the seat of government for the whole world in which he lives—what his role is to be, whether he is needed, whether any useful work is allotted to him. There is a sense of guilt everywhere, though it is never clear to what the guilt refers; there is a sense of futility, sometimes even of vindictiveness, not merely in a few in-

61

dividual scenes but as inherent qualities in the whole nature of things. And it is this which makes the horror of Kafka more than the aesthetic thrill which it is in Poe. He does not really belong with Poe at all, but with a poet like Rimbaud who lived his Season in Hell and named it for what it was. But where Rimbaud had given up poetry completely by the time he was twenty, Kafka went on for the whole of his forty-odd years in the same condition. He was "as old as the Wandering Jew," as he put it himself,[1] never at rest, always swept along like the hunter Gracchus in one of his stories, by the winds "in the lowest regions of death." It was not a season in hell but a whole lifetime. Yet the paradox remains, that like many men and women of religion who have believed themselves damned,[2] Kafka was all the more strongly convinced of the supremacy and perfection of heaven. "If it were conceivable," wrote Simone Weil, "that in obeying God one should bring about one's own damnation, whilst in disobeying him one could be saved, I should still choose the way of obedience," [3] and very similar thoughts might be quoted from St. Francis of Sales, St. Catherine of Siena, and St. Ignatius Loyola.[4] There is a sense in which Kafka, despite his reticence in expressing any religious beliefs, and his isolation from all community of worship, is linked with such experiences and affirmations as these. He differs, however, in that it was not through the traditional exercises of prayer but through writing that he ventured.

While he was alive, Kafka published only a few short stories, making a volume of about three hundred pages in all. For the rest—hundreds of fragments, several uncompleted novels—he gave instructions, which were disregarded, that they should be burned (and that none of his work should be re-issued). Today, when almost every word he wrote has been published, he is known in almost every part of the non-Communist world. And there seems to be some justification for the judgment of W. H. Auden: "Had one to name the author who comes nearest to bearing the same kind of relation to our age as Dante, Shakespeare, and Goethe bore to theirs, Kafka is the first one would think of." [5] This sense of frustration, uncertainty, aimlessness, foreboding, is widespread among artists and intellectuals at least. And this is not a matter that can be cured by denunciations or exhortations to artists, poets, dramatists, to provide more edifying material. An artist paints or writes as he must, not as he ought, and if his vision becomes fragmentary, frustrating, menacing, here is a sign of the times, not a didactic lesson.

[1] G. Janouch, *Conversations with Kafka* (London, 1953), p. 90.
[2] See Kafka's diaries.
[3] Weil, *Waiting on God* (London, 1951), p. 4.
[4] See R. Knox, *Enthusiasm* (Oxford, 1950), p. 255.
[5] Quoted in Angel Flores, *The Kafka Problem*, p. 6.

It is because I believe this view of the artist to be true, and possibly fruitful, that I have chosen to consider Kafka chiefly as a writer. To write, in Kafka's sense, was to be open completely to every impression, not rejecting the worst that might be suggested to him, or the best, but setting it all down faithfully. "Open up," he wrote in his diary, "let the Man come out." [6] It was because he so seldom felt that the whole man had in fact come out that he was dissatisfied with the greater part of his work, and no doubt for this reason that he gave instructions for it to be burned. What made this opening up particularly difficult and painful for him was that his sense of evil was acute, while his belief in good was so equally intense that the two seemed irreconcilable in the limits of one personality. "The world can be regarded as good only from the place at which it was created, for only there was it said: 'And behold, it was good' . . . ." [7] This is the root of Kafka's dilemma, that not to see the world as good is to realize his guilt acutely, while to pretend to see it as good is to be guilty of hubris. As he wrote elsewhere, "Evil knows of good, but good does not know of evil" [8]—true goodness sees no division, while evil is constantly aware of it. This dilemma Kafka could not escape.

By nature, upbringing, and environment he was distrustful, isolated, prone to see the worst. The neurotic element in his work is not trivial. A Jew, he was cut off from the Germans whose language he spoke. Living in Prague, he counted as a German, and was thus cut off from the Czechs who formed the main population of the country. Physically weak, he felt himself odd man out in his family of healthy giants, and his father was at one and the same time an almost godlike authority and an object of contempt. There was no certainty in his world: he was not an orthodox Jew, or a German of either the Austro-Hungarian or the Wilhelmine Empire, or a native Czech, or even an accepted son in his own family. To be true to his own nature—one aspect of this opening up—thus meant to yield himself to the desperation which such a position in life brought with it. His normal sequences of thought were full of it—nothing was to be trusted, there was nobody to turn to, suicide often seemed the only solution. And this desperation had to find its expression in his writing—to have suppressed it would have made a sentimentalist of him: the false note would have been detectable at once. Equally, however, he was convinced that there was that point of view from which the whole world could be seen as good. This was not a matter of hope only, it was a conviction which comes through as powerfully as anything else in his writings. The whole man, completely open to experience, would be not the

[6] *The Diaries of Franz Kafka.*
[7] *Wedding Preparations,* p. 109.
[8] *Diaries.*

despairing man whom we are perhaps too ready to see in Kafka, but the
one in whom the complete affirmation would be made. He keeps himself going when his life becomes almost completely unbearable—it is hard
to think of any book so painful to read as Kafka's diaries—with thoughts
like this: "Let the iron rays penetrate you, glide along in the water that
is sweeping you away, but stay like that, and wait, erect, till the sun comes
streaming suddenly, endlessly in." [9] This would be staying true to his
experience, while at the same time maintaining his conviction that what
he saw could still be illuminated by an entirely different source of light.
And it could be done, he believed, through his writing, which he thought
of on at least one occasion as a form of prayer. In the only form of writing
he was willing to acknowledge for himself, when the whole man came
out, he foresaw the possibility of "raising the world into the pure, the
true, the immutable." [10] The real essence of human nature, as he said at
another time, could only be loved.[11]

An illustration is worth a lot of words. Here is a short story, not so
much as that, a vignette, two sentences, where Kafka's mind can be seen
working—not producing the miraculous result he looked for, perhaps,
but showing at least where he starts from. It is called "Up in the Gallery,"
and describes a young man looking down at a circus-ring: there is something tragic about it, and at the same time a kind of wry humor.

> If some frail, consumptive equestrienne in the circus were to be urged
> round and round on an undulating horse for months on end without re-
> spite by a ruthless, whip-flourishing ringmaster, before an insatiable public,
> whizzing along on her horse, throwing kisses, swaying from the waist, and
> if this performance were likely to continue in the infinite perspective of a
> drab future to the unceasing roar of the orchestra and hum of the venti-
> lators, accompanied by ebbing and renewed swelling bursts of applause
> which are really steam-hammers—then, perhaps, a young visitor to the
> gallery might race down the long stairs through all the circles, rush into
> the ring, and yell: "Stop!" against the fanfares of the orchestra still play-
> ing the appropriate music.
>
> But since that is not so; a lovely lady, pink and white, floats in between
> the curtains, which proud lackeys open before her; the ringmaster,
> deferentially catching her eye, comes towards her breathing animal de-
> votion; tenderly lifts her up on the dapple-gray, as if she were his own
> most precious granddaughter about to start on a dangerous journey; can-
> not make up his mind to give the signal with his whip, finally masters

[9] *Diaries,* 1914-1923, p. 36.
[10] *Diaries,* 1914-1923, p. 187.
[11] *Wedding Preparations,* p. 44.

himself enough to crack the whip loudly; runs along beside the horse, openmouthed; follows with a sharp eye the leaps taken by its rider; finds her artistic skill almost beyond belief; calls to her with English shouts of warning; angrily exhorts the grooms who hold the hoops to be most closely attentive; before the great somersault lifts up his arms and implores the orchestra to be silent; finally lifts the little one down from her trembling horse, kisses her on both cheeks and finds that all the ovation she gets from the audience is barely sufficient; while she herself, supported by him, right up on the tips of her toes, in a cloud of dust, with outstretched arms and small head thrown back, invites the whole circus to share her triumph—since that is so, the visitor to the gallery lays his face on the rail before him and, sinking into the closing march as in a heavy dream, weeps without knowing it.[12]

There is often a temptation to allegorize Kafka, but I do not think it is a strong temptation here. You can say, though, that the situation has rather more general implications than appear on the surface. If only there were something so clearly wrong that the young man had a great opportunity to do something about it. How dramatic it would be. Even the orchestra would recognize that right was on his side, and its fanfares would confirm him in his moment of victorious denunciation. But that is not how it is. There is no thoroughgoing viciousness about it, the ringmaster goes out of his way to show his anxiety and watchfulness, the whole act seems to be there in order to make people happy, and the rider herself invites the audience to share this happiness with her. There can be no protest in circumstances like these. Yet there is after all a falsity about the second scene. It is exaggerated, every action laid on for effect; in its way it is as much in need of a protest as the scene in the first sentence. What prevents the protest is the common assent to it, the tumultuous applause of the audience, the show of devotion, admiration, gentle attentiveness, love. Everyone would like all this to be true, and to deny its truth, point out its hypocrisy, would be to exclude yourself from the companionship of the rest. So no protest comes. But the sense of unreality shows itself in the young man as he lays his face on the parapet and weeps. He is quite unselfconscious about it—not realizing that he is weeping—and so probably not merely regretting his inability to be the center of a grand demonstration. But what else is there for him except grief?

At the same time, the keynote of the piece is not relentlessly tragic. It has more the feeling of a caricature-cartoon, especially in the way the young man is shown rushing down the long stairway, in the way the word "Stop!" rings out at the climax of the first sentence, or in the expressions of self-subdual, deference and amazement which pass in such grotesque profusion over the ringmaster's face. The picture of the ringmaster is indeed rather like something out of Dickens, for whom Kafka had a particular liking. There is the same kind of exaggeration revealing insincerity, and at least a kindred kind of humor in the portraying of it. There is not, however, as there is in Dickens, either any glimpse of generosity in the characters themselves, or any note of condescension. It is a more detached attitude in every respect. Compare for instance this passage describing Mr. Sleary's circus-company in *Hard Times:*

> There were two or three handsome young women among them, with their two or three husbands, and their two or three mothers, and their eight or nine little children, who did the fairy business when required. The father of one of the families was in the habit of balancing the father of another of the families on the top of a great pole; the father of a third family often made a pyramid of both those fathers, with Master Kidderminster for the apex, and himself for the base; all the fathers could dance upon rolling casks, stand upon bottles, catch knives and balls, twirl handbasins, ride upon anything, jump over everything, and stick at nothing. . . . They all assumed to be mighty rakish and knowing, they were not very tidy in their private dresses, they were not at all orderly in their domestic arrangements, and the combined literature of the whole company would have produced but a poor letter on any subject. Yet there was a remarkable gentleness and childishness about these people, a special inaptitude for any kind of sharp practice, and an untiring readiness to help and pity one another, deserving often of as much respect, and always of as much generous construction, as the everyday virtues of any class of people in the world.
>
> Last of all appeared Mr. Sleary: a stout man as already mentioned, with one fixed eye, and one loose eye, a voice (if it can be called so) like the efforts of a broken old pair of bellows, a flabby surface, and a muddled head which was never sober and never drunk.

Dickens is fond of these people, whom he wants to set off against the conventional uprightness of the Gradgrinds and the Bounderbys, but he is also patronizing, and the one quality seems a part of the other. Despite his admiration, he writes playfully of the circus company as though they were in some ways curious dolls, capable of the most astonishing feats, considering their stature. There is something elfish or fairy-like rather than human about them, even in their generosity and kindness, and this, perhaps, is what makes them so satisfying and amusing. Kafka, on the other hand, is not concerned with the "everyday virtues of any class of people in the world." His more stringent eye sees the humor of the circus, the fantastic skill and dexterity that achieves such hair-raising and trivial results, but without Dickens' benevolence. There is amusement in his account, but at the same time the whole scene is an implied comment on the everyday virtues. It is not soured, or sarcastic, it does not swing to the opposite extreme from condescension, but it shocks us by its calm assumption that these virtues, even the best of them, are of no account.

Kafka implies that both the pity and indignation evoked by the first scene, and the devotion and triumph of the second, are at bottom self-congratulatory shams. The young man would rather like to be indignant, and the crowd welcomes the occasion to greet the heroine of the moment, whatever her achievement. Yet there is no harsh denunciation; on the contrary, the scenes are portrayed with such a mixture of sober statement and amused caricature that one might imagine even a mild tolerance underlying the mood of the whole. That, however, would be false to the spirit of this writing. There *is* humor and tolerance, it is true, but at the same time the structure of the two sentences builds up a relentless pressure that can almost make those qualities pass unnoticed. Only at the end does this pressure relax and afford a release. Having led the reader to an intense feeling of the falsity of this circus-world, the rapid piling-up of event after event ceases, and the young man is seen sinking his head on the parapet. The rhythm changes, and with it comes the expression of grief which seems the only remaining resolution of the disharmonies. That the grief is unconscious—the last three words are quite vital—is the one thing that preserves it from being as much of a sham as the earlier expressions of emotion.[13] And isn't this, at any rate in part, the point where we see what is pure and true and immutable about the world portrayed here?

This is, as I said, where Kafka starts from. This sense of wanting to go with the rest of people in the way they are going, and of not being able to, for too deep an awareness of futility: this is his most usual mood. And because he is by nature and upbringing so compelled to see insincerity, falsity, or sheer evil in himself and most things around him, the relentless pressure builds up into these long sentences, or even into the labyrinthine construction of a whole novel. Just as a neurotic will spin on and on with the exploration of his own motives, explaining one by another, and that by another, so Kafka's compulsive need drives him to these ramified constructions, both in the individual parts and in the wholes of his works. This was his nature; he had to be true to this if he was to be a writer, and if the result is often oppressive, it also exerts a fascination simply because it is so ruthlessly faithful to Kafka's experience as it came to him. At the same time, we should not forget

[13] St. Paul may be compared here, when he says "for we know not what we should pray for as we ought: but the Spirit itself maketh intercession for us with groanings which cannot be uttered." Rom. 8:26. Like Kafka, he implies that adequate grief is beyond human reach.

what he said about the "whole man." He must have been well aware
that he was describing one aspect of himself when he wrote a short
story—or vignette rather—about a man desperately in search of a foothold, who went climbing up staircase after staircase.[14] As he mounted,
the stairs grew miraculously under his feet, so that while they never
ended, the foothold was always there. But while there was a kind of
consolation in that, since, although the search was endless, there was always security so long as it went on, it involved an everlasting disquiet and
anxiety. The whole Kafka could seldom escape such disquiet, but he
admired and wanted a normal life of peaceable simplicity.

Before I come to another short piece, let me illustrate this further.
There was nothing Kafka admired so much as ordinary everyday happiness. It has been related by his friend and editor Max Brod how he liked
Flaubert's comment on a bourgeois family living in plain domesticity—
"Ils sont dans le vrai." In a similar vein Kafka quoted the Talmud as
saying "A man without a wife is not a human being," [15] and one of the
sources of his desperation was the thought that a wife and children were
impossible ideals for him. In one of his letters, he does rate marriage
astonishingly high in the order of things. "Marrying, founding a family,
accepting all the children that come, supporting them in this insecure
world, even guiding them a little, is, I am convinced, the utmost a
human being can succeed in doing at all." [16] These are not merely the
expressions of a sentimental longing for an unknown state of being
which might after all have had its own defects when it was reached.
The ideal marriage as Kafka envisaged it had something like a sacramental value, so that he speaks of it as a means to religious knowledge.
To have a wife who would understand him, he wrote, would be to have
God.[17] Thus, far from seeing human life as a temporal evil, Kafka
envisaged it, under certain circumstances, as a means of realizing holiness
here and now. This was consistent with his basic belief in the absolute
supremacy of good.

These beliefs of his throw some light on one small incident hidden
away in his diaries at no very conspicuous place.[18] He is writing about
his fiancée, Felice Bauer, whom he genuinely wanted to marry, though
his inescapable sense of inadequacy never allowed him to come so far.
And although she was never his wife, he feels that there have been
moments when she has understood him, with all the vast implications

[14] "Advocates," see *Description of a Struggle*, pp. 141-3.
[15] *Diaries*, 1910-13, p. 162.   [17] *Diaries*, 1914-23, p. 126-7.
[16] *Wedding Preparations*, p. 204.   [18] *Diaries, loc. cit.*

which such an understanding must have had. I quote this passage from the diary because it affords a contrast to that hectic image of Kafka's in the story I have just mentioned, desperately climbing stair after stair to reach he doesn't know what. Here again he is climbing stairs, but in real life—in fact, he has just left the underground train in a Berlin station and is rushing up to the surface to meet Felice Bauer. But the understanding she had for him had somehow prompted her to wait for him down below, on the platform, and he found his desperation to have been unnecessary after all.

> "Sometimes, I have thought that she understood me without knowing it. For instance, that time when I was longing for her unbearably, when she was waiting for me in the underground station;—I, in my desire to get to her as quickly as possible, thinking she was upstairs, was about to run past her, and she took me quietly by the hand."

The despair in Kafka, the urgent haste to be somewhere else, beyond, is illuminated by his recognition of this simple gesture of restraint. It must have needed tact in Felice Bauer to make it without affectation or showing too clearly that she "understood." Kafka would have been quick to notice condescension or any other form of superiority. Yet the fact that he could accept it, if only for a moment, is an illustration of what the whole of him was really like. He might with one part of himself be almost constantly rushing on to enter the castle or protest his innocence to the court, but all the assurance he needed could be given in an everyday event like a hand placed on his. At the same time, however, he makes a qualification. If he admits that his fiancée ever understood him, it is at most "without knowing it." The genuine understanding, like the genuine grief of the young man at the circus, is not something that enters consciousness. It is above or below the conscious frames of mind that, in Kafka's view, falsify the emotions which really link men together.

Against this background it will be easier to feel the full sense of another short piece, rather in contrast to "Up in the Gallery," though once again not immediately obvious in its implications. It is not a story, rather a word sketch, akin to a pencil drawing. It begins with the picture of Kafka himself in his most usual frame of mind, utterly at a loss, and goes on to describe a simple event of no apparent further consequence. But just as a drawing, placing some small part of reality apart on a sheet of paper, can also illuminate it in an extraordinary way, making the insignificant meaningful, so it is here.

On the Tram

I stand on the end platform of the tram and am completely unsure of my footing in this world, in this town, in my family. Not even casually could I indicate any claims that I might rightly advance in any direction. I have not even any defense to offer for standing on this platform, holding on to this strap, letting myself be carried along by this tram, nor for the people who give way to the tram or walk quietly along or stand gazing into shop windows. Nobody asks me to put up a defense, indeed, but that is irrelevant.

The tram approaches a stopping-place and a girl takes up her position near the step, ready to alight. She is as distinct to me as if I had run my hands over her. She is dressed in black, the pleats of her skirt hang almost still, her blouse is tight and has a collar of white fine-meshed lace, her left hand is braced flat against the side of the tram, the umbrella in her right hand rests on the second top step. Her face is brown, her nose, slightly pinched at the sides, has a broad round tip. She has a lot of brown hair and stray little tendrils on the right temple. Her small ear is close-set, but since I am near her I can see the whole ridge of the whorl of her right ear and the shadow at the root of it.

At that point I asked myself: How is it that she is not amazed at herself, that she keeps her lips closed and makes no such remark? [19]

It needs the introductory part about Kafka's uncertainty to make sense of this, just as it needs some awareness of what he was like in real life to see the significance of Felice Bauer's putting her hand on his. Without the introduction, the description of the girl on the platform would not matter. With it, every detail is important for its own sake—the round, broad nose, the stray hairs, the umbrella on that particular step are all clean-cut, vivid, and related in such a way that you can't forget that hand placed flat against the upright: it matters, is an essential part of the sketch. And then the last sentence of all suggests amazement at this ordinariness, and at the same time suggests how in the end the living woman matters more than the art which enhances her for the moment. Kafka the writer unobtrusively withdraws and leaves you with a sense of being left with all that really does count—not his art, but the woman herself as she was forty years ago in Prague.

This is a kind of mood which is worth looking out for in Kafka. I have no time to indicate how it comes in his novels, and in any case, with works of greater length I could only tell of, not actually give the sense I am talking about. But I am certain it is there, for example, in the last chapters of *The Castle*. This novel is, fundamentally, a widening out of

[19] *The Penal Colony*, p. 33.

the situation in the piece called "On the Tram." It is the story of a man who appears in a strange village, overshadowed by a castle whose resident officials seem to have almost the power of divinities in the eyes of the villagers themselves. The man, K., has been summoned to the place as a land-surveyor, but almost at once discovers that there is no certainty to be had from the Castle authorities, whether in fact this summons came from them, whether there is any such job for him to do now that he has come. He is, in short, in the position of the tramway passenger with his complete uncertainty about his position in the world. The remainder of the story relates his attempts at entering the castle to find some confirmation that he *is* the person he takes himself to be, that he has some foothold in the society of the village, and is not condemned, as Kafka himself was, to an utterly rootless existence of insecurity. Every attempt is frustrated, either by his own weariness, the unreliability of other people, or the indifference or even active hostility which K. supposes to exist among the Castle authorities. The one thing K. does maintain is his "natural truth," his *Naturwahrheit,* which never allows him to deny experience as it comes to him, as Kafka the writer sought to remain faithful to the whole man whenever he should emerge. The result is painful and oppressive for the greater part of the novel as frustration succeeds frustration and K. becomes increasingly weary. In fact, so far as he is aware, there is never any respite from the search, there is never any moment when the cry of "Stop!" rings out as it did in the circus ring. But there is an extraordinary transformation in K. in the last two or three chapters, where he does come to see the world dominated by the Castle as essentially a world of good, and there is, strangely enough, the possibility of rereading the novel in the light of this insight, and of finding this new view confirmed in every detail. To show this I would need to take your time for many hours. But a single illustration must be enough. Throughout the novel, K. finds himself opposed, as he believes, by the official Klamm, the supreme official of the whole hierarchy of officials so far as it comes within K.'s range of knowledge. He is jealous of Klamm, believes him indifferent to his own—K.'s—fate, is glad to wrest his mistress Frieda from him, and looks for nothing better than to score a complete victory over him. Nor is this wholly unreasonable, for the picture of Klamm as it is presented to K. by the villagers gives him justification for his enmity. The pretense of the villagers, their hushing-up of what seems self-evidently wrong, their superstitious veneration for the Castle authorities, makes it essential for K. to revolt as he does. But in the final pages, through a subtle transformation, he comes to see the Castle and Klamm in an entirely different light. Should he? Has he any right to? Remembering the scene in the circus ring by way of a parallel, can you say that it *can* be seen differently? These are questions I can't answer briefly. But I can ask you to listen to the way K. talks at the end. He is speaking to one of the girls in the village, Pepi, the rival of Frieda who was once his own mistress, telling her about the official Klamm for whom he had formerly only bitter hostility and jealousy. Pepi now is jealous of Frieda's privileged position as the mistress of Klamm, and K. seeks to prize her out of this mood.

> "It is true—just as we are sitting here beside each other and I take your hand between my hands, so too, I dare say, and as though it were the most natural thing in the world, did Klamm and Frieda sit beside each other, and he came down [to see her] of his own free will, indeed he came hurrying down, nobody was lurking in the passage waiting for him and neglecting the rest of their work [as Pepi has done]; Klamm had to bestir himself and come downstairs, and the faults in Frieda's way of dressing, which would have horrified you, didn't disturb him at all. And you won't believe her! You don't know how you give yourself away by this, how precisely in this you show your lack of experience." [20]

The outward situation remains the same. Klamm still remains in the castle, K. never manages to see him face to face, as he had intended to do at the outset. There is no question now, however, of the bold advance into the middle of the circus ring, and of shouting out "Stop!" K. has no desire to put his oar in any longer. Nor is he inclined, as the young man in the gallery was, to put his face on the parapet and weep. On the contrary, while the situation does remain the same, it is seen from a changed disposition. K. is persuaded now of good will not only in the Castle but in everyone around him. The fantastically oppressive world in which he lives is illumined by this change. It has something of the quality of light and grace which was there in the piece about the tramway passenger—in a different way, because the rhythms of the novel are longer and more sustained than those of the short piece. What is said in "On the Tram" is a momentary glimpse which lengthens out in the broader scope of the novel. But there is this similarity also, that K. in *The Castle* is quite unaware of any transformation: it is not in the purview of his own consciousness, just as the miraculous presence of the girl on the step is never explicitly stated, but rather felt through the simplicity of the detailed presentation, and just as the grief of the man at the circus is not a grief of which he himself is aware. Perhaps the real virtue of Kafka's stories is just this absence of "knowingness," and all critical appreciation of them is a more or less awkward attempt at making explicit what he was content to leave in a pure and strictly un-

[20] *The Castle*, p. 377.

translatable form. The immediacy of his work itself matters, not the interpretations.

Not long before his death, Kafka spoke to a young man with whom he had made a friendship about an observation on his work by a contemporary critic, namely that he "smuggled miracles into ordinary events." Kafka's comment was this:

Of course that is a serious mistake on his part. Ordinary events are a miracle in themselves. I only write them down. Maybe I illuminate things a little too, like a projectionist on a half-darkened stage. But that's not right. In reality the stage isn't dark at all. It's full of daylight. That's why people close their eyes and see so little.[21]

To have open eyes even for the "partial horror" of Kafka's world, let alone that of the world at large, is beyond most of us. Moreover, we usually want to do more than simply write down what he saw and wrote down; we want to elucidate and comment on this apparently half-darkened stage. There is point in doing that, if only in order to gain the courage for taking another look. But Kafka's work must ultimately stand by itself and give us such light as we can see.

[21] Janouch, *Gespräche mit Kafka*, Frankfort 1951, p. 38.

Notes on Hemingway and Kafka

by *Caroline Gordon*

It is interesting to compare the literary achievement of Ernest Hemingway with that of some of the writers who were famous when, in the Twenties, he first emerged upon the literary scene. As a rule, all writers who attain popular success during their lifetimes have one thing in common: they speak for their ages; that is, they put into words thoughts and emotions of which their readers are already to some degree conscious—the little "shock of recognition" is part of the pleasure one derives from their writings.

Hemingway began to publish his stories soon after the First World War. A whole generation of young Americans had crossed the ocean and had looked upon cities and countries which they had known up to that time only by hearsay. As the song put it:

> How're you going to keep them down on the farm
> After they've seen Paree?

Young women were not privileged to serve in that war to the same extent that they served in the Second World War, but they were as restless as the returned soldiers. At that time Sinclair Lewis was one of the most widely acclaimed novelists in the English-speaking world; the heroine of *Main Street,* Carol Kennicott, seemed to embody the restlessness, the aspirations, the distaste for the known environment of the youth of that time.

But it is hard to read *Main Street* after nearly thirty years. The author displays an innocence of technical skills that would seriously handicap a first-class mystery story writer of the present time:

> On a hill by the Mississippi where Chippewa Indians camped two generations ago, a girl stood in relief against the cornflower blue of the sky. She saw no Indians now, she saw flour mills and the blinking windows

"Notes on Hemingway and Kafka," by Caroline Gordon. From the *Sewanee Review* (Spring 1949). © 1949 by The University of the South. Reprinted by permission of the publishers and the author.

of skyscrapers in Minneapolis and St. Paul. Nor was she thinking of portages, and the Yankee fur traders whose shadows were all about her. She was meditating upon walnut fudge, the plays of Brieux, and the reason why heels run over, and the fact that the chemistry instructor had stared at the new coiffure that concealed her ears.

A breeze which had crossed a thousand miles of wheatlands bellied her taffeta skirt in a line so graceful, so full of animation and moving beauty, that the heart of a chance watcher on the lower road tightened to wistfulness over her quality of suspended freedom. She lifted her arms, she leaned back against the wind, her skirt dipped and flared, a lock blew wild. A girl on a hilltop; credulous, plastic, young, drinking the air as she longed to drink life. The eternal aching comedy of expectant youth.

It is Carol Milford, fleeing for an hour from Blodgett College.

The author tries to give the scene depth by using a historical perspective. The girl is posed on the banks of a lake where Chippewa Indians once camped, but the setting remains a flimsy backdrop. We do not see the Indians engaged in any of their activities and unless we happen to have some specific knowledge of the tribe the name remains an empty word for us. The author tells us what the girl does not see and does not think of and these details negate his specifications of what she does see and think of: flour mills, walnut fudge, the plays of Brieux, and so on. In an effort to rescue his dissolving scene he introduces another viewpoint, that of the watcher on the road; but since the girl does not know of the watcher's existence, he does not function dramatically. In the end, we are not convinced that a girl stood on a hilltop, "credulous, plastic, young, drinking the air as she longed to drink life." The specifications which would have convinced us of her existence are not solid enough and the author's comment: "The eternal aching comedy of expectant youth" strikes us as a feeble attempt to tell the reader what the passage ought to contain and doesn't.

Edgar Allen Poe, in his review of Hawthorne's "Twice-Told Tales," published in *Graham's Magazine,* showed how a writer could avoid such fumbling:

> A skilful literary artist has fashioned a tale. If wise, he has not fashioned his thought to accommodate his incidents; but having conceived, with deliberate care, a certain unique or single effect to be wrought out, he then invents such incidents—he then combines such events as may best aid him in establishing this preconceived effect. If his very initial sentence tend not to the outbringing of this effect, then he has failed in the first step. In the whole composition there should be no word written, of which the tendency, direct or indirect, is not to the pre-established design.

Poe never became as great a master of the short story as Hemingway, and few contemporary critics would agree with his dictum that the tale as opposed to the novel, or the lyric as opposed to the epic, is the highest form of literary art; but any modern master of the short story has taken to heart, or discovered for himself, the fundamental principle of fictional construction laid down in this passage.

Hemingway's *A Farewell to Arms* begins:

> In the late summer of that year we lived in a house in a village that looked across the river and the plains to the mountains. In the bed of the river there were pebbles and boulders, dry and white in the sun, and the water was clear and swiftly moving and blue in the channels. Troops went by the house and down the road and the dust they raised powdered the leaves of the trees. The trunks of the trees were dusty and the leaves fell early that year and we saw troops marching along the road and the dust rising and leaves stirred by the breeze, falling and the soldiers marching and afterward the road bare and white except for the leaves.

This lyrical work, except as regards its length, meets Poe's demands. The tone of the whole book is set in the first paragraph. The tone, in this case, is a mood, a dramatization of the wistful rebellion of youth, confronted with the hard facts of life, with love and death. This mood, evoked by the very sound of the words in the first sentence: *In the late summer of that year* . . . and persisting throughout the action, swells up at the climax in a crescendo that is so perfectly timed that when one rereads the book tears spring always to the eyes at the same passage—provided that one is capable of shedding tears over the sorrows of fictional characters.

Another master, Chekhov, might have admired the rendering of the rest of the passage. The action of the sun *shows* the pebbles and boulders that lie in the bed of the river to be *dry* and *white*. The river is clear and moves swiftly; the further specification that it was blue where the water was deepest (in the channels) makes us *see* it flow. We are convinced that the troops passed the house by the fact that enough dust was raised to powder the leaves of the trees and even the trunks. The passage could stand as an amplification of some advice that Chekhov once wrote to his good-for-nothing brother, Alexander:

> Descriptions of Nature should be very brief and have an incidental character. Commonplaces like "The setting sun, bathing in the waves of the darkening sea, flooded with purple and gold. . . . The swallows, flying over the surface of the water, chirped merrily"—such commonplaces should be finished with. In descriptions of Nature one has to snatch at small details,

grouping them in such a manner that after reading them one can obtain the picture on closing one's eyes.

For instance, you will get a moonlight night if you write that on the dam of the mill a fragment of broken bottle flashed like a small bright star, and there rolled by, like a ball, the black shadow of a dog or a wolf—and so on.

One is reminded of another piece of advice that Chekhov gave: "If a gun hangs on the wall in the first paragraph of your story it must be discharged at the end"—which is only another way of saying the same thing that Poe said. The phrase, "The leaves fell early that year," is an admirable preparation for the climax of the action, that is to say: "My love died young." The whole dénouement is, in fact, both prepared for and symbolized in this passage: *We saw troops marching along the road and the dust rising and leaves, stirred by the breeze, falling and the soldiers marching and afterward the road bare and white except for the leaves.* A human heart, ravaged by grief, will ultimately become as bare and as quiet as the white road that the soldiers have passed over.

This kind of writing was rare in the Twenties and, indeed, is rare at any time. It calls for a particular kind of response to the natural world, the kind of response that Turgenev, for instance, gave. But, we sometimes say, in order to write like Turgenev one would have to be Turgenev. And that, in a measure, was true, up to Hemingway's time. Hemingway has not the range or the depth of the Russian; but possessing a sensory apparatus capable of the same exquisite response to the natural world, he is more deeply grounded in his craft, more athletic. He is, in short, the kind of writer one can learn from as distinguished from the kind of writer, like Turgenev or Tolstoy, who can be—safely—followed only at a distance. Developing a high degree of technical proficiency, Hemingway fulfilled the promise of early American realistic writers, such as Frank Norris, Ambrose Bierce, Sarah Orne Jewett, and became, with Stephen Crane, one of the first American masters of Naturalism.

But an artist's achievement is often limited, not only by his own genius, but by the temper of the age. And every age, as Edmund Wilson has shown in his *Axel's Castle,* has its characteristic tendency. The present age has two literary trends: Naturalism and Symbolism, or Symbolism based upon Naturalism.

The natural symbolism which operates in Hemingway's stories refers to a narrow range of experience, and it seems inadequate today. The world seems to have shifted under our feet. We have seen countries ravaged and populations decimated. We can hardly believe any longer in the Divinity of Man. We are more concerned today with Man's relation to God.

Hemingway, giving expression to the doubts, the anguish, the soul searchings of the men and women of the Twenties, is voicing—and perhaps unconsciously beginning to question—the belief in the Divinity of Man which has been held as an article of faith since the Renaissance. *Today Is Friday*, a short and little known piece, is the only one of his stories (it is really a little play) which attempts to treat the relation of Man to God. Three Roman soldiers are talking in a drinking place after the Crucifixion:

> 1st ROMAN SOLDIER—You see his girl?
>
> 2nd SOLDIER—Wasn't I standing right by her?
>
> 1st SOLDIER—She's a nice looker.
>
> 2nd SOLDIER—I knew her before he did. (*He winks at the wineseller.*)
>
> 1st SOLDIER—I used to see her around the town.
>
> 2nd SOLDIER—She used to have a lot of stuff. He never brought *her* no luck.
>
> 1st SOLDIER—Oh, he ain't lucky. But he looked pretty good to me in there today.
>
> 2nd SOLDIER—What became of his gang?
>
> 1st SOLDIER—Oh, they faded out. Just the women stuck by him.
>
> 2nd SOLDIER—They were a pretty yellow crowd. When they seen him go up they didn't want any of it.
>
> 1st SOLDIER—The women stuck all right.
>
> 2nd SOLDIER—Sure, they stuck all right.
>
> 1st SOLDIER—You see me slip the old spear into him?
>
> 2nd SOLDIER—You'll get into trouble doing that some day.
>
> 1st SOLDIER—It was the least I could do for him. I tell you he looked pretty good to me in there today.

Christ's Divinity is hinted at. There is even the possibility of conversion; the Second Soldier says: "Any time you show me one that doesn't want to get down off the cross when the time comes—when the times comes, I mean—I'll climb up with him," but the beautifully rendered conversation proceeds mostly by means of bashful understatements. Christ, suffering on the cross for the sins of mankind, elicits as much eloquence from the writer as a courageous but unlucky prizefighter could have called forth. At the end of the story the Second Soldier makes a comment familiar to Hemingway's readers: "You been out here too long. That's all." Man, remaining just as he is, undergoing, that is to say, no spiritual change, may yet solve his problems by going on—or going back—to a country where everything will be "fine."

Hemingway's heroes are rarely middle-aged persons. They are returned soldiers, or adolescents, or Spaniards, like the bullfighter, Manuel Garcia, or expatriates, like Jake Barnes, seeking the answer to the question they are forever asking by returning to lost innocence or taking up their abode in some foreign land.

It is instructive to compare some of Hemingway's best stories—*The Killers, The Undefeated, Big Two-Hearted River*—with the stories of Franz Kafka, who occupies somewhat the same position in regard to influence today that Hemingway had between the wars. The two men have one thing in common: they are both masters of Naturalism. Kafka, whom Austin Warren has called "a metaphysical poet in symbolist narrative," presents a surface which is strictly Naturalistic in detail, but he is dealing with a problem that is more complicated than the problem with which Hemingway deals: Man's relation to God, rather than Man's relation to Man.

There have been fiction writers in this country before him who concerned themselves with the same problem, notably Hawthorne; but Hawthorne, important as he is, was never able to bring his material to the pitch of perfection which Kafka attained in his short lifetime. He never solved the central technical problem of the point-of-view and for that reason the action in his stories is often interspersed with sententious —and undramatic—comments.

Henry James has pointed out Hawthorne's preëminence as a master of what he called "the deeper psychology." Austin Warren says that:

> The technique available to Hawthorne as a narrative writer concerning the states of the soul was, primarily, the technique of the Gothic romance. . . . Hawthorne has himself indicated his lineage within prose fiction by calling his work "romance" and by expressly distinguishing this from the realistic novel: "When a writer calls his work a Romance [Hawthorne says] it need hardly be observed that he wishes to claim a certain latitude both as to its fashion and its material."

Hawthorne, Mr. Warren holds,

> . . . does not wish to explain all at the end. He has two chief ways of giving a sense of the mysterious while offering a concurrent rationale. One is to offer alternative natural and supernatural explanations—as, for instance, with the incision of the letter *A* upon the breast of Dimmesdale—generally attaching the latter to the credulous speculations of the community, the fanciful gossip of the uneducated, yet meanwhile intimating that the gossip may be wiser than the science.

But this method does not always serve Hawthorne as well as a strict surface adherence to Naturalism serves Kafka. Too often, with Hawthorne, myth turns into allegory. Kafka's stories are more dramatic, consisting—on the surface—of action presented in convincing detail. His meaning, which constitutes another level of action, is cryptic, and must be sought in his symbols.

The Hunter Gracchus, which, though short, exhibits his fictional gifts in something like perfection, is the story of a Christ who has been crucified but has never been able to ascend into Heaven.

The viewpoint is that of the omniscient narrator. The scenes are pictorial throughout. The opening scene shows the world of men at their various occupations. Boys are shooting dice, a man is reading a newspaper, a girl is filling her bucket at a fountain, two men are drinking wine in a cafe while the proprietor dozes at a table outside. The architecture of this setting reminds one of allegorical paintings of the Fourteenth Century. In such paintings a window or a vista often opens on what artists call "infinite space." From Kafka's symbolic spatial perspective emerges the complication of the action: the man is reading a newspaper in the shadow of a hero who is flourishing a sword on high, a fruit seller is lying beside his scales, staring out to sea, where a bark is "silently making for the little harbor as if drawn by invisible means over the water."

The complication is the arrival of the dead hunter, Gracchus (Christ), in any harbor (any community). Kafka evidently thinks of Christ's passion as being continuously enacted. The boatman (the Church) transfers the bier to the shore. Doves light on the bier, as the Holy Spirt, in the form of a dove, once alighted on the head of Christ, but "nobody on the quay troubled about the newcomers . . . nobody asked them a question, nobody accorded them even an inquisitive glance."

The action proper begins when the burgomaster of the town, whose name is significantly "Salvatore," goes into the room where the body of the dead hunter lies on its bier; goes, that is, to church. He gives the boatman a glance and the boatman vanishes through a side door into another room. (Since the soul is seeking salvation in terms of a Protestant theology it dispenses with the Roman Catholic sacrament of Confession.)

Salvatore (the soul) then communes with the hunter (Christ) who deplores his condition: "It cannot be a pleasure to look at me," and relates the story of his Incarnation and Crucifixion. Pursuing his calling (the saving of souls), he fell through a precipice (became Incarnate), bled to death in a ravine (was crucified), died, but did not ascend into Heaven; his death ship "lost its way."

Salvatore expresses his attitude toward the Doctrine of Original Sin when he asks whose was the guilt. The hunter replies that it is the boatman's (the Church's), but he does not feel that the boatman has been guilty of anything more than "a wrong turn of the wheel," "a moment's absence of mind." The result of this mischance is the resolution of the action: Christ has not been able to become Christ, but remains "forever on the great stair" that leads to Heaven—sometimes up, sometimes down, but always in motion. The hunter (of souls) has been turned into a butterfly, an ancient symbol for the soul.

The artist, as such, does not defend or criticize the myth of his age, he merely uses it. Kafka's subject matter is the scheme of redemption, as set forth in neo-Calvinist theology and the "philosophy of crisis," and his allegorical symbolism is as exact, if not as full, as Dante's, but his faith is not as complete. His skepticism shows itself occasionally in wry ambiguities. (For example, the fact that the dove which warns Salvatore of Gracchus' arrival is as big as a cock brings to our minds the image of the cock which crowed to herald the betrayal of Christ.)

Kafka also achieves some of his finest effects by understatement. Salvatore asks the hunter what port he will touch at next; the hunter says that he does not know. ". . . my ship has no rudder, and it is driven by a wind that blows in the undermost regions of death." This reply seems to spring from his lips as spontaneously as the name of the nearest town; this terrible "understatement" of the spiritual plight of modern man is accomplished with Naturalistic details.

Hemingway often uses the same device of understatement for the climax of his stories: "I can't stand to think about him waiting in the room and knowing he's going to get it. It's too awful," Nick Adams says in *The Killers* when he realizes that the two men in tight overcoats and black gloves are going to kill Ole Andresen. "Well," George the counter-man says, "you better not think about it."

At first glance it may seem unfair to compare this story or *Today Is Friday* with *The Hunter Gracchus*. But all three stories have essentially the same—ineffable—subject, a crucifixion, and all three stories show the same degree of technical proficiency; each story is a marvel of dramatic economy. But Kafka, it seems to me, achieves the most powerful effect. When one reads the Hemingway stories one is reminded of what Henry James said about Maupassant:

> Nothing can exceed the masculine firmness, the quiet force of his style, in which every phrase is a close sequence, every epithet a paying piece, and the ground is completely cleared of the vague, the ready-made and the second-best. Less than anyone today does he beat the air; more than any-one does he hit out from the shoulder.

Hemingway always hits out from the shoulder, but his reach is not long enough. Again, one is reminded of something that James said about Maupassant, that he "omitted one of the items of the problem" when he "simply skipped the whole reflective part of his men and women, that part which governs conduct and produces character." Hemingway's men and women reflect, but their reflections often seem childish. In his stories, as in Kafka's, action is often symbolic—that is, symbolism provides another plane of action. But this plane of action is for him a slippery substratum glimpsed intermittently. It does not underlie the Naturalistic plane of action solidly, or over-arch it grandly, as Kafka's symbolism does. Like Maupassant, he has limited his field of observation too strictly. For all his remarkable achievement he remains what James called Maupassant, "a lion in the path." The best contemporary writers seem to take another path, into a deeper jungle.

Kafka, Gogol and Nathanael West

by Idris Parry

It is soothing to discover that a modern writer like Kafka is really quite old in essence and even in technique. It is a discovery to be matched only by the excitement of finding that a writer of former times, like Gogol, is really modern. Either discovery suggests that the writer in question is here to stay, since he appeals to elements in man which are unchanged and possibly unchangeable. Kafka seems to be in critical disrepute at the moment—perhaps because he has been so intensely overworked as the embodiment of the modern spirit. "Nothing is so dangerous as being too modern," says Wilde's Lady Markby. "One is apt to grow old-fashioned quite suddenly." And it is as true of writers as of debutantes.

But is Kafka so modern? There is a tendency to regard him as a freak among writers, a kind of novelist who could not possibly have happened before. And, some will no doubt hope, may, please God, never happen again. We speak of the Kafka influence as though it were unique. And by "Kafka influence" we usually mean something extraordinary, grotesque, nightmarish, symbolic of modern frustration. Though why we must call frustration modern, I don't know. Perhaps because it alliterates so conveniently with Freud, and we prefer not to share this distinction of ours with those simple characters who knew it as *Weltschmerz* or even did not give it a name at all. Of course, the contemporary form of frustration is different—but then, so is the contemporary world.

In Kafka's story *The Metamorphosis* Gregor Samsa wakes up in bed one morning to find himself changed into a monstrous cockroach. Yes, extraordinary. But Gregor Samsa is not essentially different from that unfortunate man Kovalev, in Gogol's story, who also wakes up (perhaps not unnaturally) in the same place (bed) and at the same time (early morning) to find that his nose has disappeared overnight, leaving a perfectly smooth patch in the middle of his face. The place and time are significant. For Gregor Samsa and Kovalev are awakening, not from a nightmare, but, reversing the normal process, *into* a nightmare, the nightmare world which is always just below the surface. Instead of finding themselves in the waking world they are in that world of dreams which, so the psychoanalysts tell us, shows us the real truth about ourselves. So they are really finding themselves, for they are in a sphere which is more truthful than the waking world. It is no coincidence that it is just as he is getting out of bed one morning that Joseph K., and Kafka's novel *The Trial,* is arrested by strangers on that charge which leads him to his fantastic pursuit of innocence.

The centenary of Gogol's death has caused little stir in England. A few conventionally polite articles, a radio adaptation of *The Inspector General,* a reading of one of his short stories. And he is buried again—presumably until the year 2009, the bicentenary of his birth. In general we seem content to classify him as the father of Russian realism and a rather crude humorist, much too remote for serious interest. The nineteenth-century Russian novel came from Gogol's beginnings, and the spirit of those novels can be traced to one of Gogol's stories, and even to one paragraph in that story. "We all come from under Gogol's 'Overcoat,' " said Dostoevsky. And this is true, but it is not the whole truth. Gogol was more than a pathetic realist. If he must be linked with anyone, it should be with Kafka, Poe, and Melville, rather than with Goncharov, Dostoevsky, and Tolstoy. And, in more recent times, with the American novelist Nathanael West. Like these, Gogol was a disappointed Romantic. And, like these, he seems to reveal to us a new level of consciousness.

The surface writing of both Gogol and Kafka is apparently flat. They love the precise detail, the pedestrian fact. Kovalev's nose, we are told, returns to its proper position in the middle of his face on the morning of April 7th. In *Dead Souls* Gogol tells us that the idle landowner Manilov always has a book lying about in his study, marked on page fourteen, which he has been reading persistently for over two years. The exact date, the exact page—all to persuade us that this is the real, observable world. And Kafka goes into such detail about the pleats in a man's clothes or the dust that lies thickly on a heap of pictures that it is difficult to believe he is not simply reporting to us on people and places we know well. But this realism is a deceptive surface. Deceptive because pitted with holes, through which we may fall into another and apparently unreal world. But, oddly enough, only the unwary (because unimaginative) can avoid these holes, for they seldom get over the intellectual shock of the initial proposition.

Spinoza starts from self-evident propositions, Gogol and Kafka from propositions which are anything but self-evident. For pure intellect they substitute pure imagination—but go on to develop it as though it were intellect. Given that a man can lose his own nose overnight, given that a man can wake up to find himself transformed into an insect—given these things, the rest follows. But only if these propositions are given, in the sense of being accepted. We must first accept this initial imaginative feat, and to do that we must approach these writers in the mood in which Alice approached the Eat-Me cake in Wonderland. It will be remembered that she

> . . . ate a little bit, and said anxiously to herself "Which way? Which way?" holding her hand on the top of her head to feel which way it was growing; and she was quite surprised to find that she remained the same size. To be sure, this is what generally happens when one eats cake; but Alice had got so much into the way of expecting nothing but out-of-the-way things to happen, that it seemed quite dull and stupid for life to go on in the common way.

Yes, we must forget that the common way of life can be so devastatingly rational. Gogol and Kafka, like Axel, would leave the tedious round of everyday life to their servants, for they are concerned with something more fundamental than daily life. Their absurdities are nothing less than an assault on the periphery of our conscious minds. They seek the way beyond, to a profounder world.

Let us take a closer look at Kovalev's elusive nose—if we can catch it before it boards that coach for Riga. Kovalev, in his misery, is astonished at the sight of his nose, his own nose, coming out of a private house, dressed in uniform. He pursues it and manages to engage it in conversation. But when he suggests it should return to its rightful place, since it is nothing but his own nose, it draws itself up haughtily and replies: "You are mistaken, sir. I am myself." This is like a dream in which a man may recognize himself in someone of entirely different outward appearance, different age, different sex even. The nose is Kovalev too, the more important part of him, since it at least is capable of serene independence. Kovalev and his nose are the hunter and the hunted, that dichotomy of the individual which we shall find fundamental in the work of Kafka.

Kafka's Gregor Samsa, on the other hand, is not independent of his cockroach form, as Kovalev is of his nose, but he too is now really himself. No longer is he the insignificant commercial traveller, the family breadwinner; his new form is the pure expression of his personality. We know that Kafka's work is an expression of fear. All his life he was obsessed with his own father-relationship. He himself was physically puny and, as he considered, a human failure; his father was a gross giant of a man, untroubled by spiritual doubt, who had fought his way up from a miserably impoverished childhood to become a relatively pros-

perous merchant. In November 1919 Kafka wrote his father a letter
which examines their relationship in detail. It was never delivered. And
it has not yet been published in full.[1] But in one of the extracts quoted
in Max Brod's biography Kafka puts into his father's mouth words
which are relevant to this Gregor Samsa transformation.

> I admit [he makes his father say], I admit we are struggling against one
> another. But there are two kinds of struggle. Chivalrous combat, in which
> independent antagonists match their powers—each remaining independent,
> losing for himself, conquering for himself alone. And the attack of the
> noxious insect, which not only bites, but also sucks blood for its own
> preservation. This is, of course, the real professional soldier—and this is
> what you are. You are unfit for life and, so that you may feel comfortable,
> without care and without reproach, you demonstrate that I have taken all
> your fitness for life away from you and hidden it in my pockets.

So in the story Samsa/Kafka (who could overlook the clear translitera-
tion?) . . . Samsa/Kafka is the noxious insect, unfit for human life, a
pathetic and (some would say) pathological confession of human inadequacy. The human Samsa stands spiritually naked in his insect form.
No human conventions shield him from the emotional tensions of the
family—father, mother, and sister. He has dropped the human mask,
and they must take him as he is. The mother and sister almost survive
the test, but the father rejects him from the start. The father, who had
become economically dependent on his commercial traveller son, is now
rejuvenated by the shift of economic importance within the family. With
his restoration to the headship of the family he regains his emotional
ascendancy; the insect son withers and dies. For this insect does not suck
blood; it is a failure even as an insect. It dies because it is dependent—
in the last resort dependent on the father. The price of life, to the insect
as to man, is personal certainty. This is what Kafka himself did not
attain until—ironically enough—the last year of his short life. He is
perpetually in that nightmare state where a man is inarticulate when he
should speak, and rooted immovably when he knows he must fly from
danger. That is the figure that he projects into his stories—the hunter and
the hunted, both in one. Joseph K. in *The Trial,* who pursues his case
energetically and yet, at the vital moment, flings himself upon the maid
Leni when he knows he should be in the next room, where important
discussions are going on about his fate. And the interminable dialectics
in both *The Trial* and *The Castle* are perfect images of Kafka's own
vacillation. This year, next year, sometime, never . . . exasperatingly,
we arrive just where we started from. His books are unfinished because,

---

[1] [See *Wedding Preparations,* pp. 157-217].

by their nature, they never could be finished. That is the ultimate horror.

In Nathanael West's Hollywood novel *The Day of the Locust* there is a character who is closely related to Kovalev and Gregor Samsa. Homer Simpson has hands which seem to have almost as independent an existence as Kovalev's nose, for they are uncontrolled by Homer's brain. When Homer gets out of bed in the morning (again that place and time) he has to plunge his hands into cold water to awaken them. And one day, says the author,

> One day, while opening a can of salmon for lunch, his thumb received a nasty cut. Although the wound must have hurt, the calm, slightly querulous expression he usually wore did not change. The wounded hand writhed about on the kitchen table until it was carried to the sink by its mate and bathed tenderly in hot water.

And when, in company, the rest of Homer is mute and unsociable, his hands begin to jump about of their own free will; he has to sit on them or trap them between his knees. For his hands are his real self; they give him away. Repression is as clearly portrayed here as in Gogol and Kafka. Again we find the initial outrageous proposition. Nathanael West summarizes the conversational method of a screen-struck girl as follows: "Without any noticeable transition, possibilities became probabilities and wound up as inevitabilites." This might be adapted for West himself, as well as for Gogol and Kafka, into the statement that in them impossibilities become possibilities, then probabilities, and wind up as inevitabilities.

But, of course, not everyone will get past the first feeling that these events are impossibilities that remain impossible. And ludicrous and unpleasant impossibilities at that. Who in his right senses can believe in Kovalev's pursuit of his wandering nose? In Gregor Samsa, with that nauseating trail of slime behind him as he crawls over the walls and ceiling of his room? Or in Joseph K., guiltily defending himself against a charge whose nature he does not know and never will know? It's all nonsense, utterly unlike life. But then, Gogol and Kafka might protest, so is life. For life, as we know it, is incomplete. What these authors create is a symbol for the whole of life, including that other realm of consciousness which lies behind appearance. No man, they might argue, is in his right sense until he can experience the whole of this reality.

In his essay *Ur-Geräusch* (*Primal Sound*), Rilke speculates on man's sensory capacities. At present, he says, each of our five senses covers its own sector, which is separate from the others. But, as long as these sense-sectors are separate, there can be no certainty that they cover all that can possibly be experienced. May there not be gaps between them, mysterious

chasms in man's perception, spaces of which we are ignorant—not be
cause there is nothing there, but because our sensory capacity is in
complete? It is these gaps in our awareness, Rilke believes, that cause
our human anxiety, for we fear the unknown. And it is to these gaps that
Gogol and Kafka lead us. They are constantly straining beyond their
known boundaries, and this (Rilke holds) is the task of the poet—to
extend the boundaries of the individual senses until they meet and
coalesce, and the writer is enabled to grasp the whole of the real world
with one five-fingered hand of the senses.

Gogol and Kafka and their like plunge into the dark regions, and we
follow as best we can—or pull back hastily from the brink, uncharitably
scolding them for leaving our firm, rational world. But are we justified
in thinking them absurd because irrational? Or should we not recognize that they deliberately abandon the rational world because it is inadequate for them, and they for it? They choose the irrational because
they must, and because they know they will find there, as in a dream,
the roots of their own human dilemma. And, if we can follow them, we
too may find that the nonsensory world is really anything but non-
sensical.

A Dissenting Opinion on Kafka

by Edmund Wilson

Franz Kafka has been looming on the literary world like the meteorological phenomenon called the Brocken specter: a human shadow thrown on the mist in such a way that it seems monstrous and remote when it may really be quite close at hand, and with a rainbow halo around it. Since the publication in English of *The Trial* in 1937 (*The Castle* came out in 1930 but did not attract much attention), Kafka's reputation and influence have been growing till his figure has been projected on the consciousness of our literary reviews on a scale which gives the illusion that he is a writer of towering stature. New translations of him are constantly appearing, an endless discussion of his writings goes on, and a new collected edition in German is being brought out in New York. This edition, under the imprint of Schocken Books, is in part a reprinting of the old German edition which the war made unavailable, but, when complete, it will include ten or eleven volumes instead of the original six, with two volumes of Kafka's diaries, two of his letters and one or two of his miscellaneous fragments, of all of which only selections were given in a single volume before. We may be proud that this admirably produced and authoritatively edited version of a modern German classic, which was begun in Berlin under Hitler and only finished in Prague on the eve of the German occupation of Czechoslovakia, should thus have been salvaged from the ruins of Central European culture and brought out in the United States. Schocken has also published, both in German and English, *Franz Kafka: A Biography*, by Max Brod, and a selection, in English translation, from Kafka's "stories and reflections" under the title *The Great Wall of China*; and it has announced some further translations. In the meantime, a translation of *The Metamorphosis*, one of the most important of Kafka's short stories, has recently been brought out by the Vanguard Press; and *A Franz Kafka Miscellany*, which contains translated scraps of Kafka as

well as essays on his work, has been published by the Twice A Year
Press. A compilation of essays and memoirs called *The Kafka Problem*
has been published by New Directions; and *Kafka's Prayer,* an interpretation by Paul Goodman, has just been brought out by Vanguard.

These last two volumes, in the first of which the editor, Mr. Angel
Flores, has assembled no less than forty-one pieces by writers of all
nationalities, oversaturate and stupefy the reader and finally give rise to
the suspicion that Kafka is being wildly overdone. One realizes that it
is not merely a question of appreciating Kafka as a poet who gives expression for the intellectuals to their emotions of helplessness and self-
contempt but of building him up as a theologian and saint who can
somehow also justify for them—or help them to accept without justification—the ways of a banal, bureaucratic and incomprehensible God to
sensitive and anxious men. Now, it may make a good deal of difference
whether one was born, like the present writer, before the end of the
nineteenth century, when stability and progress were taken for granted,
instead of in a period when upheaval and backsliding seemed the
normal conditions of life; but with much admiration for Kafka, I find it
impossible to take him seriously as a major writer and have never ceased
to be amazed at the number of people who can. Some of his short stories
are absolutely first-rate, comparable to Gogol's and Poe's. Like them,
they are realistic nightmares that embody in concrete imagery the
manias of neurotic states. And Kafka's novels have exploited a vein of
the comedy and pathos of futile effort which is likely to make "Kafkaesque" a permanent word. But the two of these novels, *The Trial* and
The Castle, which have become for the cultists of Kafka something like
sacred wrtings, are after all rather ragged performances—never finished
and never really worked out. Their themes, as far as Kafka had got, had
been developed with so little rigor that Max Brod, when he came to edit
them, found mere loose collections of episodes, which he had to piece
together as best he could so as to give them a consistent progression,
though he was not always able to tell in precisely what order they should
come. To compare Kafka, as some of the writers in *The Kafka Problem*
do, with Joyce and Proust and even with Dante, great naturalists of
personality, great organizers of human experience, is obviously quite
absurd. As for the religious implications of these books, they seem to me
to be practically nil. I agree with Mr. D. S. Savage, who contributes to
The Kafka Problem one of its most sensible essays, that the trouble with
Kafka was that he could never let go of the world—of his family, of his
job, of his yearning for bourgeois happiness—in the interest of divine
revelation, and that you cannot have a first-rate saint or prophet without
a faith of a very much higher potential than is ever to be felt in Kafka.
All that insulated and eventually nullified the spiritual charge that he

carried is indicated in Max Brod's biography. Franz Kafka was the delicate son of a self-made Jewish merchant in the wholesale women's-wear business in Prague, a vigorous and practical man, who inspired him with fear and respect, and gave him a life-long inferiority complex. The son was a pure intellectual, who derived from the rabbinical tradition of the mother's side of the family; but he yielded to the insistence of the father and, though at times reduced to thoughts of suicide, he took his place in the drygoods warehouse. His real interest had always been writing, which represented for him not merely an art but also somehow a pursuit of righteousness—he said he regarded it as a form of prayer—and he finally got himself a job in a workers' accident-insurance office, which left him his afternoons free. He wanted, or thought he ought to want, to get married, but his relationship with his father seems to have deprived him of sexual self-confidence. He became engaged to a girl whom he described as "wholesome, merry, natural, robust"; and, after five years of gruelling hesitation, developed tuberculosis, on purpose, in his own opinion, to make it impossible for him to marry. He was by this time, one supposes, too much at home in his isolation to be able to bring himself to the point of taking the risk of trying to get out of it; and he now, at the age of thirty-six, addressed to his father an enormous letter (never yet printed in full),[1] an apologia for his own life, in which he seems to have blamed his failure on him. Later he did get away to Berlin. He had found an intellectual girl who studied Hebrew with him and whom he seems really to have wanted to marry. Her orthodox Chassidic father was forbidden by the rabbi to allow it when Franz confessed that he was not a practicing Jew; but the girl, in revolt against her family tradition, set up housekeeping with him and took care of him. Though he was eager now to work and to live, his disease had left him little time, and, after less than a year of this life, he was dead at forty-one.

The connection of all this with what Kafka wrote is made plain by his friend Max Brod in a book full of understanding. Herr Brod—whom the more metaphysical Kafkians tend to accuse of Philistinism—has, it seems to me, precisely the merit of looking in Kafka's work less for divine than for human meanings. That Kafka was weak-willed, that he was psychologically crippled, Max Brod is quite ready to admit, since he had made it his task during Kafka's life to keep his friend's morale up and make him work. He did stimulate Kafka to write and to have a few of his stories published, but he was very much less successful in his efforts to get him to break with his family. Other people escape from their parents, protests Herr Brod in astonishment and sorrow, so why on

---

[1] [See p. 25 above, footnote.]

earth couldn't Kafka? Why *should* he have allowed his father so to crush
and maim his abilities? Why, the reader may second Max Brod, remembering one of Kafka's most effective stories, should this artist have
gone on past boyhood accepting the role of cockroach for which, like
the hero of *The Metamorphosis,* he had been cast by the bourgeois
businessman? Well, the cards were stacked against poor Kafka in an
overpowering way. His impotence was that of a man constitutionally
lacking in vitality and walled in by a whole series of prisons that fitted
one into the other like Chinese eggs. There was, first, the strangling
father relationship; then the pressure of the tight little group of the
Jewish orthodox family; then the constraints of the Jewish community,
incompletely emerged from the ghetto (Brod points out that the problems
of Kafka's heroes are often those of the Jew among semi-alien neighbors
—that the wanderer of *The Castle,* for example, is always trying to get
himself accepted; he might have added that Joseph K., in *The Trial,* is
constantly pursued for some crime which he is not aware of having
committed); then the boredom and the spiritual starvation of the writer
tied down to business hours—with the impression of hopelessness made
on him by the workers who came to his office in the attempt to collect
their insurance and who were met by all sorts of evasions and subjected
to endless delays ("How modest these men are," he once said to Max
Brod, "They come to us and beg, instead of storming the institute and
smashing it to little bits."); then the deep-seated inhibitions which seem
to have made his love affairs difficult; then the position of the Czechs in
the Austrian Empire as an oppressed and somewhat scorned minority;
then the privations of a defeated Central Europe, blighted, among other
plagues, by the tuberculosis that undermined Kafka. This bewildered and
darkened captivity, which may have seemed at the time rather special,
was later to become, in Europe, more or less the common lot, and Kafka's
fantasies were to gain a validity which could hardly have been foreseen—
when, under the rule of the Nazis and the Soviets, men were to find
themselves arrested and condemned on charges that had no relation to
any accepted code of morals or law, or were driven from place to place
to labor or to fight by first one then another inhuman unpetitionable
government which they hadn't the force to defy or the intellect to grasp
and disintegrate.

But must we really, as his admirers pretend, accept the plights of
Kafka's abject heroes as parables of the human condition? We can hardly
feel toward Kafka's father, whose aspect Kafka's God always wears, the
same childish awe that Kafka did—especially when the truth is that
Kafka himself cannot help satirizing this Father-God as well as his own
pusillanimity in remaining in bondage to him. A good deal has been
made of the influence on Kafka of the Danish theologian Kierkegaard:

but we learn from Max Brod that Kafka was at least equally influenced by Flaubert, and his work is full of a Flaubertian irony which the critics have tended to disregard. There is a story of Kafka's, for example, called *Investigations of a Dog* (included in *The Great Wall of China*), in which a dog is supposed to be inquiring into certain rather puzzling phenomena that are basic to the dog world. Where, he asks, does the food for dogs come from? The conventional explanation—which all right-minded dogs have been taught—is that this food comes out of the earth and is elicited by watering the earth and by singing incantatory hymns and performing ritual dances. Yet, as the scientist-dog has observed, the dogs, when they are invoking food, look not down towards the ground but up. Why *do* they look up, and is this essential? Then there are other unsolved problems: the dogs that roll over in unison and walk on their hind legs to the sound of mysterious music, and the small dandified dogs that seem to float through the air. The point is, of course, that the dogs have had their own reasons for pretending that human beings do not exist. Now, if you read the interpretations of this story which have recently been appearing, you will gather that it is simply an allegory of the relation of man to God—though the analogy does not hold, in view of the fact that the dogs *can* perfectly well see their masters, as man cannot do God, and are dependent on them in a practical way. Kafka remarked of this story, started—and never finished—not long before he died, that it was his *Bouvard et Pécuchet,* by which he must certainly have meant, not merely, as he said, that he thought it was a late work rather lacking in vitality, but also that it had something in common with Flaubert's most contemptuous indictment of the pettiness and ineptitude of the modern world. The sting of Kafka's story resides in the reluctance of the dogs to admit that they are in servitude to men—so that they have all entered into a conspiracy to conceal this fact from themselves, and even their boldest thinker cannot allow himself to find out the secret because it would rob him of his own self-respect. This is much less like an edifying allegory of the relations between God and man than like a Marxist-Flaubertian satire on the parasites of the bourgeoisie.

I do not deny that the enslaver, the master, is often given, in Kafka's stories, a serious theological meaning; but this side is never developed in anything like equal proportion to the ironical self-mocking side. Is the man condemned to death in *The Trial,* and finally convinced of his guilt for some crime which is never named, really either adapted or intended to illustrate original sin? —or is Kafka not rather satirizing the absurdities of his own bad conscience? In *The Castle,* there is also self-irony, but, besides this, a genuine wistfulness in K.'s longing to settle down and find a modest place in life for himself. But neither—unless one takes them as parodies of the Calvinist doctrine of Grace—seems to me to possess much interest as the expression of a religious point of view. The Christian of *Pilgrim's Progress* had obstacles to overcome and required moral fortitude to meet them; but all the struggling, such as it is, that is done by Kafka's K. is against an omnipotent and omniscient authority whose power and lights he can never share but to whose will he is doomed to succumb. And Dante, whose religious vision is all an exercise in control and direction, makes even his pagan Ulysses urge his men not to sleep before evening and tells them they were not made "to live like brutes but to follow virile courage and knowledge"; whereas Kafka is at his most characteristic when he is assimilating men to beasts —dogs, insects, mice, and apes—which can neither dare nor know. On the other hand, for me, these stories too often forfeit their effectiveness as satires through Kafka's rather meaching compliance, his little-boylike respect and fear in the presence of the things he would satirize: the boring diligence of commercial activity, the stuffiness of middle-class family life, the arid reasonings and tyrannous rigidities of Orthodox Judaism (which have a good deal in common with those of our old-fashioned Puritan Protestantism).

If, however, one puts Kafka beside writers with whom he may properly be compared, he still seems rather unsatisfactory. Gogol and Poe were equally neurotic, in their destinies they were equally unhappy; and if it is true, as Mr. Savage says, that there is present in Kafka's world neither personality nor love, there is no love in either Gogol or Poe, and though there are plenty of personalities in Gogol, the actors of Poe, as a rule, are even less characterized than Kafka's. But, though the symbols that these writers generate are just as unpleasant as Kafka's, though, like his, they represent mostly the intense and painful realization of emotional *culs-de-sac,* yet they have both certain advantages over Kafka—for Gogol was nourished and fortified by his heroic conception of Russia, and Poe, for all his Tory views, is post-Revolutionary American in his challenging, defiant temper, his alert and curious mind. In their ways, they are both tonic. But the denationalized, discouraged, disaffected, disabled Kafka, though for the moment he may frighten or amuse us, can in the end only let us down. He is quite true to his time and place, but it is surely a time and place in which few of us will want to linger—whether as stunned and hypnotized helots of totalitarian states or as citizens of freer societies, who have relapsed into taking Kafka's stories as evidence that God's law and man's purpose are conceived in terms so different that we may as well give up hope of ever identifying the one with the other.

"One must not cheat anybody," says Kafka, in an aphorism which has been much applauded, "not even the world of its triumph." But what are we writers here for if it is not to cheat the world of its triumph? In Kafka's case, it was he who was cheated and never lived to get his own back. What he has left us is the half-expressed gasp of a self-doubting soul trampled under. I do not see how one can possibly take him for either a great artist or a moral guide.

The World of Franz Kafka

by Erich Heller

Sometimes I feel I understand the Fall of Man better than anyone.

—FRANZ KAFKA

I

The relationship of Kafka's heroes to that truth for which they so desperately search can best be seen in the image through which Plato, in a famous passage of his *Republic,* expresses man's pitiable ignorance about the true nature of the *Ideas.* Chained to the ground of his cave, with his back toward the light, all he perceives of the fundamental reality of the world is a play of shadows thrown on to the wall of his prison. But for Kafka there is a further complication: perfectly aware of his wretched imprisonment and obsessed with a monomaniac desire to know, the prisoner has, by his unruly behavior and his incessant entreaties, provoked the government of his prison to an act of malicious generosity. In order to satisfy his passion for knowledge they have covered the walls with mirrors which, owing to the curved surface of the cave, distort what they reflect. Now the prisoner sees lucid pictures, definite shapes, clearly recognizable faces, an inexhaustible wealth of detail. His gaze is fixed no longer on empty shades, but on a full reflection of ideal reality. Face to face with the images of Truth, he is yet doubly agonized by their hopeless distortion. With an unparalleled fury of pedantry he observes the curve of every line, the ever-changing countenance of every figure, drawing schemes of every possible aberration from reality which his mirror may cause, making now this angle and now that the basis of his endless calculation which, he passionately hopes, will finally yield the geometry of truth.

In a letter (December 16, 1911) Kafka says: "I am separated from all things by a hollow space, and I do not even reach to its boundaries." In another (November 19, 1913): "Everything appears to me constructed.

. . . I am chasing after constructions. I enter a room, and I find them in a corner, a white tangle." And as late as 1921: "Everything is illusion: family, office, friends, the street, the woman, all illusion, drawing nearer and further away; but the nearest truth is merely that I push my head against the wall of a cell without doors or windows." [1] And in one of his aphorisms he says: "Our art is dazzled blindness before the truth: the light on the grotesquely distorted face is true, but nothing else." [2]

Kafka's novels take place in infinity. Yet their atmosphere is as oppressive as that of those unaired rooms in which so many of their scenes are enacted. For infinity is incompletely defined as the ideal point where two parallels meet. There is yet another place where they come together: the distorting mirror. Thus they carry into the prison-house of their violently distorted union the agony of infinite separation.

It is a Tantalus situation, and in Kafka's work the ancient curse has come to life once more. Kafka says of himself:

> "He is thirsty, and is cut off from a spring by a mere clump of bushes. But he is divided against himself: one part overlooks the whole, sees that he is standing here and that the spring is just beside him, but another part notices nothing, has at most a divination that the first part sees all. But as he notices nothing he cannot drink.[3]

Indeed, it was a curse, and not a word of light which called the universe of Kafka's novels into existence. The very clay from which it was made bore the imprint of a malediction before the creator had touched it. He builds to a splendid design, but the curse runs like a vein through every stone. In one of his most revealing parables Kafka shows himself completely aware of this:

> Everything seemed to fit the design of his edifice magnificently. Foreign workmen brought the marble, quarried for the purpose, each block fashioned for its proper place. The stones lifted themselves up and moved along in obedience to his measuring fingers. No edifice ever grew so smoothly as this temple, or rather this temple grew truly in the way in which temples ought to grow. Only that there were cut into every stone, obviously with wonderfully sharpened instruments, clumsy scribblings from the hands

[1] Franz Kafka, *Gesammelte Schriften,* edited by Max Brod (Prague, 1937), VI, p. 108. The present, rather confused, state of Kafka editions is unavoidably reflected in my references. Whenever possible, I refer to English translations of his works. Frequently, however, I had to modify the English text, partly for the sake of greater accuracy and partly for the sake of the particular emphasis required in the context of my discussion. Where my references are to the original, the translations are my own.

[2] *The Great Wall of China,* translated by Willa and Edwin Muir (London, 1946), p. 151.

[3] *Ibid.,* p. 140.

of senseless children, or perhaps inscriptions of barbaric mountain-dwellers; mischievous texts, blasphemous, or totally destructive, fixed there for an eternity which was to survive the temple.[4]

It is the reality of the curse that constitutes the ruthlessly compelling logic of Kafka's writings. They defy all attempts at rational interpretation, for Kafka is the least problematic of modern writers. He never thinks in disputable or refutable generalities. His thinking is a reflex movement of his being and shares the irrefutability of all that is. He thinks at an infinite number of removes from the Cartesian *cogito, ergo sum.* Indeed, it sometimes seems that an unknown "It" does all the thinking that matters, the radius of its thought touching the circumference of his existence here and there, causing him infinite pain, bringing his life into question and promising salvation on one condition only: that he should expand his being to bring it within the orbit of that strange Intelligence. The formula has become: "It thinks, and therefore I am not," with only the agony of despair providing overpowering proof that he is alive. He says of himself that he *is* the problem, and "no scholar to be found far and wide." [5]

There is, outside this agony, no reality about which he could entertain or communicate thoughts, nothing apart from the curse of his own separation from that Intelligence. Yet it is a complete world that is to be found within that pain, the exact pattern of creation once more, but this time made of the stuff of which curses are made. Like sorrow in the tenth of Rilke's *Duino Elegies,* despair is given a home of its own in Kafka's works, faithfully made in the image of customary life, but animated by the blast of the curse. This gives to Kafka's writings their unique quality. Never before has absolute darkness been represented with so much clarity, and the very madness of desperation with so much composure and sobriety. In his work an intolerable spiritual pride is expressed with the legitimate and convincing gesture of humility, disintegration finds its own level of integrity, and impenetrable complexity an all but *sancta simplicitas.* Kafka established the moral law of a boundlessly deceitful world, and performs in a totally incalculable domain ruled by evil demons, the most precise mathematical measurements.

Small wonder at the pathetic plight of critics in the face of Kafka's novels. It was with incredulous amazement that I noticed extracts from reviews which appear as advertisements of the English translation of Kafka's *The Castle*: "One reads it as if one were reading a fairy tale . . ." —"What a lovely, moving, memorable book!"—"A book of curious and

---

[4] *Gesammelte Schriften,* VI, p. 237.
[5] *The Great Wall of China,* p. 145.

original beauty." All this, attributed by the publishers to critics of some repute, is, of course, perverse. A nightmare is not a lovely fairy-tale, and a torture-chamber of the spirit is not full of original beauty. More serious, however, are the misinterpretations of Kafka by those who have undoubtedly made an honest effort to understand him. In the introduction to his own (and Willa Muir's) translation of *The Castle* Edwin Muir describes the subject-matter of this novel (very much in keeping with Max Brod's interpretation) as "human life wherever it is touched by the powers which all religions have acknowledged, by divine law and divine grace," and suggests that it should, with some reservations, be regarded "as a sort of modern *Pilgrim's Progress*," the reservation being that "the progress of the pilgrim here will remain in question all the time." According to him "*The Castle* is, like the *Pilgrim's Progress*, a religious allegory." [6]

From a great number of similar attempts to elucidate the darkness of Kafka's world I am choosing these sentences as a starting-point for a discussion of the work of this writer, and of *The Castle* in particular, because they express most succinctly what seems to me a disquieting misconception of its nature, the more disquieting because it is harbored by men of letters who are seriously concerned with literature and have —like Max Brod, Kafka's lifelong friend and editor of his writings, and Edwin Muir, his English translator—grasped the religious relevance of their author. Thus their misapprehension would seem to reflect a very profound religious confusion, so profound indeed that one can scarcely hold the individual critic responsible for it. It is the very spiritual uprootedness of the age which has deprived us of all sureness of religious discrimination. To men suffering from spiritual starvation, even a rotten fruit of the spirit may taste like bread from Heaven, and the liquid from a poisoned well like the water of life. If the critic is, moreover, steeped in psychology and comparative religion (as we all unwittingly are) the difference may appear negligible to him between Prometheus clamped to the rock, and the martyrdom of a Christian saint; between an ancient curse, and the grace that makes a new man.

The Castle is as much a religious allegory as a photographic likeness of the devil could be said to be an allegory of Evil. Every allegory has an opening into the rarefied air of abstractions, and is furnished with signposts pointing to an ideal construction beyond. *The Castle,* however, is a terminus of soul and mind, a *non plus ultra* of existence. In an allegory the author plays a kind of guessing game with his reader, if he does not actually provide the dictionary himself; but there is no key to *The Castle*. It is true that its reality does not precisely correspond to

---

[6] *The Castle,* translated by Willa and Edwin Muir (London, 1947), p. 6.

what is commonly understood in our positivist age as real, namely, neutral sense-perception of objects and, neatly separated from them, feelings; hence our most authentic and "realistic" intellectual pursuits: natural sciences and psychology; and our besetting sins: the ruthlessness of acquisitive techniques and sentimentality. In Kafka's novels there is no such division between the external sphere and the domain of inwardness, and therefore no such reality.

Kafka's creations are at the opposite pole to the writings of that type of Romantic poet, the true poetical representative of the utilitarian age, who distills from a spiritually more and more sterile external reality those elements which are still of some use to the emotions, or else withdraws from its barren fields into the greenhouse vegetation of inwardness. The author of *The Castle* does not select for evocative purposes, nor does he project his inner experience into a carefully chosen timeless setting. He does not, after the manner of Joyce, give away, in the melodious flow of intermittent articulation, the secret bedroom conversations which self conducts with self. There are no private symbols in his work, such as would be found in symbolist writing, no crystallized fragments of inner sensations charged with mysterious significance; nor is there, after the fashion of the Expressionists, any rehearsing of new gestures of the soul, meant to be more in harmony with the "new rhythm" of modern society. Instead of all this, the reader is faced with the shocking spectacle of a miraculously sensitive soul incapable of being reasonable, or cynical, or resigned, or rebellious, about the prospect of eternal damnation. The world which this soul perceives is unmistakably like the reader's own; a castle that is a castle and "symbolizes" merely what all castles symbolize: power and authority; a telephone exchange that produces more muddles than connections; a bureaucracy drowning in a deluge of forms and files; an obscure hierarchy of officialdom making it impossible ever to find the man authorized to deal with a particular case; officials who work overtime and yet get nowhere; numberless interviews which never are to the point; inns where the peasants meet, and barmaids who serve the officials. In fact, it is an excruciatingly familiar world, but reproduced by a creative intelligence which is endowed with the knowledge that it is a world damned for ever. Shakespeare once made one of his characters say:

> They say miracles are past, and we have our philosophical persons, to make modern and familiar things supernatural and causeless. Hence it is that we make trifles of terrors, ensconcing ourselves in seeming knowledge when we should submit ourselves to an unknown fear.

In Kafka we have the abdication of the philosophical persons.

In his work the terror recaptures the trifles, and the unknown **fear** invades all seeming knowledge—particularly that of psychology. Any criticism of the current religious interpretation of Kafka (which, at least, meets the religious aspect of his work on its own plane) is, I think, well advised to avoid the impression that it sides surreptitiously with other equally well-established dogmas about this writer. One of them, the psychological, is laid down by critics fascinated by Kafka's indubitably strained relationship with his father. But to interpret Kafka's novels in the perspective of the Oedipus complex is about as helpful to our understanding of his work as the statement that Kafka would have been a different person (and perhaps not a writer at all) if he had had another father; a penetrating thought, of which even psychologically less initiated ages might have been capable if they had deemed it worth thinking. This kind of psychology can contribute as much to the explanation of a work of art as ornithological anatomy to the fathoming of a nightingale's song. But so deeply ingrained is positivism in the critics of this age that even when they are genuinely moved by the symbolic reality which the author has created, they will soon regain the balance of mind required for the translation of the symbol into what it "really" means; and by that they mean precisely that meaningless experience which the artist has succeeded in transcending through his poetic creation. If, for instance, to the author the *meaning* of his senselessly tormenting feud with his father has been revealed through the discovery (which, in creating his work, he has made) that what he is *really* called upon to find is his place within a true spiritual order of divine authority, the interpreter will insist that what the author "really" means by talking about God, is that the quarrels with his father should stop.

In Kafka we have before us the modern mind, seemingly self-sufficient, intelligent, sceptical, ironical, splendidly trained for the great game of pretending that the world it comprehends in sterilized sobriety is the only and ultimate reality there is—yet a mind living in sin with the soul of Abraham. Thus he knows two things at once, and both with equal assurance: that there *is* no God, and that there *must* be God. It is the perspective of the curse: the intellect dreaming its dream of absolute freedom, and the soul knowing of its terrible bondage. The conviction of damnation is all that is left of faith, standing out like a rock in a landscape the softer soil of which has been eroded by the critical intellect. Kafka once said: "I ought to welcome eternity, but to find it makes me sad." [7]

This is merely an exhausted echo of the fanfares of despair with which Nietzsche (in many respects a legitimate spiritual ancestor of Kafka) welcomed his vision of eternity. In one of the posthumously published

[7] *Gesammelte Schriften*, VI, p. 231.

notes on *Zarathustra,* he says about his idea of the Eternal Recurrence: "We have produced the hardest possible thought—now let us create the creature who will accept it lightheartedly and blissfully!" [8] He conceived the Eternal Recurrence as a kind of spiritualized Darwinian test to select for survival the spiritually fittest. This he formulated with the utmost precision: "I perform the great experiment: who can bear the idea of Eternal Recurrence?" [9] And an ever deeper insight into the anatomy of despair we gain from his posthumous aphorisms and epigrams which were assembled by his editors in the two volumes of *The Will to Power,* many of which refer to the idea of Eternal Recurrence: "Let us consider this idea in its most terrifying form: existence, as it is, without meaning or goal, but inescapably recurrent, without a finale into nothingness. . . ." [10] Nietzsche's Superman is the creature strong enough to live forever a cursed existence, even to derive from it the Dionysian raptures of tragic acceptance. Nietzsche feels certain that only the Superman could be equal to the horror of a senseless eternity, and perform the great metamorphosis of turning "this most terrifying knowledge" into the terror of superhuman delight. And Kafka? On most of the few occasions when, in his diary, he speaks of happiness, he registers it as the result of a successful transformation of torture into bliss. This is one of his most horrible entries (November 21, 1911): "This morning, after a long time, I again took pleasure in imagining that a knife is turned in my heart." And in 1921, in the account of a dream: "There was bliss in my welcoming, with so deep a sense of freedom, conviction and joy, the punishment when it came." [11] If Nietzsche's Superman is the aesthetic counterbalance to the weight of the curse, then Kafka is its chosen victim. What some of his critics interpret as signs of religious achievement in his later writings, is merely the all-engulfing weariness of a Nietzschean Prometheus, which Kafka expressed in the fourth of his Prometheus legends: "Everyone grew weary of the meaningless affair. The gods grew weary, the eagles grew weary, the wound closed wearily." [12]

Thus Kafka's work, as much as Nietzsche's, must remain a stumbling-block to the analysing interpreter to whom, in the enlightened atmosphere of modern Europe, the word "curse" comes only as a faint memory of Greek tragedy, or as a figurative term for a combination of ill-luck and psychological maladjustment. Yet the gray world of Kafka's novels is luminous with its fire. Perhaps one cannot expect from modern man that, when he sees light, he should be able to distinguish between

[8] *Menschliches, Allzumenschliches,* XIV, p. 179.
[9] *Ibid.,* XIV, p. 187.
[10] *Ibid.,* XVIII, p. 45.
[11] *Gesammelte Schriften,* VI, p. 108.
[12] *The Great Wall of China,* p. 129.

burning sulphur and the radiance of Heaven. And although Mr. Muir is right in saying that Kafka's novels are about life in the grip of a power "which all religions have acknowledged," this power is certainly not "divine law and divine grace," but rather one which, having rebelled against the first and fallen from the second, has, in its own domain, successfully contrived the suspension of both. Undoubtedly, the land surveyor K., hero of *The Castle,* is religiously fascinated by its inscrutably horrid bureaucracy; but again it is a word from Nietzsche, and not from the Gospels, that sums up the situation: "Wretched man, your god lies in the dust, broken to fragments, and serpents dwell around him. And now you love even the serpents for his sake."

II

The Castle is not an allegorical, but a symbolic novel. A discussion of the difference could easily deteriorate into pedantry, the more so as, in common and literary usage, the terms are applied rather arbitrarily and have established themselves as meaning more or less the same thing. It will, however, help our understanding of Kafka's work if we distinguish, in using these two terms, two different modes of experience and expression. I shall therefore define my own—probably not less arbitrary—use of the terms.

The symbol *is* what it represents; the allegory represents what, in itself, it is *not.* The terms of reference of an allegory are abstractions; a symbol refers to something specific and concrete. The statue of a blindfolded woman, holding a pair of scales, is an *allegory* of Justice; bread and wine are, for the Christian communicant, *symbols* of the Body and Blood of Christ.[13] Thus an allegory must always be rationally translatable; whether a symbol is translatable or not depends on the fundamental agreement of society on the question of what kind of experience (out of the endless range of possible human experience) it regards as significant. The possibility of allegorizing will only vanish with the last man capable of *thinking in abstractions,* and of forming *images* of them; yet the validity of symbols depends not on rational operations, but on complex experiences in which thought and feeling merge in the act of spiritual comprehension. The sacramental symbols, for instance, would become incommunicable among a race of men who no longer regard the life,

---

[13] At this point I would like to beg the indulgence of the reader for disregarding the established theological terminology. The following discussion will, I hope, to some extent justify my apparent arbitrariness, which I do not wish to maintain outside the scope of this particular argument.

death, and resurrection of Christ as spiritually relevant *facts*. An allegory, being the imaginary representation of something abstract, is, as it were, doubly unreal; whereas the symbol, in being what it represents, possesses a double reality.

Goethe, summing up in one line at the end of *Faust II* the mature experience of his life, attributes whatever permanent reality there may be in a transient world to its symbolic significance. What is, is only *real* in so far as it is symbolic. Earlier in his life he defined the "true symbol" as "the representation of the general through the particular, not, however, as a dream or shadow, but as the revelation of the unfathomable in a moment filled with life."

The predicament of the symbol in our age is caused by a split between "reality" and what it signifies. There is no more any commonly accepted symbolic or transcendent order of things. What the modern mind perceives as order is established through the tidy relationship between things themselves. In one word: the only conceivable order is positivist-scientific. If there still is a—no doubt, diminishing—demand for the fuller reality of the symbol, then it must be provided for by the unsolicited gifts of art. But in the sphere of art the symbolic substance, dismissed from its disciplined commitments to "reality," dissolves into incoherence, ready to attach itself to any fragment of experience, invading it with irresistible power, so that a pair of boots, or a chair in the painter's attic, or a single tree on a slope which the poet passes, or an obscure inscription in a Venetian church, may suddenly become the precariously unstable center of an otherwise unfocused universe. Since "the great words from the time when what *really* happened was still visible, are no longer for us" (as Rilke once put it in a Requiem for a young poet), the "little words" have to carry an excessive freight of symbolic significance. No wonder that they are slow in delivering it. They are all but incommunicable private symbols, established beyond any doubt as symbols by the quality and intensity of artistic experience behind them, but lacking in any representative properties. Such is the economy of human consciousness that the positivist impoverishment of the one region produces anarchy in the other. In the end, atomic lawlessness is bound to prevail in both.

The intellectual foundation of every human society is a generally accepted model of reality. One of the major intellectual difficulties of human existence is, I think, due to the fact that this model of reality is in every single case a mere *interpretation* of the world, and yet exerts, as long as it seems the valid interpretation, the subtly compelling claim to being accepted as the only true picture of the universe, indeed as truth itself. This difficulty, manifesting itself in the deeper strata of doubt, by which, at all times, certain intellectually sensitive men have been affected, develops easily into a mental epidemic in epochs in which a certain model of reality crumbles and collapses. It seems that we have lived in such an epoch for a long time.

One of its main characteristics was the uncertainty, steadily increasing in the minds and feelings of men, about the relation between mundane and transcendental reality; or, in other words, about the meaning of life and death, the destiny of the soul, the nature and sanction of moral laws, the relative domains of knowledge and faith. As far as Christianity was the representative religion of the Middle Ages, their model of reality was essentially sacramental. A definite correspondence prevailed between the mundane and transcendental spheres. Faith was not established in any distinct "religious experience," nor, as a particular "mode of comprehension," kept apart from "knowledge." It was an element in *all* experience, indeed its crystallizing principle. Only within a mold and pattern determined by faith did experiences make sense and impressions turn to knowledge. This correspondence between the two spheres was so close that at every important stage of man's life they met and became one in the Sacraments.

The sacramental model of reality, intermittently disputed and questioned throughout the whole development of Christian theological thought, was upset in an historically decisive fashion at the time of the Reformation. During that period an intellectual tension, inherent in Christian dogma, developed into a conflagration of vast historical consequences. It produced an articulate climax—which was, however, a mere symptom of a more inarticulate, yet more comprehensive process—at a particularly exposed point of dogmatic faction: the sacramental dispute between Luther and Zwingli. Luther, despite his divergent interpretation of the traditional dogma, represents in it the essentially medieval view, whereas Zwingli, disciple of the humanist Pico della Mirandola, is the spokesman of modernity. To Luther the Sacrament of the Last Supper *is* Christ (the bread and the wine *are* what they represent), while Zwingli reduces it to the status of an allegory (as merely representing what, in itself, it is not). From then onwards the word "merely" has been attaching itself ever more firmly to the word "symbol," soon gaining sufficient strength to bring about a complete alienation between the two spheres. Finally a new order of things emerged. Within it the transcendental realm is allotted the highest honors of the spirit, but, at the same time, skilfully deprived of a considerable measure of reality; the mundane, on the other hand, is recompensed for its lowering in spiritual stature by the chance of absorbing all available reality and becoming more "really" real than before.

The sudden efflorescence of physical science in the seventeenth century is the positive result of this severance. Its successes have further contributed to the "lower realm" setting itself up as the only "really" real one, and as the sole provider of relevant truth, order, and lawfulness. Scientific and other positivist pursuits owe the unchallenged dominion, which they have wielded ever since over the intellectual life of Europe, to the ever more exclusive fascination which the new model of reality has had for the European mind.

As an unavoidable corollary of this state of affairs, religion and art lost their unquestioned birthright in the homeland of human reality, and turned into strange messengers from the higher unreality, admitted now and then as edifying or entertaining songsters at the positivist banquet. What had once been a matter-of-fact expression of life, became a "problem," worthy of a great deal of intellectual fuss and a negligible assignment of reality. As far as the arts are concerned, it is most revealing that the only *distinctive* artistic achievement of Europe since the end of the seventeenth century was accomplishd by the art with the least claim to "reality," music; while the most "real" of all arts, architecture, degenerated more and more until it gained new vitality as the unashamed functional servant of technology.

In Germany, a country which, for historical reasons too complex ever to be unravelled, suddenly rose in the eighteenth century to the heights of European consciousness and to the fulfillment of the most extravagant intellectual aspirations (without any gradual transition from the Middle Ages), the plight of the poet within the new model of reality is most conspicuous. The artist as an exile from reality—this is one of the most authentic themes of German literature, from Goethe's *Tasso* and Grillparzer's *Sappho* to Thomas Mann's *Tonio Kröger*. Kleist, Hölderlin, Nietzsche are the greatest among the victims of a hopeless collision between the minority demand for a realization of the spirit and a spiritualization of reality on the one hand, and, on the other, the inexorable resistance of a safely established spirit-proof view of life. Hölderlin is the greatest poet among those involuntary desperadoes of the spirit. His work is one continuous attempt to recapture the lost reality of the symbol and the sacramental experience of life. And for Goethe, to preserve his life, exposed at every point to the revengeful blows of the banished spirit, was, from beginning to end, a terrible struggle, entailing the most precarious maneuvers of compromise, irony and resignation. It was only— ironically enough—in his scientific activities that he gave vent to his unrestrained fury against the analytical-positivist view of the world and its scientific exposition through mathematics and Newtonian physics. How gloriously he blundered into physical science, determined to meet the enemy on his own ground, and how stubbornly convinced he was of being right! He once said to Eckermann (February 19, 1829):

> Whatever I have achieved as a poet is nothing to be particularly proud of. Excellent poets are my contemporaries, still better poets lived before me, and others will come after me. But in my own century I am the only man who knows what is right in the difficult science of colors; and this is something that gives me real satisfaction and a feeling of superiority over many.

His own idea of science was based on the *Urphänomen,* a striking assertion of the symbol as the final and irreducible truth of reality.

Goethe lost the battle for the symbol. In the century that stretches between his death and Kafka's writing, reality has been all but completely sealed off against any transcendental intrusion. But in Kafka's work the symbolic substance, forced back in every attempt to attack from above, invades reality from down below, carrying with it the stuff from hell. Or it need not even invade: Kafka writes at the point where the world, having become too heavy with spiritual emptiness, begins to sink into the unsuspected demon-ridden depths of unbelief. In this cataclysm, the more disastrous because it overtakes a world which has not even believed in its own unbelief, Kafka's heroes struggle in vain for spiritual survival. Thus his creations are symbolic, for they are infused with (and not merely allegorical of) negative transcendence.

Kafka knew the symbolic relevance of his work; he knew, too, of the complete alienation of modern man from the reality of the symbol. One of his profoundest meditations runs as follows:

> Many complain that the words of the wise are always merely symbols and of no use in daily life, which is the only life we have. When the wise man says: "Go over," he does not mean that we should cross to some actual place, which we could do anyhow if it were worth the effort; he means some miraculous beyond, something unknown to us, something that he too cannot define more precisely, and therefore cannot help us here in the least. All these symbols merely express that the incomprehensible is incomprehensible, and we have known that before. But the cares we have to struggle with every day: that is a different matter.
>
> Concerning this a man once said: Why such reluctance? If you only followed the symbols you would become symbols yourselves, and thus rid of all your daily cares.
>
> Another said: I bet this is also a symbol.
>
> The first said: You have won.
>
> The second said: But unfortunately only symbolically.
>
> The first said: No, in reality; symbolically you have lost.[14]

[14] *The Great Wall of China,* p. 132.

III

There are, however, allegorical elements to be found in *The Castle:* for instance, the names of many of the characters. The hero himself, who is introduced to us with the bare initial K. (undoubtedly an autobiographical hint,[15] and at the same time, through its very incompleteness, suggesting an unrealized, almost anonymous personality) is a land-surveyor. Kakfa's choice of this profession for his hero clearly has a meaning. The German for it is *Landvermesser,* and its verbal associations are significant. The first is, of course, the land-surveyor's professional activity, consisting precisely in what K. desperately desires and never achieves: to produce a workable order within clearly defined boundaries and limits of earthly life, and to find an acceptable compromise between conflicting claims of possession. But *Vermesser* also alludes to *Vermessenheit,* "hubris"; to the adjective *vermessen,* "audacious"; to the verb *sich vermessen,* "commit an act of spiritual pride," *and* also, "apply the wrong measure," "make a mistake in measurement." The most powerful official of the Castle (for K., the highest representative of authority) is called *Klamm,* a sound producing a sense of anxiety amounting almost to claustrophobia, suggesting straits, pincers, chains, clamps, but also a person's oppressive silence. The messenger of the Castle (as it turns out later, self-appointed and officially never recognized) has the name of *Barnabas,* the same as that man of Cyprus who, though not one of the Twelve, came to rank as an apostle; "Son of Consolation," or "Son of Exhortation," is the Biblical meaning of his name, and it is said of him that his exhortation was of the inspiring kind, and so built up faith. And the Barnabas of the novel is indeed a son of consolation, if only in the desperately ironical sense that his family, whom the curse of the Castle has cast into the lowest depths of misery and wretchedness, in vain expects deliverance through his voluntary service for the authority. To K., however, his messages, in all their obscurity and pointlessness, seem the only real link with the Castle, an elusive glimmer of hope, a will-o'-the-wisp of faith. Barnabas' counterpart is *Momus,* the village secretary of Klamm, and namesake of that depressing creature, the son of Night, whom the Greek gods had authorized to find fault with all things. In the novel it is he whose very existence seems the denial of any hope which Barnabas may have roused in K. *Frieda* ("peace") is the girl through whose love K. seeks to reach the goal of his striving; *Bürgel* (diminutive of *Bürge,* "guarantor") , the name of the little official who offers the solution, with-

---

[15] The first draft of the novel was written in the first person.

out K. even noticing the chance; and the secretary through whom K. does expect to achieve something and achieves nothing, is called *Erlanger* ("citizen of the town of Erlangen," but also suggestive of *erlangen*, "attain," "achieve").

This discussion of names provides an almost complete synopsis of the slender plot of *The Castle*. Someone, a man whose name begins with K., and of whom we know no more, neither whence he comes nor what his past life has been, arrives in a village which is ruled by a Castle. He believes that he has been appointed land-surveyor by the authorities. The few indirect contacts that K. succeeds in establishing with the Castle—a letter he receives, a telephone conversation he overhears, yet another letter, and above all the fact that he is joined by two assistants whom the rulers have assigned to him—*seem* to confirm his appointment. Yet he himself is never fully convinced, and never relaxes in his efforts to make quite sure of it. He feels he must penetrate to the very center of authority and wring from it a kind of ultra-final evidence for his claim. Until then he yields, in paralyzed despair, broken by only momentary outbursts of rebellious pride, to the inarticulate, yet absolutely self-assured refusal of the village to acknowledge him as their land-surveyor:

> You've been taken on as land-surveyor, as you say, but, unfortunately, we have no need of a land-surveyor. There wouldn't be the least use for one here. The frontiers of our little estates are marked out and all neatly registered. . . . So what would be the good of a land-surveyor? [16]

says the village representative to him.

K.'s belief appears, from the very outset, to be based both on truth and illusion. It is Kafka's all but unbelievable achievement to force—indeed, to frighten—the reader into unquestioning acceptance of this paradox, presented with ruthless realism and irresistible logic. Truth and illusion are mingled in K.'s central belief in such a way that he is deprived of all order of reality. Truth is permanently on the point of taking off its mask and revealing itself as illusion, illusion in constant danger of being verified as truth. It is the predicament of a man who, endowed with an insatiable appetite for transcendental certainty, finds himself in a world robbed of all spiritual possessions. Thus he is caught in a vicious circle. He cannot accept the world—the village—without first attaining to absolute certainty, and he cannot be certain without first accepting the world. Yet every contact with the world makes a mockery of his search, and the continuance of his search turns the world into a mere encumbrance. After studying the first letter from the Castle, K. contemplates his dilemma:

[16] *The Castle*, p. 79.

. . . whether he preferred to become a village worker with a distinctive but merely apparent connection with the Castle, or an ostensible village worker whose real occupation was determined through the medium of Barnabas." [17]

From the angle of the village all K.'s contacts with the Castle are figments of his imagination:

"You haven't once up till now come into real contact with our authorities. All those contacts are merely illusory, but owing to your ignorance of the circumstances you take them to be real." [18]

The Castle, on the other hand, seems to take no notice whatever of the reality of K.'s miserable village existence. In the midst of his suffering the indignity of being employed as a kind of footman to the schoolmaster, he receives the following letter from Klamm:

"The surveying work which you have carried out thus far has my recognition. . . . Do not slacken in your efforts! Bring your work to a successful conclusion. Any interruption would displease me. . . . I shall not forget you." [19]

From all this it would appear that it is, in fact, the village that disobeys the will of the Castle, while defeating K. with the powerful suggestion that he misunderstands the intentions of authority. And yet the authority seems to give its blessing to the defiance of the village, and to punish K. for his determination to act in accordance with the letter of its orders. In his fanatical obedience it is really he who rebels against the Castle, whereas the village, in its matter-of-fact refusal, lives the life of the law.

Kafka represents the absolute reversal of German idealism. If it is Hegel's final belief that, in the Absolute, truth and existence are one, for Kafka it is precisely through the Absolute that they are forever divided. Truth and existence are mutually exclusive. From his early days onwards it was the keenest wish of Kafka the artist to convey this in works of art; to write in such a way that life, in all its deceptively convincing reality, would be seen as a dream and a nothing before the Absolute:

Somewhat as if one were to hammer together a table with painful and methodical technical efficiency, and simultaneously do nothing at all, and not in such a way that people could say: "Hammering a table together is

[17] *Ibid.*, p. 38.
[18] *Ibid.*, p. 95.
[19] *Ibid.*, p. 150.

really nothing to him," but rather "Hammering a table together is really hammering a table together to him, but at the same time it is nothing," whereby certainly the hammering would have become still bolder, still surer, still more real and, if you will, still more senseless.[20]

This is how Kafka describes the vision of artistic accomplishment which hovered before his mind's eye when, as a young man, he sat one day on the slopes of the Laurenziberg in Prague. Has he, in his later works, achieved this artistic justification of nonentity? Not quite; what was meant to become the lifting of a curse through art, became the artistically perfect realization of it, and what he dreamed of making into something as light as a dream, fell from his hands with the heaviness of a nightmare. Instead of a vindication of nothingness, he achieved the portrayal of the most cunningly vindictive unreality. He had good reason for decreeing that his writings should be burned.

It is hard to see how *The Castle* can possibly be called a religious allegory with a pilgrim of the type of Bunyan's as its hero. Pilgrimage? On the contrary, the most oppressive quality of Kafka's work is the unshakable stability of its central situation. It takes place in a world that knows of no motion, no change, no metamorphosis. Its caterpillars never turn into butterflies, and when the leaves of a tree tremble it is not due to the wind: it is the stirring of a serpent coiled round its branches. There is, in fact, no pilgrimage to be watched in *The Castle,* and the progress not merely "remains in question all the time," but is not even possible, unless we agree to call progress what Kafka once described in his fable of the mouse:

> "Alas," said the mouse, "the world is growing smaller every day. At the beginning it was so big that I was afraid, I kept running and running, and I was glad when at last I saw walls far away to the right and left, but these long walls have narrowed so quickly that I am in the last chamber already, and there in the corner stands the trap that I must run into." "You only need to change your direction," said the cat, and ate it up.[21]

Of the two points on which Kafka and Bunyan, according to Edwin Muir's introduction, are agreed: "that the goal and the road indubitably exist, and that the necessity to find them is urgent," only the second is correct, and indeed, to find them is so urgent for Kafka that life is impossible unless they are found. But do they exist? "There is a goal, but no way; what we call way is only wavering," [22] is what Kafka says about it. And *is* there really a goal for him? This is Kafka's self-reply:

[20] *The Great Wall of China,* p. 136.
[21] *Ibid.,* p. 133.
[22] *Ibid.,* p. 145

He feels imprisoned on this earth, he feels constricted; the melancholy, the impotence, the sickness, the feverish fancies of the captive afflict him; no comfort can comfort him, since it is merely comfort, gentle, head-splitting comfort glozing the brutal fact of imprisonment. But if he is asked what he actually wants he cannot reply, for—that is one of his strongest proofs—he has no conception of freedom.[23]

Kafka's hero is the man who *believes* in absolute freedom, but cannot have any conception of it because he *exists* in a world of slavery. Therefore it is not grace and salvation that he seeks, but either his right or—a bargain with the powers. "I don't want any act of favor from the Castle, but my rights," [24] says K. in his interview with the village representative. But convinced of the futility of this expectation, his real hope is based on Frieda, his fiancée and former mistress of Klamm, whom he is obviously prepared to hand back to him "for a price."

In K.'s relationship to Frieda the European story of romantic love has found its epilogue. It is the solid residue left behind by the evaporated perfume of romance, revealing its darkest secret. In romantic love, as it has dominated a vast section of European literature ever since the later Middle Ages, individualism, emerging from the ruins of a communal order of the spirit, has found its most powerful means of transcendence. The spiritually more and more autonomous, and therefore more and more lonely individual worships Eros (and his twin deity within the romantic imagination: Death) as the only god capable of breaking down the barriers of his individualist isolation. Therefore love becomes tragedy: overcharged with unmanageable spiritual demands it must needs surge ahead of any human relationship. In its purest manifestations, romantic love is a glorious disaster of the soul, carrying frustration in its wake. For what the romantic lover seeks is not really the beloved. Intermixed with his erotic craving, inarticulate, diffuse, and yet dominating it, is the desire for spiritual salvation. Even a "happy ending" spells profound disillusionment for the romantic expectation. Perhaps it is Strindberg who wrote the last chapter of its history. It is certainly Kafka who wrote its postscript.

For K. loves Frieda—if he loves her at all—entirely for Klamm's sake. This is not only implied in the whole story of K. and Frieda, but explicitly stated by Kafka in several—afterwards deleted—passages of the book. It is contained in the protocol about K.'s life in the village which Momus has drawn up, and in which K. is accused of having made up to Frieda merely because he believed that in her he would win a mistress of Klamm "and so possess a hostage which could only be redeemed at

[23] *Ibid.,* p. 135.
[24] *The Castle,* p. 98.

the highest price." [25] On the margin of the protocol there was also "a childishly scrawled drawing of a man holding a girl in his arms; the girl's face was hidden in the man's breast, but he, being much taller, was looking over her shoulders at a paper in his hand on which he was gleefully entering some figures." [26] But perhaps still more conclusive than Momus' clearly hostile interpretation is another deleted passage giving K.'s own reflections on his love for Frieda:

> . . . And soon afterwards—and there was not even time to think—Frieda had entered his life, and with her the belief (a belief which he was quite unable to abandon completely even now) that through her there was established an almost physical connection with Klamm, intimate to the point of whispered communications; perhaps, for the time being, it was only K. who knew of it, but it needed a mere touch, a word, a raising of eyes, to reveal itself first to Klamm, but then to everybody, as something unbelievable but yet self-evident by virtue of the irrefutability of life itself, the irrefutability of the embrace of love. . . . What was he without Frieda? A nonentity, staggering after glittering will-o'-the-wisps. . . . [27]

The desperate desire for spiritual certainty is all that is left of romantic love. K. *wills* his love for Frieda because he *wills* his salvation. He is a kind of Pelagius believing that he "can if he ought," yet living in a relentlessly predestined world. This situation produces a theology very much after the model of Gnostic and Manichean beliefs. The incarnation is implicitly denied in an unmitigated loathing of "determined" matter, and the powers which rule are perpetually suspected of an alliance with the devil because they have consented to the creation of such a loathsome world. Heaven is at least at seven removes from the earth, and only begins where no more neighborly relations are possible. There are no real points of contact between divinity and the earth, which is not even touched by divine emanation. Reality is the sovereign domain of strangely unangelic angels, made up of evil and hostility. The tedious task of the soul is, with much wisdom of initiation and often with cunning diplomacy, gradually to bypass the armies of angels and the strong-points of evil, and finally to slip into the remote kingdom of light. The Castle of Kafka's novel is, as it were, the heavily fortified garrison of a company of Gnostic demons, successfully holding an advanced position against the maneuvers of an impatient soul. I do not know of any conceivable idea of divinity which could justify those interpreters who see in the Castle the residence of "divine law and divine grace." Its

[25] *Ibid.*, p. 316, in Max Brod's "Additional Note."
[26] *Ibid.*, p. 317.
[27] *Gesammelte Schriften*, IV, pp. 380, 381.

officers are totally indifferent to good if they are not positively wicked. Neither in their decrees nor in their activities is there discernible any trace of love, mercy, charity, or majesty. In their icy detachment they inspire certainly no awe, but fear and revulsion. Their servants are a plague to the village, "a wild, unmanageable lot, ruled by their insatiable instincts . . . their shamelessness knows no limits," [28] an anticipation rather of the blackguards who were to become the footmen of European dictators than the office-boys of a divine ministry. Compared to the petty and apparently calculated torture of this tyranny, the gods of Shakespeare's indignation who "kill us for their sport" are at least majestic in their wantonness.

From the very beginning there is an air of indecency, indeed of obscenity, about the inscrutable rule of the Castle. A newcomer in the village, K. meets the teacher in the company of children. He asks her whether she knows the Count and is surprised at the negative answer:

> "What, you don't know the Count?" "Why should I?" replied the teacher in a low tone, and added aloud in French: "Please remember that there are innocent children present." [29]

And, indeed, what an abhorrent rule it is! The souls of women seem to be allowed to enter the next realm if they surrender, as a sort of pass, their bodies to the officials. They are then married off to some nincompoop in the village, with their drab existence rewarded only by occasional flashes of voluptuously blissful memories of their sacrificial sins. Damnation is their lot if they refuse, as happened in the case of Amalia, Barnabas' sister, who brought degradation upon herself and her family by declining the invitation of the official Sortini.

The unfathomable depths of nonsense into which an interpretation can be lured by its own mistaken assumptions is revealed in Max Brod's critical dealings with that crucial point in the story of Barnabas' family. In his epilogue to *The Castle* Max Brod writes:

> The connection between the Castle—that is divine guidance—and the women . . . may appear mysterious and even inexplicable in the Sortini episode, where the official (Heaven) requires the girl to do something obviously immoral and sordid; here a reference to Kierkegaard's *Fear and Trembling* may be of value. . . . The Sortini episode is literally a parallel to Kierkegaard's book, which starts from the fact that God required of Abraham what was really a crime, the sacrifice of his child; and which uses this paradox to establish triumphantly the conclusion that the categories of morality and religion are by no means identical.[30]

[28] *The Castle*, p. 269.
[29] *Ibid.*, p. 21.
[30] *Ibid.*, p. 317.

This is, for the believer, downright blasphemy, and a critical insult to the intelligence of a reader able to read for himself the Bible, Kierkegaard, and Kafka. The comparison between Kierkegaard and Kafka would indeed be relevant. It might bring home, even to a modern reader, the difference between Purgatory and Hell. For this is the precise relationship between Kierkegaard's *Fear and Trembling* and Kafka's *The Castle*. The sacrifice of Isaac a parallel to Sortini's designs on Amalia? But this means, without any polemical exaggeration, to ascribe to the God of Abraham a personal interest in the boy Isaac, worthy rather of a Greek demi-god. Moreover, He having tested Abraham's absolute obedience, did not accept the sacrifice. Yet Sortini (who conveys to Max Brod the idea of divine guidance and Heaven itself) can, to judge by the example of his colleagues, be relied upon not to have summoned Amalia to his bedroom merely to tell her that one does not do such a thing.

To return from the comic escapades of literary criticism to Franz Kafka's novel: the Castle represents neither divine guidance nor Heaven. It is for K. something that is to be conquered, something that bars his way into a purer realm. K.'s antagonism to the Castle becomes clear from the very first pages of the book. This is how he responds to the first telephone conversation about his appointment which, in his presence, is conducted between the Village and the authorities:

> K. pricked up his ears. So the Castle had recognized him as the land-surveyor. That was unpropitious for him, on the one hand, for it meant that the Castle was well-informed about him, had estimated all the probable chances and was taking up the challenge with a smile. On the other hand, however, it was quite propitious, for if his interpretation were right they had underestimated his strength, and he would have more freedom of action than he had dared to hope.[31]

The correspondence between the spiritual structure of *The Castle* and the view of the world systematized into Gnostic and Manichean dogma is indeed striking. There is, however, no reason to assume that Kafka had any special knowledge of those ancient heresies. In their radical dualism they are merely the model systems of a deep-rooted spiritual disposition, asserting itself over and over again in individuals and whole movements. That which is Gnostic and Manichean is, above all, "the face that is filled with loathing and hate" at the sight of physical reality. Kafka refrains from any dealings with nature. There is, apart from the mention of a starry sky, wind and snow, not one description of nature in *The Castle*. Within the human sphere everything that is of the flesh is treated with a sense of nausea and disgust. All the habita-

[31] *Ibid.,* p. 15.

tions of men are lightless, airless, and dirty. The nuptial embrace between K. and Frieda takes place amidst puddles of beer on the floor of a public bar, the room still filled with the stale smells of an evening's business, while mass prostitution is carried on in the stable of the inn.

But Kafka has also found subtler means of conveying his revolt against the "real." One evening K. is waiting in the dark courtyard of the inn for Klamm to emerge from his village room and enter his sleigh. The coachman, noticing K., encourages him to wait inside the sleigh and have a drink from one of the bottles kept in the side pockets. K. opens the bottle and smells:

> Involuntarily he smiled, the perfume was so sweet, so caressing, like praise and good words from someone whom one loves very dearly, yet one does not quite know what they are about and has no desire to know, and is simply happy in the knowledge that it is he who is saying them. "Can this be brandy?" K. asked himself doubtfully, and tasted out of curiosity. Yes, surprisingly enough, it was brandy, and it burned and warmed. How strangely it transformed itself, as he drank, from something which was hardly more than a medium of sweet perfume, into a vulgar drink, fit for a coachman![32]

Whether intentional or not, this profanation of the perfume of a spirit in the process of being "realized," is a wonderfully subtle symbol of a Manichean perspective of the world. And the most telling formula of this Manichean disposition Kafka once found after finishing one of his stories:

> I can still derive some temporary satisfaction from a work of this kind . . . but happiness only if I ever succeed in lifting the world into a sphere pure, true, unchangeable." (Diary note of September 25, 1917)[33]

Is his Castle of that sphere? It is, no doubt, the highest realm K. is capable of perceiving. This is what misled the critics, but not Kafka himself, into equating it with God. But it is certainly not quite irrelevant that in his personal confessions Kafka never, not once, utters the belief that the incessant striving of his spirit was directed towards God, or prompted by *amor Dei*. All the time his soul is preoccupied with the power of Evil; a power so great that God had to retreat before it into purest transcendence, forever out of reach of life. Life itself is the incarnation of Evil: "Knowledge of the diabolical there can be, but not

---

[32] *Ibid.*, pp. 132, 133.
[33] Quoted by Max Brod as motto to *Franz Kafka, A Biography*, translated by G. Humphreys Roberts (London, 1947).

belief in it, for there is nothing more diabolical than what exists." [34]
And then again the reality of life, still identified with Evil, is denied completely: "There is only a spiritual world; what we call the physical world
is the evil in the spiritual one. . . ." [35] Thus the idea of final authority,
merely by assuming the shape of physical reality in *The Castle,* falls,
without the author either willing it or being able to help it, under the
spell of Evil. It is the paradox of spiritual absolutism that the slightest
touch of concreteness will poison the purest substance of the spirit, and
one ray of darkness blot out a world of light.

Yet Kafka is neither a dogmatic follower of the Gnosis nor a Manichee;
he is an artist, and although the cursed rule of the Castle is the farthest
point of the world to which his wakeful mind can reach, there dawns, at
its extreme boundaries, a light, half-suspectingly perceived, half-stub-
bornly ignored, that comes from things outside the scope of Klamm's
authority. K. knows only one thing: that he must come to grips with
Klamm; yet at the same time he knows that his very obsession with this
thought precludes him from reaching what he mistakenly believes only
Klamm can give. He senses dimly that humility and humor would
bring him the possession of which he deprives himself by his very striving
for it. In Pepi who, for a short time, was promoted to the rank of bar-
maid in the local inn (and thus to the opportunity of serving beer to
Klamm), now trembling at the prospect of losing her position again, K.
meets the caricatured embodiment of his own ambition. In giving advice
to her he shows a remarkable knowledge of his own disease:

> It is a job like any other, but for you it is the kingdom of Heaven. There-
> fore you set about your business with exaggerated zeal . . . you tremble
> for your position, feel constantly persecuted, try by overdoing your friend-
> liness, to win over those who you believe could help you; but you merely
> annoy and repel them; for what they look for in a bar is peace, and not, on
> top of their own cares, the anxiety of a barmaid. [36]

And later:

> If I compare myself to you, I suspect that both of us have tried, in too
> noisy, too childish, too inexperienced a fashion, to get something which is to
> be had easily and simply through Frieda's matter-of-factness. We are crying
> and scratching and tossing about, like little children who tug at the table-

[34] *The Great Wall of China,* p. 157. [Editor's Note: This aphorism is rendered in the
Definitive Edition, "There can be knowledge of the diabolical, but no belief in it, for
more of the diabolical than there is does not exist." *Wedding Preparations,* p. 51.
(". . . *denn mehr Teuflisches, als da ist, gibt es nicht"*).]
[35] *Ibid.,* p. 149.
[36] *Gesammelte Schriften,* IV, p. 353.

cloth, but gain nothing, only cause all the nice things to tumble down, making them unobtainable for ever.[37]

But it is in K.'s adventure with the Castle official Bürgel that this insight finds its most striking parable. K., summoned in the middle of the night to an interview with the official Erlanger, has, in his weariness and exhaustion, forgotten the number of the right door, and enters (more in the hope of finding an empty bed there than an official of the Castle) another room. There he encounters, lying in bed, the official Bürgel. The ensuing dialogue, or monologue rather, is one of Kafka's greatest feats in the art of melting the solid flesh of a grotesque reality and revealing behind it the anatomic structure of the miraculous. Bürgel promises K. to settle once and for all his affairs in the Castle. K. is not in the least impressed by this offer. He waves it aside as the boast of a dilettante:

> Without knowing anything of the circumstances in which K.'s appointment had been made, and nothing of the difficulties which it met in the Village and in the Castle, and of the complications which had either already arisen or were in the air; without knowing anything of all this, indeed without even showing—and might one not take that for granted with a secretary?—that he had at least a faint notion of it, he offered, by sleight-of-hand, and with the help of a little pad of notepaper, to settle the matter up there.[38]

It is the unbelief of a labyrinthine mind in the very existence of simplicity. And while K. grows ever more weary, Bürgel delivers, in a rapturous crescendo, the message of the miracle: if a man takes a secretary of the Castle by surprise; if, in the middle of the night, the applicant, almost unconscious of what he does, slips, like a tiny grain through a perfect sieve, through the network of difficulties that is spread over all approaches to the center of authority, then the Castle, in the person of this one secretary, must yield to the intruder, indeed must almost force the granting of the request upon the unsuspecting subject: "You believe it cannot happen? You are right, it cannot happen at all. But one night—who can vouch for everything?—it does happen after all." It is an event so rare that it seems to occur merely by virtue of rumor, and even if it does occur, one can, "as it were, render it innocuous by proving to it—and this proof is easy enough—that there is no room for it in this world." [39] And Bürgel goes on with his rhapsody, describing the shattering delight with which a secretary responds to this situation. But when he ends, K. is sound asleep, and, with the conditions of the miracle fulfilled before

---

[37] *Ibid.*, p. 355.
[38] *Ibid.*, p. 300.
[39] *Ibid.*, 308, 309.

his eyes, as oblivious of its possibility as he had been in his tortured wakeful pursuit of it.

Indeed, no comfort can be found *within* this world. Yet the power, not only to experience, but poetically to create this world, must have its source *outside*. Only a mind keeping alive in at least one of its recesses the memory of a place where the soul is truly at home, is able to contemplate with such creative vigor the struggles of a soul lost in a hostile land; and only an immensity of goodness can be so helplessly overcome by the vision of the worst of all possible worlds. This is the reason why we are not merely terrified by the despair of this book, but also moved by its sadness, the melancholy of spiritual failure carrying with it a subtle promise.

In one of his most Manichean sayings Kafka speaks of the power of a single crow to destroy the heavens; but, he adds, this "proves nothing against the heavens, for the heavens signify simply: the impossibility of crows." [40] And although these birds swarm ceaselessly around *The Castle*, its builder built it from the impulse to render them impossible. Is it, one wonders, yet another phantom hope in a deluded world that prompts, in the book, a child, a simple girl and a wretched family to turn with a mysteriously messianic expectation to the land-surveyor K.? And makes, on a deleted page of the unfinished manuscript, a mother invite the homeless stranger to her house with the words: "This man should not be allowed to perish"? [41] Or is it perhaps the reflection of a faith, maintained even in the grip of damnation, which Nietzsche once expressed: "Whosoever has built a new heaven has found the strength for it only in his own hell." [42]

[40] *The Great Wall of China*, p. 146.

[41] *Gesammelte Schriften*, IV, p. 428.

[42] Long after this essay was written, I found the following passage in an as yet unpublished letter of Kafka's: "No people sing with such pure voices as those who live in deepest hell; what we take for the song of angels is their song."

Franz Kafka

by *Austin Warren*

Kafka's novels evoke a world as self-coherent and characteristic as that of Dickens, of Dostoevsky, of Proust, of Poe, of Hawthorne. Like Hawthorne's and Poe's, Kafka's is a limited, a lyric, world. Kafka is a metaphysical poet in symbolist narrative.

His is a city world. Like Dickens' London, it flourishes in grotesques. But they have not the vigor, the delight in their own salt being, of Quilp and Miss Mowcher; and they are chiefly unnamed and seen but momentarily. Old women look out of inquisitive windows; in the gutters sit leering, irreverent, mocking children; a young lad, his nose half-eaten away, scrutinizes arrivals; the warden wears a gross body, ill-adjusted to his "dry bony face, with a great nose twisted to one side."

It is an overcrowded, airless world, within which it is difficult to sustain faith in the weight and worth of the individual. In Georg Salter's illustration to *The Trial,* most persons except the introspective hero are but shapes of shadow. Kafka's solipsism is intelligible, is defensible, as necessary to sustaining, in a city of the anonymous, the belief that the soul and its choices matter.

Even Kafka's imagined America is not a land of broad cornfields shining in the sun but a chiefly metropolitan affair, already stratified, weary, and hopeless—a land of hotels and of slums.

> Karl thought of the east end of New York which his uncle had promised to show him where it was said that several families lived in one little room and the house of a whole family consisted of one corner where many children clustered around their parents.

Kafka read Franklin's *Autobiography,* we are told, and admired Walt Whitman, and liked the Americans because he believed them to be "healthy and optimistic." But his imagination does not so present them. A sort of WPA theater opens hospitably at the end, to be sure; yet the novel follows Dickens, not Alger. Karl is the young Copperfield, the young Oliver Twist, the sensitive boy ejected from home on charges which puzzle him. He finds America gleaming but hard. Before landing, he encounters social injustice in the case of "The Stoker"; his uncle, who suddenly appears and assumes his support, as suddenly and less plausibly renounces responsibility; he is deceived and maltreated by his chance travelling companions: for no fault of his own, he is discharged from the hotel; he comes near to ending as a slavey in a delirious apartment. America is a world in which elevators whiz up and down, phonographs play incessantly without anyone's listening, political candidates get lost in the crowds which are to elect them. It offers the image of the ascent to Brunelda's apartment: long stairs moving up into squalid darkness; beside the stair-railing, a little girl weeps, then rushes up the steps gasping for breath.

Kafka's is a world known in nightmares—a rational, unnatural world in which unnatural situations are rationally worked out—in which everyone is able, like Lewis Carroll's creatures, to argue long, ingeniously, and convincingly. It is a nightmare world in which the "I," all innocent and eager to submit, all desirous to propitiate, is pushed about, pursued, regimented by potencies veiled of visage—in which one is forever being orally examined by dignitaries who forever flunk one. The self and the world are juxtaposed in opposition. If one is not being pursued by the world or carried off by the world, one is running after it. There is the image of the old father trying to catch the ear of the Castle dignitaries—trying in vain, for the officials go at a gallop, their carriages "race like mad." It is the world of a Mack Sennett comedy—one of chase and pursuit, of intense movement, horizontal and vertical: of running and climbing. It is a world of uncertainty and insecurity, of fear and trembling.

It is a world of hierarchy, created by Kafka in the parodic imitation of the Austrian bureaucracies under which he lived, within which, as underofficial, he worked. In its chief traits it could be a feudal estate or it could be an American department store or a chain of restaurants or a metropolitan public library. Hierarchy provides, negatively, for deferment of responsibility or infinite regress. One's complaint always reaches the wrong office; one is passed on from office to office, in general moving up the scale of delegated authority, only to find that the proper official to handle the complaint is out of town, or the necessary documents are lost, or by delay one's claim is outlawed. Wonderful is the efficiency of an order so complexly graduated that every expert is inexpert at satisfying the simple need for justice.

There are other difficulties. Hierarchic order is necessary in a universe densely populated, whether with atoms or souls; yet, in an order so intricate, instrumentalities must, almost unavoidably, turn into ends: readers exist in order that librarians may make card catalogs, pupils in order that educationalists may publish books on Methods of Teaching, worshipers in order that janitors may sweep and lock churches. Underofficials, those who administer the rules to the public, can scarcely be expected to understand the spirit of the rules or what, as formulated by unseen and doubtless long dead "higher-ups," the rules aimed at. A teeming universe must, of course, be a "planned," even if an ill-planned, or a too fussily planned, society. The easy improvisation which fits the New England village cannot be transported to the city. Indeed, by one of his most brilliant audacities, Kafka imagines that even the village cannot really be a village, for if its multiple needs are adequately to be taken care of, there will be business enough to require busy attention from a whole caste of officials.

Kafka's novels can be taken as burlesques of bureaucracy. Satiric, of course, they are. Yet they lack satiric norm, a contrasting model of elegance and humanity. The hero is too uncertain of himself to sit in judgment on duly constituted authorities and too intent upon learning their ways to have leisure for criticizing them. As for bureaucracy, it is even at its worst a corruption of order; and order is a state so blessed, so indispensable, that even its parodies deserve respect. As for bureaucrats, the common charge against them is that they are too insistent upon the importance of their work, too narrow in their conception of it; but surely it is the duty of officials to be officious, and narrowness and even scrupulosity are marks of their being dedicated to their profession. The work of the world is carried on by experts, not by gentlemen; and if we want to deepen the sense of "work" and "world," we must add, "strait is the gate and narrow the way"; the price of salvation is the forced sale of all that one has.

Hierarchy is pyramidal. Is there, for Kafka, any Reason, any Supreme Will, at the top and the end? Or is hierarchy a staircase which ends not in a dome or a tower but in a fall into darkness? The answer is uncertain. Of a chief justice we never hear, nor of a head-manager of a hotel. In *The Castle,* we hear for a preliminary moment of the "Count West-west," but soon he and any direct view of the Castle itself are lost or forgotten. Doubtless there is an ultimate authority, but we never reach it except through its intermediaries: there is no direct vision. In "Before the Law," the lowest doorkeeper can see a few doors ahead of him into what he believes to be a vast series of ascents: "From hall to hall keepers stand at every door, one more powerful than the other. Even the third of these has an aspect that even I cannot bear to look at." Of the ascending series we can say that there is no point at which we observe it to stop. Olga explains to K.:

"Who is it that Barnabas speaks to there [in the Castle] I have no idea—
perhaps the clerk is lowest in the whole staff; but even if he is lowest he
can put one in touch with the next man above him, and if he can't even do
that he can refer to somebody who can give the name."

They are men set under authority; and "Does not the least degree of
authority contain the whole?"

In both *The Trial* and *The Castle,* underofficials, advocates, and villagers spend much time in speculating upon the ways of the "higher-
ups." In the latter we hear Amalia ask, "Is it Castle gossip you're at? . . .
There are people in the village who live on it; they stick their heads
together just like you two and entertain each other by the hour"; to
which K. replies that he is just such a person, "and moreover people who
don't care for such gossip and leave it all to others don't interest me
particularly." So the talk goes on. We "gossip" or speculate about Klamm,
attempting to adjust to coherence the glimpses we catch. A man like
Klamm "who is so much sought after and rarely seen is apt to take different shapes in people's imaginations"—to give rise to theophanies
very diverse each from the other.

Yet Kafka's officials, however otherwise various, have in common a
certain obtrusive perversity: their lack of elegance. So, too, the rooms
in which the courts sit have none of the grandeur or even decent neat-
ness we might anticipate, and the Castle is unimpressive, disappointing to
strangers. Instead of being better balanced and more humanistic than
the villagers, the officials are officious, pompous, and pedantic. But the
"virtues of the pagans are splendid vices": "officious, pompous, and
pedantic" are dyslogistic terms to be transvaluated as "conscientious,
dignified, and properly accurate."

These paper-reading officials are scholars, intellectuals; and their
scholarly life bears no discernible relation to their biological and effective
lives: they have their mistresses; and they have their papers.

"Papers," we see, both bless and curse. They are not only the records
of law and the ledgers of business but the annals of history and the
memory of the race, the possibility of preserving and interpreting our
past experience. They represent the effort of the intellect to understand
by dissection, arrangement, systemization. "Papers" constitute civilization; without them we remain barbarians. Yet they clutter up the world
and menace our freedom. They may be "busywork" to amuse old children, to keep scholars from thinking and the timid from knowing themselves afraid. The academic vice is the substitution of "research" for
existential thinking; to preserve records without selection, to multiply
discriminations until one is incapable of singleness of mind and simplicity
of action. Papers assemble, by the most laudable of intentions, into

libraries; yet for every man who, like Arnold, fears he may know more than he feels, a great library must be an object of terror—a monument to the futility of past speculation, a deterrent to future action.

There are some rich, fantastic scenes in which Kafka's papers become objects in themselves, figures in a Disney cartoon: in *The Castle* the search through the superintendent's bedroom for a missing document—in the process of which papers half cover the floor and go on mounting—or the description of Sordini's office, every wall of which is covered with columns of documents tied together, piled on top of one another:

> those are only the documents that Sordini is working on at the time, and as bundles of papers are continually being taken away and brought in, and all in great haste, those columns are always falling on the floor, and it's just those perpetual crashes, following fast on one another, that have come to distinguish Sordini's workroom.

The copiousness of the papers has an approximate correspondence in the volubility of official speech. Ready argument characterizes almost all Kafka's people—not merely his lawyers and secretaries. In these novels all are dialecticians: all are conscious of *pro et contra,* fertile in "various lections." Unlike Mann's controversialists, Naphtha and Settembrini, who argue in abstract terms, Kafka's are existential thinkers and deploy their subtlety on the obscure and difficult matter of how to live aright.

The Trial and *The Castle* are composed very largely of dialogues, and dialogues dialectic. Indeed, the characteristic excitement of these later novels, written by a student of Plato and Kierkegaard, lies in the wit and intellectual suspense of the dialogue. No more than the papers in Sordini's office do the thoughts stand still; like the action in a murder mystery, they move by sudden shifts of direction, convincing evasions of the foregone conclusion.

What does Kafka intend us to make of his argumentation? Is it ridiculously specious, or—so far as it goes—true: "Both," would have to be the answer. It is absurd to speculate about the nature of the highest, for of course we cannot know; we cannot even know how near we come to knowing. Yet it is man's true nature and highest function to engage himself upon these speculative questions concerning the nature of reality; and there can be no delegation of this duty to others.

Kafka's world is one of mystery. In stories like *The Country Doctor* and *The Metamorphosis,* the unnatural thrusts itself into the orderly sequence of nature. The redaction of a young clerk into a bug neither allows of allegorical sterilization, nor is presented as a dream. It is the chief horror of the story, perhaps, that no one within it sees what happens as "impossible"; it is horrible, to be sure, but in various ways these people, obviously sane and simple, adjust themselves to a painful situation. There are occasional bits of near or even sheer magic in Kafka: in *The Castle*, Barnabas disappears with the rapidity of an elf or a thought; the first day passes and it grows night, within an hour or two after morning; after a few days of living with K., Frieda, formerly "unnaturally seductive," is withering in his arms. But it is not Kafka's ordinary or best practice thus to deal in legerdemain. He secures his sense of mystery chiefly through his device of multiple interpretation.

His method offers a superficial analogy with that of Hawthorne. But Hawthorne offers alternatives—usually supernaturalism and some form of naturalism. Thus, at the elaborate ending of *The Scarlet Letter*, we are tendered the preliminary option of supposing that there was, or was not, a scarlet letter imprinted upon the breast of the minister, and then a choice of three methods for the possible production of the stigmata: by the natural means of penance; by means of magic and drugs; or by the outgoing operation of the spirit. "The reader," says Hawthorne, "may choose among these theories."

It is not Kafka's method thus to contrast a supernatural with a natural reading. It is, for him, in and through the natural that the supernatural operates and—with whatever intermittence and illusion—is revealed.

Kafka's world is neither the world of the average sensual man nor yet fantasy. It is the world seen slightly askew, as one looks through his legs or stands on his head, or sees it in a distorting mirror. Nor does his adjustment take, like Swift's in *Gulliver*, the method of segregation. With Swift, the fantastic is safely corralled and tucked away in the initial assumption; with Kafka, realism and fantasy move in more close and sensitive relation. In *The Trial* and *The Castle* the whole sequence is so improbable as to suggest some kind of pervasive allegory, but at no point (or almost no point) does one encounter downright impossibility. It is improbable that any law courts of a wealthy city should be lodged high up in dingy tenement houses or that a village should require the service of a vast staff of busy, hurrying officials, or that, upon looking into a lumber-room in one's own office building, one should discover two court-wardens being flogged. Yet these things "could be"; they are not like centaurs, oceans flowing with lemonade, and trees growing greenbacks. And Kafka's multiple interpretations are all possible options within one world. They represent the same fact or situation read from successive views, as the operations of a mind which keeps correcting itself.

Kafka offers a convincing interpretation; then, with rapidity, substitutes another, yet more convincing. A scene in *America* shows Robinson, his face and arms swathed in manifold bandages. "It was horrible to see him lift his arms to his eyes to wipe away his tears with the bandages—tears of pain or grief or perhaps even of joy at seeing Karl again." Then we see the horror dissolve. "The trivial nature of his wounds could be seen from the old rags of bandages with which the lift-boys, obviously in jest, had swathed him round."

The Castle abounds in more subtle shifts. A woman sits in a chair in a kitchen. The pale light gives a "gleam of silk" to her dress; she seems to be an aristocrat, "although of course illness and weariness give even peasants a look of refinement." To a question from K., the woman replies disdainfully, but "whether contemptuous of K. or of her own answer was not clear." If one is self-conscious or otherwise fearful, it is necessary and difficult to interpret the looks of others. Thus K. sees the peasants gazing fixedly at him; he thinks it done out of malice—yet perhaps they really wanted something from him but could not express it, or, perhaps, on the other hand, they were simply childish. But if the first view of the peasants and their attitude was mistaken, what about the first view of Barnabas? One doubt, one disillusionment, infects the judge with a general mistrust of his judgment. "Perhaps K. was as mistaken in Barnabas' goodness as in the malice of the peasants." Frieda's hands "were certainly small and delicate, but they could quite as well have been called weak and characterless." After Olga's account of Amalia's defiance of Sortini, K. says, "Amalia's act was remarkable enough, but the more you say about it the less clearly can it be decided whether it was noble or petty, clever or foolish, heroic or cowardly." Longer, more structural examples are the discussion between K. and the Superintendent concerning the meaning of Klamm's letter, and K.'s talk with Frieda about the landlady, and Olga's discussion with K. regarding the nature of Barnabas' relation to the Castle.

Kafka's "mystery" is, then, the apparent sign of how elusive is the truth. What happens is tolerably easy to ascertain, but what it means is precarious as well as important.

Such scrupulosity of interpretation recalls a characteristic feature of hierarchy everywhere prominent in Kafka's novels—the connection between promotion, pleasing, and propitiation. Kafka's worlds are patriarchies or theocracies. One's success or failure depends on one's skill in divining the wishes of the great man; and among underlings there develops a necessary skill in calculating his mood by his complexion, step, tone of voice. Cases there naturally are in which the signs allow of differing interpretation between experts.

The interpretative complexity recalls also the elaborations of rabbinic and patristic commentary. John Mason Neale's commentary on the Song of Songs offers, out of innumerable Fathers, Doctors, and Saints, all manner of conflicting yet severally edifying glosses: on the text "his left hand is under my head, and his right hand doth embrace me," for example. What is the distinction between the hands, and why their positions? According to some, the hands distinguish temporal from spiritual goods; according to another view, the left hand equates the law, the right hand the gospel; according to another, the left hand indicates punishment, the right blessings and rewards. Other comments differentiate mystical states—the left being the Illuminative as the right is the Unitive Way. And "the loveliest interpretation of all," says Neale, is that which sees in the left the Manhood of Christ, and in the right his Godhead.

Not until late in his life did Kafka begin to study the Talmud; but already, in the priest's discourse at the Cathedral (*The Trial*), Kafka shows his ingenuity and depth as the exegete of a given fable. The priest cites the studies of innumerable rabbis who had already concerned themselves with the story. "I am only showing you different opinions about it," he says. "You mustn't have too much regard for opinions. The text is unchangeable and opinions are often only an expression of doubt about it." Like Kierkegaard, whose *Fear and Trembling* starts from and repeatedly returns to the story of Abraham and Isaac, so Kafka, delighting in speculation, yet offers his story as a mythic fable the meaning of which is anterior to and unexhausted by any included commentary.

Myth is not allegory; and Kafka is not an allegorist. An allegory is a series of concepts provided with a narrative or a narrative accompanied by a conceptual parallel. Strictly, it is a philosophical sequence which systematically works itself out in images. But allegory is rarely as pure as *Pilgrim's Progress*, or *The Romance of the Rose*: it deviates from purity in two directions—by losing its systematic character, becoming a series of intermittent symbolisms; or by keeping its system but abstaining from offering a conceptual key to its parable.

The novels of Kafka are not, in any exact sense, allegorical. From his diaries and aphorisms and his friend Brod's commentaries, we know that he intended the novels to give creative expression to the mysteries of Justice and Grace; that they are "metaphysical" novels we should surely have discerned without aid. But Kafka provided them with no conceptual chart; they require none; and it is their special richness that they have much particularity untranslatable into generality. We need not systematically recall that the Castle is Heaven or that K.'s disappointments show the mysterious ways in which God moves. The ways of men are, for men who seek to understand them, baffling enough.

Kafka's symbols are, indeed, capable of more than the religious interpretation. According to Brod, K. symbolizes the Jew, in his exclusion from society and his eagerness for inclusion, as well as the seeker after the Kingdom of Heaven. But K. is also the bachelor in search of marriage and companionship; and K. is also every man in respect to his final aloneness.

The novels all, significantly, remained unfinished. Of them Kafka wrote:

> What sense would there be in reviving such . . . bungled pieces of work? Only if one hoped to create a whole out of such fragments, some complete work to which one could make a final appeal. . . .

We have for each novel, however, a notion of the ending. *America* was to conclude with the young hero's finding, within the Nature Theatre of Oklahoma, his freedom, "even his old house and his parents." *The Trial* is of Brod's assembling, and a chapter like "The Whipper" could only vaguely be placed. Parts of the novels—for example, "The Stoker" and "Before the Law"—were published separately.

With some plausibility, one might call these books novels of the spiritual picaresque. Yet they are not completely episodic: even in the loosest, *America,* the two rascals, Delamarche and Robinson, reappear after we suppose ourselves to have seen the last of them; and in *The Castle* there is a very considerable integration of the materials: one notes in particular the fashion in which the matter of Chapter One (the teacher, the Lasemann family, Hans Brunswick and his mother) is subsequently developed. Each novel begins in substantially the same way: the hero breaks with his past. In two of them he has left his home, and we meet him as he enters a new world; in a third his thirtieth birthday and his summons collaborate to start a new life.

The question of method is: Can there be a logic of composition when one's theme is the irruption of the irrational? There might, of course, be a psychological unwinding; the episodes might grow more complex, deeper, or more wry. In the unfinished state of the novels, no such progress is obvious. If one compares these novels with the mystical documents of SS. Teresa and John of the Cross, he finds no such obvious symmetry and development as that of *The Interior Mansions.* Such systematic structure was too rational for Kafka.

It is Kafka's narrative method (with occasional lapses) to write from within the mind of the hero. The introspective hero, through whose eyes we have glimpses of other persons, static figures, is man alone, man hunted and haunted, man confronted with powers which elude him and with women with whom he is never at ease, man prosecuted and persecuted. He is the man eager to do right but perpetually baffled and thwarted and confused as to what it is to do right—the man for whom the sense of duty, of responsibility, the irreducibility of "ought," has survived the positive and particular codes of religions and moral systems—the man in search of salvation.

A narrow, moving writer, Kafka is both an artist and a symbol. The appeal of this symbol has been extraordinarily wide to Europeans and Americans in the past decade. One secular hope after another has failed. Kafka can be the symbol for what is left. He is illiberal, unrelenting, unsentimental; as Spender has said, he combines the power of the visionary with the self-criticism of the skeptic, so that he communicates the sense of their being something to believe without the claim of being able to define what it is. It is difficult today to believe in the reality of a world of comfort, good sense, and progress; we doubt that we shall ever see such a world again; we think it wise to prepare ourselves spiritually for worlds more exacting and metaphysical; and of such worlds Kafka is initiate.

Kafka's Distorted Mask

by *Eliseo Vivas*

If one may judge by much of the criticism of Kafka, the Kafka problem arises from the confused demands made by the readers and not from any unusual difficulty inherent in Kafka's work. This is most clearly seen in those egregious compounds of homemade psycho-analysis and facile sociology of art of a purely speculative nature, which —without any inductive evidence to support them—find Kafka's meaning in his psychological or political history, and in so doing explain it utterly away. The sociological critic takes Kafka's fables to be the expression of the social conditions which allegedly motivated them. For him the question is not, What does the author say? but rather, Why does he say what he does? The psychoanalytic critic shares with the sociological the assumption that the content of Kafka's vision of the world is of no importance, but differs in that what he considers of importance is the way in which the work of art expresses an allegedly pathological condition of the author. Neither sociologist nor psychoanalyst finds the answer by reading the objective, public content of the work; they find it by applying to it a theory devised prior to the reading of it, regarding the relation said to hold between either social or psychological conditions and artistic expression. Now even granting that this kind of genetic analysis of art is valid, and that artistic symbols may indeed point to psychic conditions or to social determinants, it is nevertheless at least possible that the objective traits to which they refer are of interest to the reader as they are without doubt to the artist (or the latter would not have struggled as he did with the problem of choosing them and organizing them into the artistic work). This does not deny the therapist's right to use the work of art as diagnostic evidence. Psychoanalytic criticism is, however, seldom practiced by properly trained therapists for their purposes; it is as a rule written by amateur psychoanalysts whose insensibility to the

"Kafka's Distorted Mask." From *Creation and Discovery*, by Eliseo Vivas. © 1948 by Eliseo Vivas. Reprinted by permission of the author and Noonday Press, Inc.

aesthetic values and indifference to the philosophic content of the work
is hardly camouflaged by their pseudoscientific interest in it.[1]

The reader who considers that the critic's most urgent task is to lead
attention to those aspects of the world which are expressed by his subject is justified in passing by these highly speculative psychologistic or
pseudo-sociological constructions. He must devote his efforts to exhibiting
his subject's objective contribution and to essaying an evaluation of it.
Inadequately supported speculations about the causes of the complicated
difficulties which Kafka had with his father or his women or his job
must necessarily be relegated to a relatively unimportant place until the
work of objective criticism is finished and a working consensus obtains
as to what is to be found in Kafka's fables. But when at last we turn
our attention to psychogenetic questions we should do so with a greater
respect than the majority of these fanciful speculations show for the
demands of inductive verification. The biographical data that we have
on Kafka are inadequate because Brod, who was their chief gatherer,
interprets Kafka in his own terms and seems incapable of distinguishing
his own personal interest in his gifted friend from his interest in the
objective meaning of his friend's fables. Brod's book does not enable us
to check our fanciful psychoanalytic constructions against reliable and
sufficient facts. But even if it did, it would still leave us with the chief
problems of Kafka on hand, with the question of Kafka's aesthetic
achievement and of the objective meaning and validity of his vision of
the world. We have Freud's word, although we do not need it, for the
insight that the analysis of aesthetic values is not within the reach of
his analytic method. But psychological and sociological criticism—and
Freud's own is to be included in it—systematically rides the genetic
fallacy when it assumes that the discovery of the complete psychological
or social sources of the artist's experience invalidate the objective meaning which is expressed by his art.

Although a large number of Kafka's critics avoid the fanciful constructions of his psychological or his sociological interpreters, they share with
these the inability simply to take Kafka seriously as an artist at the
objective level. Aware that art performs a very important function in
elucidating objective experience but not clear as to how it does it, they
have in one of two ways assumed that the key to his work is to be
found, not within it, but beyond it. Some find it in some ready-made
philosophical conception of the world, usually in Kierkegaard, as if all

---

[1] When I wrote this essay in 1948, I was so outraged by a number of fanciful and
irresponsible essays on Kafka, that I overlooked what I then knew perfectly well, namely
that Freud has deepened our comprehension of literary texts by giving us an awareness of the meaning of symbols that pre-Freudian man does not seem to have pos-
sessed.

the artist had to do was to dress up in a dramatic costume a philosophic skeleton. Others, taking Kafka to be merely an allegorical writer, consider the task of criticism accomplished when the more or less superstructural allegorical features of his fables are translated into that for which they stand—or, as I shall call it, employing I. A. Richards' convenient terminology, into the "tenor" of the extended metaphor that is the allegory. The objective of these critics becomes then the translation of what Kafka meant by the Castle, or the Court or by an advocate conveniently called "Grace," or by the Chinese emperor and his wall, or by the elaborate burrow built by the digger obsessed with a need to seek safe refuge from a predatory world. Although the difference in practice between these two modes of interpretation is important enough to notice, in principle they share the same assumption, namely, that the meaning of Kafka's work is to be found beyond the fables themselves and can therefore be better expressed in other terms than those which Kafka himself used.

Sharing the same assumption, these two modes of extrinsic interpretation also share a basic error consisting of a misconception of what the artist does and how he does it. The philosophic interpreters ignore the fact that the creative process involves a complete digestion of all the material on which the artist feeds so that what he finally produces is essentially different from what went into its makeup. They also ignore the fact that the poet, in the measure in which he is indeed a maker, does not seek to "imitate" or "represent" a reality which, independently of his poetic activity, possesses already a formal structure which anyone can discover. If this is true, it should be easy to see why the assumption that Kafka's meaning is to be found in a ready-made system of philosophy such as Kierkegaard's or anyone else's even in a more or less systematic set of abstract ideas of his own, is a disparagement of his achievement. Artistically Kafka failed to a considerable extent. But his was the failure of a man who was an artist of major pretensions. His meaning is something not to be better stated abstractly in terms of ideas and concepts, to be found beyond the fable, but within it, at the dramatic level, in the interrelationships thus revealed to exist among the characters and between them and the universe. The fallacy of finding his meaning in abstract ideas inverts the relationship between philosophy and art, for it is the philosopher who must go to art for the subject-matter which the poet has organized at the dramatic level, in order to abstract from it the systematic relationships which it is his business to formulate.

The allegorical interpreter fails for a similar reason. He translates the allegory into its "tenor" by supplying—not Kafka's own grasp of reality in dramatic terms—but a more or less commonplace version of it in abstract terms, and one which does not possess any of those traits which, in the fable, we discern to be the most distinctively Kafkian. But if Kafka had a contribution to make, it was not to be found in the ingenuity of his allegorical "vehicle" (again in Richards' terminology), nor even in a version of a cockeyed world whose absurdity at the human level had its source in the unqualified irrationality of transcending factors lying beyond human reach and beyond human comprehension. These conceptions of existence had already been expressed in one way or another in literature and in philosophy. What Kafka had to say was something else, involving as much freshness and originality as one has a right to expect in literature. It is something which, so far as I know, he could not have borrowed from philosophy, for no thinker one hears of in standard histories of philosophy has ever viewed the world in quite the way in which Kafka viewed it. There are, undeniably, allegorical features in Kafka's vision of the world, but they are obvious and relatively unimportant. What is important is the concrete dramatic world exhibited in his fables under the allegorical "vehicles" which he uses to capture it. Kafka, as Brod points out, even when trying to think conceptually, thinks in images and not in conceptual structures. But his vision has a coherence and meaningful interrelatedness lacked by the vision of the nonartistic mind, since the latter is distracted by the multifarious demands made on it and it is not driven by the need to organize and unify its experience. The picture of the world as it presented itself to Kafka was a mythopoetical one and if it is our business as readers to discover its meaning for us, in our own terms, we cannot do so until we are reasonably clear as to what was its own intrinsic meaning. Miss Magny puts the point so effectively that it is worth transcribing her own words:

. . . we ought not to . . . provide dialectical constructions for the unfolding of events which should be taken as a *real* account. Otherwise Kafka is quickly converted into a kind of frustrated philosopher who needs to be explained to himself and to others for lack of sufficient power of analysis and abstraction. . . . That would imply a gratuitous insult.[2]

In spite of her depth and acuity, however, I believe that Miss Magny's interpretation of Kafka's conception of existence can be objectively shown to miss a very essential element. She says:

. . . the world for Kafka is essentially *turmoil*, something that is not *rational* and whose essence therefore only a fantastic tale can express. . . . Only the gratuitousness of the event itself, of the *contingit,* can reveal the essential absurdity of things.

[2] G.-E. Magny, "The Objective Depiction of Absurdity," from *The Kafka Problem,* edited by A. Flores (New York, 1946), p. 76.

At another place Miss Magny speaks of "Kafka's predilection for the infraconceptual, the infrarational." But Kafka's world was not merely absurd. Indeed what constituted for him the problem which he sought to resolve through his art—and of course the only manner in which an artist resolves his problem is through a statement of it in mythopoetic terms—was that certain transcending aspects of the universe envisaged through experience and seen to be those on which normal visible existence depends, blatantly proclaimed an irrationality which, upon the most casual glimpse, appeared to be at the same time rational.

But the Magny essay has at least this value, that it poses the Kafka problem correctly and reveals one aspect of our author without a grasp of which no understanding of him is possible. In Kafka, as she puts it, "the irrational . . . the horrible . . . the grotesque . . . are never induced for the sake of literary effect . . . but to express a depth of reality." Our problem therefore is to inquire as to what conception of existence is found in Kafka's fables. The answer must of course be couched in abstract terms, but it is not to be taken as a translation of Kafka's meaning but as a means of pointing to it within the fables themselves. The validity of the interpretation is to be judged by checking to see whether what I claim to be found in Kafka is indeed there and whether I do not neglect important factors which are there. The allegorical features must of course be translated into their "tenors" but this goes without saying and rather than constituting a difficult task—as in fact it does for critics like Rahv when they try to translate Kafka into Kierkegaardian philosophy—it is a relatively easy one.[3] The labor of criticism however begins at that point and what it has to accomplish is a reading of Kafka. After that one may express one's own opinion as to whether Kafka's conception of existence is valid or not.

II

In order to offer inductive evidence in favor of the preceding argument we must turn to an analysis of Kafka's works in search of his conception of existence. But since an exhaustive analysis of all of his works is not here possible, I propose that we turn our attention to *The Trial* and *The Castle* which embody his most ambitious efforts to integrate his various discoveries about the world. Let us first turn to *The Trial*. We must first remember that Joseph K.'s arrest is sudden and seems to him so unjustified that never between the period of his arrest and of his execution does he admit his guilt. But while verbally denying it,

[3] In his notes to *The Great Wall of China*. Rahv has also published psychoanalytic and sociological interpretations of Kafka in the *Kenyon Review* and *Southern Review*.

unconsciously Joseph K. betrays his sense of guilt from the very first day of his arrest in numerous small ways. Let only one instance suffice: During the preliminary examination that took place the morning of his arrest Joseph K. said to the Inspector in anger and seemingly irrelevantly, "But this is not the capital charge yet." In a more important way Joseph K. gives evidence of his sense of guilt: the outward circumstances of his life do not at first change very radically but gradually Joseph K. gets more and more absorbed in his case and finally finds out that his job is suffering from his preoccupation with it. If he truly were convinced of his innocence he would have laughed at the whole absurd business, as he tried to do the first Sunday at the preliminary investigation when he told the Magistrate that his could not be a trial unless he recognized it as such. To the reader it is quite clear that Joseph K. did not want to admit to himself when he made that statement that he had already through action eloquently yielded the recognition that his lips withheld.

Remember next that while Joseph K. realizes that the Court is a formidable organization he insists nevertheless on his belief that its purposes are absurd, and the evidence for that is to be found, as he believes, in all that he discovers about it at the lower level. Thus Joseph K. seems to be justified in his conviction, expressed angrily to the Magistrate, that the organization is interested in condemning innocent victims and doing so while keeping them in ignorance of what action is brought against them. This belief is strengthened by the result of his efforts to gain information about the higher officials of the Court.

But is Joseph K. really justified in his belief that the Court is an utterly aimless, absurd institution? A formidable organization with a code of law and with such a large number of employees, with traditions and equipment, an organization that will punish its employees on occasion upon the complaint of a man under arrest—such an organization is simply not aimless. Its aims may not be knowable or may not seem to be intelligible to us but the evidence—without denying Joseph K.'s conviction of its absurdity—points at the very same time to a rationality all its own. Joseph K. does not want to admit this to himself and insists on judging the organization and its charges against him by his own criterion of rationality. But all his actions proclaim that he is not altogether ignorant of the limitations of his own criterion. In view of his stiffnecked attitude towards the evidence, the counsel which Joseph K. gives himself on the way to the execution has a tremendous ironic force. "The only thing for me to do now . . . is to keep my intelligence calm and discriminating to the end." He therefore resigns himself. But it has been precisely the failure of his discriminating intelligence that led him to the impasse in which he found himself. For it was not resignation that the situation required of him; what it required was admission of his guilt and genuine contrition. This is precisely what the priest tried in vain to tell him in the Cathedral. But Joseph K. was too discriminatingly intelligent and too proud of the primacy of his intelligence to listen.

The Castle is a much more complex book than *The Trial*. Indeed it represents the most ambitious effort on Kafka's part to gather together all the important aspects of his vision of the world into one coherent fable. For this reason the unfinished condition in which it was left suggests a radical criticism of the validity of Kafka's conception of existence. In this book his preoccupations are given a different organization from that which he gave them in *The Trial*. A problem with which *The Trial* is concerned only obliquely is here brought forward, namely the problem of man's place in the scheme of things and, as a corollary of this more comprehensive problem, the question as to the nature of the bond between man and his fellow beings. In *The Trial* that bond, after the crisis of the arrest, is somehow unhealthy; for instance, for the normal relationship between his mistress and himself Joseph K. substitutes the relationship with Huld's maid, Leni, which does not involve either the fulfilment of genuine love or even the gratification which purely sexual relations can yield. In *The Castle* the emphasis seems to change but both the human and the merely sexual relations result in the same vague frustration. Again the question of guilt which is central in *The Trial* is subordinated in *The Castle* by being presented through the episode of Barnabas and his family. But the cause of the guilt, which in *The Trial* is only indirectly and ambiguously suggested, is in the latter explicitly traced to Amalia's refusal of Sortini's invitation to visit him in his room at the Inn; the guilt is caused, that is, by the pride of those who will not serve and is thus connected with the most ancient of guilts, the guilt that led to the fall before man's. The cause is brought out with sufficient clarity by the contrast between Amalia's attitude towards Sortini and the attitude of the landlady and of Frieda towards Klamm. K. is himself relatively free from a sense of guilt but he is dominated by a need to find a place for himself in the scheme of things. The need, baffled, develops into anxiety as his efforts lead him to discover the nature of the organization that he has to contend with.

From Olga, and from the superintendent who receives K. in bed, the land-surveyor gains important information about the organization of the Castle. K. tries to make his informants admit that the organization is quite absurd and leaves much to be desired. But the superintendent does not admit that the organization lacks order or is subject to error. The apparatus works with great precision; in the Castle nothing is done without thought and the very possibility of error on the part of the Head Bureau must be ruled out. The superintendent admits that he is convinced that in respect to K. an error has been committed. But who can tell what the first Control Officials will say, and the second, and the third, and the rest? However, if there has been one, the error is not established by the evidence K. has from Klamm, for Klamm's letter to K. is not official, and as to the telephone calls, these mean nothing. If Huld in *The Trial* is an advocate without legal standing, Klamm in *The Castle* is a protector seemingly helpless to protect his man—that is, if there is a Klamm and if it is K. and not someone else in whom Klamm is interested.

I have purposely said in a vague way that K. was trying "to find his place in the scheme of things" because I do not find that K. is anxious about obtaining a livelihood or solving any other purely secular problem but only about finding a place in the village which would give him status not only in respect to the village itself but, more importantly even, in respect to the inaccessible powers of the Castle. K. wants an unambiguous statement of his position before the authorities of the Castle. This involves documents, proofs, something to which he could refer that could not be gainsaid, like the letters from Klamm, but containing of course an official appointment and a definition of his place. He starts with large demands and ends up by offering to take anything that will be given him so long as it brings him the needed nod of recognition for which he craves. But his efforts to get into direct touch with the officials of the Castle are no less pathetically useless than those of Barnabas' father who wants his crime defined. No one can be certain of anything beyond the elementary fact that there must be a Castle which is visible above the village and from which officials and servants constantly come and go. One also suspects that it must have its method, no matter how absurd that method may seem and how deeply it may outrage the feeling of what we take to be fitness or justice or rationality. But beyond that all is doubt and incertitude.

Between *The Trial* and *The Castle* there are important differences, but to me none seems as important as the fact that Joseph K. never learns anything whatever about the invisible Judges, while K. knows the name of the Lord of the Castle, Count West-west, and receives indications, however unsatisfactory, that between the Castle and himself there is some sort of nexus. He first tries to get into touch with the Count, then with the Castellan and, when he sees the impossibility of his ambition, he tries to reach Klamm. K.'s relations with Klamm are more baffling than those of Joseph K. with his Judges in *The Trial* because there is more teasing evidence of Klamm's existence and therefore the evidence is more unintelligible. K. thinks he once saw Klamm but it turns out later that that is very doubtful. Was it Klamm who wrote the letter to K.? The signature is illegible and Olga later tells K. that the letters that her brother Barnabas has brought him were not received from Klamm but from a clerk. Even if they were from Klamm it is doubtful whether Klamm is well enough posted on K. really to be his patron or protector as the second letter that K. receives from Klamm clearly shows. The question is even more difficult since, if you press it, it turns out that there are all kinds of contradictory reports about Klamm, and some people go so far as to say that Momus, the Secretary, is Klamm. Who then is Klamm? Some sort of fluctuating image of him has been constructed but, as Olga tells K., perhaps it does not fluctuate as much as Klamm's real appearance does. However, in *The Trial* not even such a deceptive hope ever urges Joseph K. on and he conducts his defense in a state of unrelieved and increasing enervation.

It is not necessary to demonstrate in detail that the various aspects of the conception of existence that were integrated in these two novels are separately expressed in a large number of his stories and sketches: in *Investigations of a Dog, The Great Wall of China, The Burrow* and *The Giant Mole,* for instance, as well as in some of his shorter pieces like *The Problem of Our Laws.* But it is necessary to state frankly that there are a number of more or less important stories which could not be susceptible of this interpretation; for example, *Josephine the Songstress, Blumfeld, an Elderly Bachelor, The Penal Colony* and *The Judgment.* In some of these, what Kafka was trying to do is not difficult to guess. He was exploring psychological reality strictly at the human level. The result of Kafka's psychological exploration, it seems to me, contradicts the purely hedonistic conception of man which is found deeply imbedded in the liberal, secularistic tradition of our Western world and which is true only of what Kierkegaard called the "aesthetic stage" of human development. Kafka's discoveries ally him with the tradition which Freud himself joined as a result of his metapsychological speculations and to which Dostoevsky and Kierkegaard belong—men who repudiate the shallow optimism which controls the conception of human destiny at the "aesthetic stage." For Kafka's psychological conceptions we must go to stories like *The Metamorphosis, The Judgment* and *The Penal Colony.* With some diffidence I venture the opinion that an analysis of his contributions to the understanding of the purely psychological problems of contemporary men would hardly be worth the trouble it would involve.

America, begun only a few months before *The Trial,* seems to represent, as I read it, an unsuccessful experiment of Kafka's, for in it he views his problem as imbedded in a purely social context. *America* seems therefore to constitute very little more than social criticism of his temporal world and we find in it only faint and incomplete indications of the insights into the transcending aspects of experience which we identify as Kafka's central focus of interest and the elucidation of which constitutes his contribution.

III

We are now able to put together Kafka's conception of existence. Note first that what Kafka undertook was a stubbornly empirical exploration of experience, beyond which he discovered a constellation of factors for which evidence is found within the texture of experience itself. For this reason allegory must be employed to point to these factors not directly revealed. But the "tenor" of the allegory, being itself beyond direct grasp, must be expressed in mythopoetic terms drawn from ordinary life. Kafka, with whom Brod read Plato in his university days, could have invoked Plato as precedent for his use of myth, for the Greek used it to elucidate the structure which he glimpsed as lying beyond experience through evidence found within it. Kafka's discovery involves an ordered process which we can more or less adequately capture in the following formula: a crisis leads either to a sense of guilt or to a condition of alienation. In either case the crisis generates a struggle which expresses itself, among other ways, in the arrogant demands made by the hero. As he begins to feel the effects of the crisis the hero gradually trims his demands but he never altogether ceases to press them. The reduction of demands results from the hero's gradual discovery of a transcending organization which seems beyond his power either to look into, control, or understand. His discovery is based not upon unwarranted assumptions or gratuitous hypotheses but on more or less direct empirical evidence, and although what is discovered seems unintelligible to him, the evidence is ambivalent and points not only to the irrationality of the organization but to its rationality as well. The anguished doubt into which the victim of the crisis is plunged is the result of the fact that the antinomy he faces cannot be resolved since it does not occur to him to transcend his perspective or go beyond his empirical method. But what other method is there? For Kafka's heroes there seems to be no other.

It is of the utmost importance, however, to note that Kafka's "empiricism" differs radically from that which is fashionable today—that which constitutes the foundations of scientific naturalism—since the latter has been devised in order to deny the evidence which experience presents of its lack of self-sufficiency, while Kafka through an empirical examination of human existence is led to assert its dependence on transcending factors.

We do not find in Kafka an assertion of a world made up of two aspects such as we find in the traditional dualism of Western philosophy; for in these the two terms, the visible and the transcending, are said to bear certain intelligible relations toward one another and in the major tradition the transcending term is taken as the ground of the rationality of the other. Nor do we have in Kafka a dramatized version of Schopenhauerian dualism in which a pure irrational factor is taken to be the ground of our world of experience. What we find is something quite different, something to a large degree fresh and original, expressing in challenging terms the novel conditions and predicaments of modern man. These predicaments generate anguish. But unlike Kierkegaard, who mastered his "sterile anguish" through faith, or Dostoevsky, who suggested that it could be mastered through faith and love in the way in which the Russian monk, Father Zossima, mastered it, Kafka's man never succeeds in surpassing human anguish. Face to face with what many of his critics recognize as a metaphysical problem —in a vague sense of this conveniently ambiguous word—Kafka tried to solve it empirically. But what he was up against was the problem of theodicy and not in the Leibnizian sense but in the fuller, in the Cartesian sense. The problem that Kafka faced was not primarily the conventional need to find a satisfactory human account of evil once it has been discovered that its roots lie beyond the human level. Neither was it the problem of discovering what attitudes we may be expected to take towards an invisible agent on which we depend and which we know to be infinite—this was the Kierkegaardian problem. Rather, it was the problem of discovering the ground of rationality. He went so far as to grasp clearly that that ground transcends human experience. But he could not go beyond this relatively elementary discovery because the stubborn empirical attitude which he assumed is helpless before questions of the magnitude he was raising.

This is not to say, however, that personally Kafka resigned himself to the monstrous predicament into which his discoveries plunged him. And least of all is it to say that the reader must himself be plunged into a pessimistic attitude by contemplating Kafka's picture of the world. Those readers who find him merely depressing have not read him carefully. Brod quotes a trenchant statement in his *Biography* of Kafka which suggests the precise way in which Kafka himself avoided a purely enervating pessimism and in which the reader may also avoid it. "Our art," it reads, "consists of being dazzled by Truth. The light which rests on the distorted mask as it shrinks from it is true, nothing else is." The light is Truth but the mask on which it shines, the artifact of the maker, is "distorted"—and the rich contextual ambiguities of the statement are precisely what gives it density of suggestive meaning and confirms the reader's hunch that in the ambiguities which Kafka systematically exploits is to be found the comic dimension of his picture of the world and the means of purging oneself from effects generated by its arbitrariness and irrationality. Kafka's artistry makes this comic feature compatible with the sense of anguish and even of terror that is the defining quality of existence in it. But it is not merged with or sacrificed to the latter. And in the reader its perception generates enough detachment to enable him to assimilate all the absurdity and pervasive anguish presented without surrendering to it.

The comical quality of Kafka's world is expressed in the way in which he treats the antinomous nature of existence. Generally speaking, a comic grasp of the world rests on the perception by the writer of a moral duality which elicits from the reader a "comic" response as the only means of freeing himself from the conflict towards values to which he is attached and yet towards which he cannot justify his attachment satisfactorily. It is not merely a moral duality but, if you will allow it, a cosmological duality that we find in Kafka's world, and its perception involves a disparagement of the means which reveal it, a disparagement of the mind as a rational tool of analysis. There is no gaiety in Kafka's irony as there is in Rabelais' satire; nor a deep sense of moral outrage and the bitter laughter arising from the fact that at least you know you cannot be fooled which we find in Swift. But there is nevertheless the essential element of the comic in Kafka: the transparent error involved in any statement that can be made of the world. Such a world, a world about which nothing can be said that cannot in the same breath be as plausibly contradicted, is a quintessentially comic world. You cannot of course expect its victims to find it so but you cannot, either, be expected by them to take them at their own asking value and in your mind you are ready with a discount. A world towards which one cannot develop any kind of attachment, however ideal and prospective, is a world in which the pain it creates, the terror it inspires, the cruelty it shows is not utterly crushing pain or terror or cruelty, because it crushes with its absurdity the piety it generates. The only response to it therefore is the ironic.

In the light of the foregoing it is not difficult to see in concrete terms that the differences between Kierkegaard and Kafka are essential and the affinities superficial. For the one thing one could not impute to Kierkegaard is the empirical attitude. He starts with it but he soon soars away into a region where intuition and faith, free from the demands of empirical evidence, allow him to ignore the insoluble problems which for the thorough-going empiricist stand in the way of accepting a historical or even a personal religious view of man and the world. Kierkegaard is therefore not at all baffled by the nature of those elements which he found to transcend experience. He does not claim that he is able to "know" them; but the proper response towards them is not for him that of the pure knower, the abstract ratiocinator in search of verified "truth." The existentialist is a man of flesh and bones—as Unamuno put it—who, disregarding the artificial limitations and restrictions of the pure knower, makes a total human decision and wills the act of belief; and not in the pragmatic sense of William James, either, but in a passionate, affirmative, plenary manner. For this reason Kierkegaard would have pooh-poohed the parallelism which has been found to exist between himself and Kafka. A man who tries to reach plenary conviction as to the transcending structure that subtends human experience by "cognitive" means places himself as the very opposite pole of Kierkegaardian existentialism. Furthermore, because for Kierkegaard the object of faith was infinite, man must be in the wrong and as a result must endure anguish. But this is his highest condition. By contrast, the anguish that at times almost chokes Kafka's characters—the stagnant, the oppressive atmosphere of Barnabas' home or the claustrophobic closedness of Titorelli's room, the terrifying searches, the endless corridors—is the result of insecurity which arises from lack of knowledge. In Kafka anguish issues from doubt, in Kierkegaard from certitude.

There is, however, a modicum of justification for the coupling of the Danish philosopher with the Jewish novelist, since the reading of the former does make us aware of the importance of anguish, of the crisis and of absolute disjunctions in human experience. Without a full appreciation of these factors as inherent in the human situation, the effort to understand Kafka turns into a diagnostic hunt for signs of neuroses. It is important to keep in mind however the different way in which these factors function in philosopher and poet although it is impossible to undertake here specifications of the differences.

IV

There is need to make explicit some hints I have given about what I take to be the validity of Kafka's conception of existence. Let us disregard the fact of his failure to bring any of his major works to completion, although such a failure may legitimately be taken as the basis for the most devastating criticism that may be leveled against Kafka's version of reality. Still it must be noted that Kafka's conception of existence is defective because it is inherently unstable. It seems to me that Kafka's picture constitutes a decided advance over that given us by contemporary naturalism, for Kafka has no desire to deny the evidence of experience which points to dimensions of existence which transcend it. But he could not or would not surrender his method to the demands of rationality and left us with a vision of the world which both artistically and philosophically represents an impasse. The change of attitude generated by the crisis opens to the subject large ranges of hitherto unsuspected possibilities as to the nature of existence. But these cannot be realized unless the new attitudes brought about by the crisis are accepted as revealing factors which experience itself cannot explore, but in which one must believe nevertheless, even without a basis that those who have not gone through the crisis would be willing to accept as adequate evidence. And this is what the empiricist will not, cannot do. I believe it would be relatively easy to prove from his work that Kafka saw clearly the root of the difficulty. But his intellectual grasp of his perplexity was useless since his difficulty arose precisely from his insistence on the use of the intelligence beyond its legitimate range.

There is therefore a profound justification to Kafka's own remark that he expressed the negative tendencies of his age. Note however that he does so in the sense that he grasped clearly the meaning of certain phenomena as constitutive of normal human development in its break from what Kierkegaard called the "aesthetic" stage. But he was not able to concede what is demanded in order to reach the "ethico-religious" stage. Having been thrust from the aesthetic his heroes stop before they reach the next stage. And they stop because they refuse— or are unable to bring themselves—to solve their problems by the only means that such problems can be solved: in the manner in which Plato solved his, through the recognition of the valid claims of religious intuition in certain ranges of experience; or in the manner in which Kant did, by supplying the terms required to complete a rational picture of the world as postulates made necessary by the objective demands of practical reason. It is this leap, taken by the greatest number of the major philosophers of our West, that Kafka, faithful to the limitations of his empiricism, will not take. In that refusal Kafka is at one with the negative tendencies of his age and remains impaled on the horns of a brutal antinomy.

Hope and the Absurd in the Work of Franz Kafka

by Albert Camus

The whole art of Kafka consists in forcing the reader to reread. His endings, or his absence of endings, suggest explanations which, however, are not revealed in clear language but, before they seem justified, require that the story be reread from another point of view. Sometimes there is a double possibility of interpretation, whence appears the necessity for two readings. This is what the author wanted. But it would be wrong to try to interpret everything in Kafka in detail. A symbol is always in general and, however precise its translation, an artist can restore to it only its movement: there is no word-for-word rendering. Moreover, nothing is harder to understand than a symbolic work. A symbol always transcends the one who makes use of it and makes him say in reality more than he is aware of expressing. In this regard, the surest means of getting hold of it is not to provoke it, to begin the work without a preconceived attitude and not to look for its hidden currents. For Kafka in particular it is fair to agree to his rules, to approach the drama through its externals and the novel through its form.

At first glance and for a casual reader, they are disturbing adventures that carry off quaking and dogged characters into pursuit of problems they never formulate. In *The Trial,* Joseph K. is accused. But he doesn't know of what. He is doubtless eager to defend himself, but he doesn't know why. The lawyers find his case difficult. Meanwhile he does not neglect to love, to eat, or to read his paper. Then he is judged. But the courtroom is very dark. He doesn't understand much. He merely assumes that he is condemned, but to what, he barely wonders. At times he suspects just the same and he continues living. Some time later, two well-dressed and polite gentlemen come to get him and invite him to follow them. Most courteously they lead him into a wretched suburb,

"Hope and the Absurd in the Work of Franz Kafka." From *The Myth of Sisyphus,* by Albert Camus. © 1955 by Alfred A. Knopf, Inc. Reprinted by permission of Alfred A. Knopf, Inc. and Hamish Hamilton, Ltd.

put his head on a stone and slit his throat. Before dying the condemned man says merely: "like a dog."

You see that it is hard to speak of a symbol in a tale whose most obvious quality just happens to be naturalness. But naturalness is a hard category to understand. There are works in which the event seems natural to the reader. But there are others (rarer, to be sure) in which the character considers natural what happens to him. By an odd but obvious paradox, the more extraordinary the character's adventures are, the more noticeable will be the naturalness of the story: it is in proportion to the divergence we feel between the strangeness of a man's life and the simplicity with which that man accepts it. It seems that this naturalness is Kafka's. And precisely, one is well aware what *The Trial* means. People have spoken of an image of the human condition. To be sure. Yet it is both simpler and more complex. I mean that the significance of the novel is more particular and more personal to Kafka. To a certain degree, he is the one who does the talking, even though it is us he confesses. He lives and he is condemned. He learns this on the first pages of the novel he is pursuing in this world, and if he tries to cope with this, he nonetheless does so without surprise. He will never show sufficient astonishment at this lack of astonishment. It is by such contradictions that the first signs of the absurd work are recognized. The mind projects into the concrete its spiritual tragedy. And it can do so solely by means of a perpetual paradox which confers on colors the power to express the void and on daily gestures the strength to translate eternal ambitions.

Likewise, *The Castle* is perhaps a theology in action, but it is first of all the individual adventure of a soul in quest of its grace, of a man who asks of this world's objects their royal secret and of women the signs of the god that sleeps in them. *The Metamorphosis,* in turn, certainly represents the horrible imagery of an ethic of lucidity. But it is also the product of that incalculable amazement man feels at being conscious of the beast he becomes effortlessly. In this fundamental ambiguity lies Kafka's secret. These perpetual oscillations between the natural and the extraordinary, the individual and the universal, the tragic and the everyday, the absurd and the logical, are found throughout his work and give it both its resonance and its meaning. These are the paradoxes that must be enumerated, the contradictions that must be strengthened, in order to understand the absurd work.

A symbol, indeed, assumes two planes, two worlds of ideas and sensations, and a dictionary of correspondences between them. This lexicon is the hardest thing to draw up. But awaking to the two worlds brought face-to-face is tantamount to getting on the trail of their secret relationships. In Kafka these two worlds are that of everyday life on the one hand, and, on the other, that of supernatural anxiety.[1] It seems that we are witnessing here an interminable exploitation of Nietzsche's remark: "Great problems are in the street."

There is in the human condition (and this is a commonplace of all literatures) a basic absurdity as well as an implacable nobility. The two coincide, as is natural. Both of them are represented, let me repeat, in the ridiculous divorce separating our spiritual excesses and the ephemeral joys of the body. The absurd thing is that it should be the soul of this body which it transcends so inordinately. Whoever would like to represent this absurdity must give it life in a series of parallel contrasts. Thus it is that Kafka expresses tragedy by the everyday and the absurd by the logical.

An actor lends more force to a tragic character the more careful he is not to exaggerate it. If he is moderate, the horror he inspires will be immoderate. In this regard Greek tragedy is rich in lessons. In a tragic work fate always makes itself felt better in the guise of logic and naturalness. Oedipus' fate is announced in advance. It is decided supernaturally that he will commit the murder and the incest. The drama's whole effort is to show the logical system which, from deduction to deduction, will crown the hero's misfortune. Merely to announce to us that uncommon fate is scarcely horrible, because it is improbable. But if its necessity is demonstrated to us in the framework of everyday life, society, state, familiar emotion, then the horror is hallowed. In that revolt that shakes man and makes him say: "That is not possible," there is an element of desperate certainty that "that" can be.

This is the whole secret of Greek tragedy, or at least of one of its aspects. For there is another which, by a reverse method, would help us to understand Kafka better. The human heart has a tiresome tendency to label as fate only what crushes it. But happiness likewise, in its way, is without reason, since it is inevitable. Modern man, however, takes the credit for it himself, when he doesn't fail to recognize it. Much could be said, on the contrary, about the privileged fates of Greek tragedy and those favored in legend who, like Ulysses, in the midst of the worst adventures, are saved from themselves. It was not so easy to return to Ithaca.

What must be remembered in any case is that secret complicity that joins the logical and the everyday to the tragic. This is why Samsa, the hero of *The Metamorphosis,* is a travelling salesman. This is why the

[1] It is worth noting that the works of Kafka can quite as legitimately be interpreted in the sense of a social criticism (for instance, in *The Trial*). It is probable, moreover, that there is no need to choose. Both interpretations are good. In absurd terms, as we have seen, revolt against men is *also* directed against God: great revolutions are always metaphysical.

only thing that disturbs him in the strange adventure that makes a
vermin of him is that his boss will be angry at his absence. Legs and
feelers grow out of him, his spine arches up, white spots appear on his
belly and—I shall not say that this does not astonish him, for the effect
would be spoiled—it causes him a "slight annoyance." The whole art
of Kafka is in that distinction. In his central work, *The Castle,* the
details of everyday life stand out and yet in that strange novel in which
nothing concludes and everything begins over again, it is the essential
adventure of a soul in quest of its grace that is represented. That
translation of the problem into action, that coincidence of the general
and the particular are recognized likewise in the little artifices that belong to every great creator. In *The Trial* the hero might have been
named Schmidt, or Franz Kafka. But he is named Joseph K. He is not
Kafka and yet he is Kafka. He is an average European. He is like everybody else. But he is also the entity K. who is the *x* of this flesh and
blood equation.

Likewise if Kafka wants to express the absurd, he will make use of
consistency. You know the story of the crazy man who was fishing in a
bathtub. A doctor with ideas as to psychiatric treatments asked him "if
they were biting," to which he received the harsh reply: "Of course not,
you fool, since this is a bathtub." That story belongs to the baroque
type. But in it can be grasped quite clearly to what a degree the absurd
effect is linked to an excess of logic. Kafka's world is in truth an in-
describable universe in which man allows himself the tormenting
luxury of fishing in a bathtub, knowing that nothing will come of it.

Consequently I recognize here a work that is absurd in its principles.
As for *The Trial,* for instance, I can indeed say that it is a complete
success. Flesh wins out. Nothing is lacking, neither the unexpressed
revolt (but *it* is what is writing), nor lucid and mute despair (but *it*
is what is creating), nor that amazing freedom of manner which the
characters of the novel exemplify until their ultimate death.

. . . .

Yet this world is not so closed as it seems. Into this universe devoid
of progress, Kafka is going to introduce hope in a strange form. In this
regard *The Trial* and *The Castle* do not follow the same direction.
They complement each other. The barely perceptible progression from
one to the other represents a tremendous conquest in the realm of
evasion. *The Trial* propounds a problem which *The Castle,* to a certain
degree, solves. The first describes according to a quasiscientific method
and without concluding. The second, to a certain degree, explains. *The
Trial* diagnoses, and *The Castle* imagines a treatment. But the remedy
proposed here does not cure. It merely brings the malady back into

normal life. It helps to accept it. In a certain sense (let us think of Kierkegaard), it makes people cherish it. The land-surveyor K. cannot imagine another anxiety than the one that is tormenting him. The very people around him become attached to that void and that nameless pain, as if suffering assumed in this case a privileged aspect. "How I need you," Frieda says to K. "How forsaken I feel, since knowing you, when you are not with me." This subtle remedy that makes us love what crushes us and makes hope spring up in a world without issue, this sudden "leap" through which everything is changed, is the secret of the existential revolution and of *The Castle* itself.

Few works are more rigorous in their development than *The Castle*. K. is named land-surveyor to the Castle and he arrives in the village. But from the village to the Castle it is impossible to communicate. For hundreds of pages K. persists in seeking his way, makes every advance, uses trickery and expedients, never gets angry, and with disconcerting good-will tries to assume the duties entrusted to him. Each chapter is a new frustration. And also a new beginning. It is not logic but consistent method. The scope of that insistence constitutes the work's tragic quality. When K. telephones to the Castle, he hears confused, mingled voices, vague laughs, distant invitations. That is enough to feed his hope, like those few signs appearing in summer skies or those evening anticipations which make up our reason for living. Here is found the secret of the melancholy peculiar to Kafka. The same, in truth, that is found in Proust's work or in the landscape of Plotinus: a nostalgia for a lost paradise. "I become very sad," says Olga, "when Barnabas tells me in the morning that he is going to the Castle: that probably futile trip, that probably wasted day, that probably empty hope." "Probably"—on this implication Kafka gambles his entire work. But nothing avails; the quest of the eternal here is meticulous. And those inspired automata, Kafka's characters, provide us with a precise image of what we should be if we were deprived of our distractions[2] and utterly consigned to the humiliations of the divine.

In *The Castle* that surrender to the everyday becomes an ethic. The great hope of K. is to get the Castle to adopt him. Unable to achieve this alone, his whole effort is to deserve this favor by becoming an inhabitant of the village, by losing the status of foreigner that everyone makes him feel. What he wants is an occupation, a home, the life of a healthy, normal man. He can't stand his madness any longer. He wants to be reasonable. He wants to cast off the peculiar curse that makes him a

---

[2] In *The Castle* it seems that "distractions" in the Pascalian sense are represented by the assistants who "distract" K. from his anxiety. If Frieda eventually becomes the mistress of one of the assistants, this is because she prefers the stage setting to truth, everyday life to shared anguish.

stranger to the village. The episode of Frieda is significant in this regard.
If he takes as his mistress this woman who has known one of the Castle's
officials, this is because of her past. He derives from her something that
transcends him—while being aware of what makes her forever unworthy
of the Castle. This makes one think of Kierkegaard's strange love for
Regina Olsen. In certain men, the fire of eternity consuming them is
great enough for them to burn in it the very heart of those closest to
them. The fatal mistake that consists in giving to God what is not God's
is likewise the subject of this episode of *The Castle*. But for Kafka it
seems that this is not a mistake. It is a doctrine and a "leap." There is
nothing that is not God's.

Even more significant is the fact that the land-surveyor breaks with
Frieda in order to go toward the Barnabas sisters. For the Barnabas
family is the only one in the village that is utterly forsaken by the Castle
and by the village itself. Amalia, the elder sister, has rejected the shame-
ful propositions made her by one of the Castle's officials. The immoral
curse that followed has forever cast her out from the love of God. Being
incapable of losing one's honor for God amounts to making oneself unworthy of His grace. You recognize a theme familiar to existential philosophy: truth contrary to morality. At this point things are far-reaching.
For the path pursued by Kafka's hero from Frieda to the Barnabas sisters
is the very one that leads from trusting love to the deification of the
absurd. Here again Kafka's thought runs parallel to Kierkegaard. It is
not surprising that the "Barnabas story" is placed at the end of the book.
The land-surveyor's last attempt is to recapture God through what negates him, to recognize him, not according to our categories of goodness
and beauty but behind the empty and hideous aspects of his indifference,
of his injustice, and of his hatred. That stranger who asks the Castle to
adopt him is at the end of his voyage a little more exiled because this
time he is unfaithful to himself, forsaking morality, logic, and intellectual truths in order to try to enter, endowed solely with his mad
hope, the desert of divine grace.[3]

. . . .

The word "hope" used here is not ridiculous. On the contrary, the
more tragic the condition described by Kafka, the firmer and more
aggressive that hope becomes. The more truly absurd *The Trial* is, the
more moving and illegitimate the impassioned "leap" of *The Castle*
seems. But we find here again in a pure state the paradox of existential
thought as it is expressed, for instance, by Kierkegaard: "Earthly hope

---

[3] This is obviously true only of the unfinished version of *The Castle* that Kafka
left us. But it is doubtful that the writer would have destroyed in the last chapters
his novel's unity of tone.

must be killed; only then can one be saved by true hope" [4] which can be translated: "One has to have written *The Trial* to undertake *The Castle.*"

Most of those who have spoken of Kafka have indeed defined his work as a desperate cry with no recourse left to man. But this calls for review. There is hope and hope. To me the optimistic work of Henri Bordeaux seems peculiarly discouraging. This is because it has nothing for the discriminating. Malraux' thought on the other hand is always bracing. But in these two cases neither the same hope nor the same despair is at issue. I see merely that the absurd work itself may lead to the infidelity I want to avoid. The work which was but an ineffectual repetition of. a sterile condition, a lucid glorification of the ephemeral, becomes here a cradle of illusions. It explains, it gives a shape to hope. The creator can no longer divorce himself from it. It is not the tragic game it was to be. It gives a meaning to the author's life.

It is strange in any case that works of related inspiration like those of Kafka, Kierkegaard, or Chestov; those, in short, of existential novelists and philosophers completely oriented towards the absurd and its consequences, should in the long run lead to that tremendous cry of hope.

They embrace the God that consumes them. It is through humility that hope enters in. For the absurd of this existence assures them a little more of supernatural reality. If the course of this life leads to God, there is an outcome after all. And the perseverance, the insistence with which Kierkegaard, Chestov, and Kafka's heroes repeat their itineraries are a special warrant of the uplifting power of that certainty.[5]

Kafka refuses his god moral nobility, evidence, virtue, coherence, but only the better to fall into his arms. The absurd is recognized, accepted, and man is resigned to it, but from then on we know that it has ceased to be the absurd. Within the limits of the human condition, what greater hope than the hope that allows an escape from that condition? As I see once more, existential thought in this regard (and contrary to current opinion) is steeped in a vast hope. The very hope which at the time of early Christianity and the spreading of the good news inflamed the ancient world. But in that leap that characterizes all existential thought, in that insistence, in that surveying of a divinity devoid of surface, how can one fail to see the mark of a lucidity that repudiates itself? It is merely claimed that this is pride abdicating to save itself. Such a repudiation would be fecund. But this does not change that. The moral value of lucidity cannot be diminished in my eyes by calling it sterile like all pride. For a truth also, by its very definition, is sterile. All facts are. In

[4] Kierkegaard: *Purity of Heart.*
[5] The only character without hope in *The Castle* is Amalia. She is the one with whom the land-surveyor is most violently contrasted.

a world where everything is given and nothing is explained, the fecundity of a value or of a metaphysic is a notion devoid of meaning.

In any case, you see here in what tradition of thought Kafka's work takes its place. It would indeed be intelligent to consider as inevitable the progression leading from *The Trial* to *The Castle*. Joseph K. and the land-surveyor K. are merely two poles that attract Kafka.[6] I shall speak as he does and say that his work is probably not absurd. But that should not deter us from seeing its nobility and universality. They come from the fact that he managed to represent so fully the everyday passage from hope to grief and from desperate wisdom to intentional blindness. His work is universal (a really absurd work is not universal) to the extent to which it represents the emotionally moving face of man fleeing humanity, deriving from his contradictions reasons for believing, reasons for hoping from his fecund despairs, and calling life his terrifying apprenticeship in death. It is universal because its inspiration is religious. As in all religions, man is freed of the weight of his own life. But if I know that, if I can even admire it, I also know that I am not seeking what is universal but what is true. The two may well not coincide.

This particular view will be better understood if I say that truly hopeless thought just happens to be defined by the opposite criteria and that the tragic work might be the work that, after all future hope is exiled, describes the life of a happy man. The more exciting life is, the more absurd is the idea of losing it. This is perhaps the secret of that proud aridity felt in Nietzsche's work. In this connection, Nietzsche appears to be the only artist to have derived the extreme consequences of an aesthetic of the absurd, inasmuch as his final message lies in a sterile and conquering lucidity and an obstinate negation of any supernatural consolation.

The preceding should nevertheless suffice to bring out the capital importance of Kafka in the framework of this essay.[7] Here we are carried to the confines of human thought. In the fullest sense of the word, it can be said that everything in that work is essential. In any case it propounds the absurd problem altogether. If one wants to compare these conclusions with our initial remarks, the content with the form, the secret meaning of *The Castle* with the natural art in which it is molded, K.'s passionate, proud quest with the everyday setting against which it takes place, then one will realize what may be its greatness. For if nostalgia is the mark of the human, perhaps no one has given such flesh and volume to these phantoms of regret. But at the same time will be sensed

      [6] On the two aspects of Kafka's thought, compare *The Penal Colony* "Guilt ["of man" is understood] is never doubtful" and a fragment of *The Castle* (Momus' report): "The guilt of the land-surveyor K. is hard to establish."
      [7] [i.e. *The Myth of Sisyphus,* from which this contribution is reprinted.]

what exceptional nobility the absurd work calls for, which is perhaps not found here. If the nature of art is to bind the general to the particular, ephemeral eternity of a drop of water to the play of its lights, it is even truer to judge the greatness of the absurd writer by the distance he is able to introduce between these two worlds. His secret consists in being able to find the exact point where they meet in their greatest disproportion.

And to tell the truth, this geometrical locus of man and the inhuman is seen everywhere by the pure in heart. If Faust and Don Quixote are eminent creations of art, this is because of the immeasurable nobilities they point out to us with their earthly hands. Yet a moment always comes when the mind negates the truths that those hands can touch. A moment comes when the creation ceases to be taken tragically; it is merely taken seriously. Then man is concerned with hope. But that is not his business. His business is to turn away from subterfuge. Yet this is just what I find at the conclusion of the vehement proceedings Kafka institutes against the whole universe. His unbelievable verdict is this hideous and upsetting world in which the very moles dare to hope.[8]

[8] What is offered above is obviously an interpretation of Kafka's work. But it is only fair to add that nothing prevents its being considered, apart from any interpretation, from a purely aesthetic point of view. For instance, B. Groethuysen in his remarkable preface to *The Trial* limits himself, more wisely than we, to following merely the painful fancies of what he calls, most strikingly, a daydreamer. It is the fate and perhaps the greatness of that work that it offers everything and confirms nothing.

Kafka and Judaism

by *Martin Buber*

The periods of Christian history can be classified according to the degree in which they are dominated by Paulinism, by which we mean of course not just a system of thought, but a mode of seeing and being which dwells in the life itself. In this sense our era is a Pauline one to a particular degree. In the human life of our day, compared with earlier epochs, Christianity is receding, but the Pauline view and attitude is gaining the mastery in many circles outside that of Christianity. There is a Paulinism of the unredeemed—one, that is, from which the abode of grace is eliminated: like Paul, man experiences the world as one given into the hands of inevitable forces, and only the manifest will to redemption from above, only Christ, is missing. The Christian Paulinism of our time is a result of the same fundamental view, although it softens down or removes that aspect of the demonocracy of the world: it sees, nevertheless, existence divided into an unrestricted rule of wrath and a sphere of reconciliation, from which point indeed the claim for the establishment of a Christian order of life is raised clearly and energetically enough, but *de facto* the redeemed Christian soul stands over against an unredeemed world of men in lofty impotence. Neither this picture of the abyss spanned only by the halo of the Savior nor that of the same abyss covered now by nothing but impenetrable darkness is to be understood as brought about by changes in subjectivity: in order to paint them, the retinas of those now living must have been affected by an actual fact, by the situation now existing.

I will illustrate my position from two books, which are very different from each other; I choose them because the view of which I am speaking comes to light clearly in them. For this reason I have chosen one from the literature of modern Christian theology, because I do not know of any other in which the Pauline view of God is expressed so directly; it is *The Mediator* by Emil Brunner. The other, one of the few authentic similes which our age has produced, is the work of a non-Christian poet, a Jew, Franz Kafka's novel *The Castle*.

I am only concerned in Brunner's book with what he has to say about God, and not about Christ; that is, with the dark foil and not the image of glory which stands out against it. We read: "God cannot allow His honor to be impugned"; "the law itself demands from God the reaction"; "God would cease to be God if He allowed His honor to be impugned." This is said of the Father of Christ; therefore it does not refer to one of the gods and rulers, but to Him of Whom the "Old Testament" witnesses. But neither in this itself nor in any Jewish interpretation is God spoken of in this way; and such a word is unimaginable from the lips of Jesus as I believe I know him. For here in fact "with God all things are possible"; there is nothing which He "could not." Of course the rulers of this world cannot allow their honor to be impugned; what would remain to them if they did! But God—to be sure, prophets and psalmists show how He "glorifies His Name" to the world, and Scripture is full of His "zeal," but He Himself does not assume any of these attitudes otherwise than remaining superior to them; in the language of the interpretation: He proceeds from one *middah* to the other, and none is adequate to Him. If the whole world should tear the garment of His honor into rags, nothing would be done to Him. Which law could presume to demand anything from Him?—surely the highest conceivable law is that which is given by Him to the world, not to Himself:[1] He does not bind Himself and therefore nothing binds Him. And that He would cease to be God —"God" is a stammering of the world, the world of men, He Himself is immeasurably more than "God" only, and if the world should cease to stammer or cease to exist, He would remain. In the immediacy we experience His anger and His tenderness in one; no assertion can detach one from the other and make Him into a God of wrath Who requires a mediator.

In the Book of Wisdom, scarcely later than a hundred years before Christ, God is addressed in this fashion: "But Thou hast compassion upon all, since Thou canst do all things"—He is able to have compassion even upon us, as we are!—"and Thou dost overlook the sins of men up to their turning"—He overlooks them, not that we should perish, but turn to Him; He does not wait until we have turned (this is significantly

[1] Brunner explains: "The law of His being God, on which all the lawfulness of the world is based, the fundamental order of the world, the consistent and reliable character of all that happens, the validity of all standards. . . ." Precisely this seems to me to be an inadmissible derivation of the nature of the world from the nature of God, or rather the reverse. Order and standards are derived from the act of God, which sets the world in being and gives it the law, and not from a law which would determine His being. *Cf.* E. Brunner, *The Mediator* (1934), p. 444.

the opposite of the Synoptic characterization of the Baptist's preaching: not repentance for the remission of sins, but the remission of sins for repentance)— ". . . for Thou lovest all creatures and abhorrest nothing that Thou hast made"—here the Creation is obviously taken more seriously than the Fall—". . . Thou sparest all things because they are Thine, O Lord, Who willest good to the living. For Thine incorruptible Spirit is in all." It is as if the author wished to oppose a doctrine current in Alexandria about the Jewish God of wrath.

Kafka's contribution to the metaphysics of the "door" is known: the parable of the man who squanders his life before a certain open gateway which leads to the world of meaning, and who vainly begs admission until just before his death it is communicated to him that it had been intended for him, but is now being shut. So "the door" is still open; indeed, every person has his own door and it is open to him; but he does not know this and apparently is not in a condition to know it. Kafka's two main works are elaborations of the theme of the parable, the one, *The Trial,* in the dimension of time, the other, *The Castle,* in that of space; accordingly, the first is concerned with the hopelessness of man in his dealings with his soul, the second with the same in his dealings with the world. The parable itself is not Pauline but its elaborations are— only, as we have said, with salvation removed. The one is concerned with the judgement under which the soul stands and under which it places itself willingly; but the guilt, on account of which it has to be judged, is unformulated, the proceedings are labyrinthine and the courts of judicature themselves questionable—without all this seeming to prejudice the legality of the administration of justice. The other book, which especially concerns us here, describes a district delivered over to the authority of a slovenly bureaucracy without the possibility of appeal, and it describes this district as being our world. What is at the top of the government, or rather above it, remains hidden in a darkness, of the nature of which one never once gets a presentiment; the administrative hierarchy, who exercise power, received it from above, but apparently without any commission or instruction. A broad meaninglessness governs without restraint; every notice, every transaction is shot through with meaninglessness, and yet the legality of the government is unquestioned. Man is called into this world, he is appointed in it, but wherever he turns to fulfill his calling he comes up against the thick vapors of a mist of absurdity. This world is handed over to a maze of intermediate beings —it is a Pauline world, except that God is removed into the impenetrable darkness and that there is no place for a mediator. We are reminded of the Haggadic account (Aggadat Bereshit IX) of the sinful David, who prays God that He Himself may judge him and not give him into the hands of the seraphim and cherubim, for "they are all cruel." Cruel also are the intermediate beings of Kafka, but in addition they are disorderly and stupid. They are extremely powerful bunglers, which drive the human creature through the nonsense of life—and they do it with the full authority of their master. Certain features remind us of the licentious demons into which the archons of Paul's conception of the world have been changed in some Gnostic schools.

The strength of Pauline tendencies in present-day Christian theology is to be explained by the characteristic stamp of the time, just as that of earlier periods can explain that at one time the purely spiritual, the Johannine tendency was emphasized, and at another the so-called Petrine one, in which the somewhat undefined conception "Peter" represents the unforgettable recollection of the conversations of Jesus with the disciples in Galilee. Those periods are Pauline in which the contradictions of human life, especially of man's social life, so mount up that they increasingly assume in man's consciousness of existence the character of a fate. Then the light of God appears to be darkened, and the redeemed Christian soul becomes aware, as the unredeemed soul of the Jew has continually done, of the still unredeemed concreteness of the world of men in all its horror. Then to be sure, as we know indeed from Paul, too, the genuine Christian struggles for a juster order of his community, but he understands the impenetrable root of the contradiction in the view of the threatening clouds of wrath, and clings with Pauline tenacity to the abundant grace of the mediator. He indeed opposes the ever-approaching Marcionite danger, the severing not only of the Old and New Testaments, but that of creation and salvation, of Creator and Savior, for he sees how near men are, as Kierkegaard says of the Gnosis, "to identifying creation with the Fall," and he knows that a victory for Marcion can lead to the destruction of Christianity; but—this seems to me to be more strongly recognized again in Christendom today—Marcion is not to be overcome by Paul.

Even Kierkegaard, a century ago, gave expression to the fact that there is a non-Pauline outlook—that is, one superior to the stamp of the age —when he wrote in his Journal a prayer, in which he says: "Father in Heaven, it is indeed only the moment of silence in the inwardness of speaking with one another." That to be sure is said from the point of view of personal existence ("When a man languishes in the desert, not hearing Thy voice there"), but in this respect we are not to distinguish between the situation of the person and that of man or mankind. Kierkegaard's prayer, in spite of his great belief in Christ, is not from Paul or from John, but from Jesus.

A superficial Christian considering Kafka's problem can easily get rid of him by treating him simply as the unredeemed Jew who does not reach after salvation. But only he who proceeds thus has now got rid of him; Kafka has remained untouched by this treatment. For the Jew, insofar as he is not detached from the origin, even the most exposed Jew like Kafka, is safe. All things happen to him, but they cannot affect him. He is not, to be sure, able any longer to conceal himself "in the covert of Thy wings" (Psalms 61:4), for God is hiding Himself from the time in which he lives, and so from him, its most exposed son; but in the fact of God's being only hidden, which he knows, he is safe. "Better the living dove on the roof than the half-dead, convulsively resisting sparrow in the hand." He describes, from innermost awareness, the actual course of the world, he describes most exactly the rule of the foul devilry which fills the foreground; and on the edge of the description he scratches the sentence: "Test yourself on humanity. It makes the doubter doubt, the man of belief believe." His unexpressed, ever-present theme is the remoteness of the judge, the remoteness of the lord of the castle, the hiddenness, the eclipse, the darkness; and therefore he observes: "He who believes can experience no miracle. During the day one does not see any stars." This is the nature of the Jew's security in the dark, one which is essentially different from that of the Christian. It allows no rest, for as long as you live, you must live with the sparrow and not with the dove, who avoids your hand; but, being without illusion, it is consistent with the foreground course of the world, and so nothing can harm you. For from beyond, from the darkness of heaven the dark ray comes actively into the heart, without any appearance of immediacy. "We were created to live in Paradise, Paradise was appointed to serve us. Our destiny has been changed; that this also happened with the appointment of Paradise is not said." So, gently and shyly, anti-Paulinism speaks from the heart of this Pauline painter of the foreground-hell: Paradise is still there and it benefits us. It is there, and that means it is also here where the dark ray meets the tormented heart. Are the unredeemed in need of salvation? They suffer from the unredeemed state of the world. "Every misery around us we too must suffer"—there it is again, the word from the shoot of Israel. The unredeemed soul refuses to give up the evidence of the unredeemed world from which it suffers, to exchange it for the soul's own salvation. It is able to refuse, for it is safe.

This is the appearance of Paulinism without Christ which at this time when God is most hidden has penetrated into Judaism, a Paulinism therefore opposed to Paul. The course of the world is depicted in more gloomy colors than ever before, and yet Emunah[2] is proclaimed anew,

[2] [Editor's Note: This term is defined by the author elsewhere in his book, as follows: "The origin of the Jewish Emunah is in the history of a nation, that of Christian Pistis in that of individuals.

"Emunah originated in the actual experiences of Israel, which were to it experiences of faith. Small, then great numbers of people, first in search of open pastureland,

with a still deepened "in spite of all this," quite soft and shy, but unambiguous. Here, in the midst of the Pauline domain, it has taken the
place of Pistis.[3] In all its reserve, the late-born, wandering around in the
darkened world, confesses in face of the suffering peoples of the world
with those messengers of Deutero-Isaiah (Isaiah 65:15): "Truly Thou art
a God Who hides Himself, O God of Israel, Savior!" So must Emunah
change in a time of God's eclipse in order to persevere steadfast to God,
without disowning reality. That He hides Himself does not diminish the
immediacy; in the immediacy He remains the Savior and the contradiction of existence becomes for us a theophany.

---

then of land for a free settlement, make their journey as being led by God. This fact,
that Israel experienced its way to Canaan, which was its way into history, already in
the days of the 'Fathers' as guidance, sensually as guidance through wilderness and
dangers—this fact which took place historically once only is the birth of Emunah.
Emunah is the state of 'persevering'—also to be called trust in the existential sense
—of man in an invisible guidance which yet gives itself to be seen, in a hidden but
self-revealing guidance; but the personal Emunah of every individual remains embodied in that of the nation and draws its strength from the living memory of generations in the great leadings of early times."]

[3] [Editor's Note: This term is defined by the author elsewhere in his book, as
follows: "Christian Pistis was born outside the historical experiences of nations, so to
say in retirement from history, in the souls of individuals, to whom the challenge
came to believe that a man crucified in Jerusalem was their savior. Although this
faith, in its very essence, was able to raise itself to a piety of utter devotedness and
to a mysticism of union with him in whom they believed, and although it did so, yet
it rests upon a foundation which, in spite of its 'irrationality,' must be described
as logical or noetic: the accepting and recognizing as true of a proposition pronounced
about the object of faith. All the fervor or ecstasy of feeling, all the devotion of life,
grew out of the acceptance of the claim and of the confession made both in the soul
and to the world: 'I believe that it is so.' "]

Recent Kafka Criticism (1944-1955)—A Survey

by H. S. Reiss

The high tide of enthusiasm for Kafka has undoubtedly ebbed away. Recent critics no longer think it necessary to push him at any cost, and scholars, now less influenced by the latest fashion in literary taste, are turning to a more sober appraisal of his work so that, in the end, he should find a more secure place in the history of German literature. It is perhaps not surprising that interest in Kafka has been so widespread and sensational; for, since anxiety is the keynote of his writing, many critics have found in his work an imaginative representation of the anxieties which they themselves have known in our troubled times and have thus identified their own emotions with the fears and obsessions experienced by his characters. In addition, Kafka is often so obscure, his imagery so vague, his language so ambiguous, the reasoning of his characters so involved and his situations capable of being interpreted so variously, that his work lends itself to endless speculation. Others have considered Kafka not as a creative writer, but as a metaphysician and completely misunderstood his artistic intention. Heinz Politzer[1] and Friedrich Beissner[2] are, therefore, right in attacking those who seek to subordinate the events and sayings in his work to their own preoccupations. Although this kind of approach is invalid and has damaged Kafka's reputation as a serious writer it has, however, also aroused interest in his work and extended his reading public. Time should prove that Kafka is too significant a writer not to survive the vicissitudes of his literary reputation.

"Recent Kafka Criticism (1944-1955)—A Survey," by H. S. Reiss. From *German Life and Letters*, James Boyd, Leonard Forster, and C. P. Magill, eds. © 1953 by H. S. Reiss. Reprinted by permission of Basil Blackwell & Mott, Ltd.

[1] Heinz Politzer, "Problematik und Probleme der Kafka-Forschung" in *Monatshefte für Deutschen Unterricht, Deutsche Sprache und Deutsche Literatur* (quoted as *MDU*), XLII (Wisconsin, 1950).

[2] Freidrich Beissner, *Der Erzähler Franz Kafka* (Stuttgart, 1952), p. 5.

There have been various brands of Kafka enthusiasts. The most influential ones have been those who interpreted Kafka entirely in quasi-theological and quasimetaphysical terms. Foremost among them has been Max Brod. The debt which all students of Kafka owe to Brod is so great that all his observations deserve the most sympathetic attention. After all, but for him, at least four-fifths of Kafka's work would have been destroyed. Had he burned the posthumous papers Kafka would scarcely be remembered, or if he were, he would probably be ranked as a writer of promise who composed some startling short stories, the full significance of which might easily have escaped us. It is, therefore, unfortunate that it should have become almost a habit among critics to disparage Brod.[3] His picture of Kafka is undoubtedly colored by his friendship for Kafka, by what Kafka means to him, and by his belief that Kafka had a message for our times. This view has misled those who listened to Brod's comments rather than Kafka's writings. To Brod's belief in Kafka as a prophet and exemplary figure must be added the reverence with which he testifies to Kafka's personality. In this respect, Kafka's influence on his friends is borne out by their reminiscences and, notably, by Gustav Janouch's remarkable conversations with Kafka.[4] We may, indeed, view Kafka differently from Brod; for Brod is, in the last resort, not concerned with Kafka's works as literary works of art, but with his ideas. The titles of Brod's last two books on Kafka reveal this clearly, for he called them *Franz Kafkas Glauben und Lehre* (Winterthur, 1948; Munich, 1951) and *Franz Kafka als wegweisende Gestalt* (St. Gallen, n.d.). Those whose main concern is literary criticism or literary history are, of course, unable to assent to this approach on methodological grounds. Much of what Brod says is thus on the fringe of our interest in Kafka. Brod's contribution to our knowledge of Kafka's life is, however, always valuable, constantly throwing new light on Kafka the man, as an additional chapter to his biography shows.[5] Doubts have, however, been cast on Brod's editorial competence. He has been accused of negligence in the actual task of editing the works[6] and even of a radically mistaken arrangement of some of the posthumous works.[7] His recollection of dates of composition

[3] For instance, Erich Heller, "The World of Franz Kafka" in *The Disinherited Mind* (Cambridge, 1952), especially p. 177.

[4] Gustav Janouch, *Gespräche mit Kafka*, Frankfurt/Main, 1951. (Translated as *Conversations with Kafka*, by Goronwy Rees, London, 1953.)

[5] Max Brod, "Neue Züge zu Kafkas Bild," in *Franz Kafka, eine Biographie*, 3rd edition (Frankfurt/Main, 1954).

[6] Friedrich Beissner, *op. cit.*, pp. 44-8.

[7] Herman Uyttersprot, *Zur Struktur von Kafkas 'Der Prozess'. Versuch einer Neuordnung. Langues Vivantes*, XLII (Brussels, 1953), and "Zur Struktur von Kafkas Romanen" in *Revue des Langues Vivantes*, XX, 5 (Brussels, 1954). [Also *Eine neue Ordnung der Werke Kafkas?* (Antwerp, 1957). (Ed.)]

and his comments on Kafka's artistic intentions have been subjected to severe scrutiny. The result of this has been to prove him guilty of, at least, contradictory statements.

Edwin Muir has greatly influenced English and American Kafka criticism. Kafka's principal English translator has similarly stressed Kafka's spiritual message.[8] Many other commentators have followed in the wake of Brod and Muir, either elaborating their views or seeking to refute them. It must here suffice to draw attention to a few of the more outstanding contributions to that strand of Kafka criticism, most of which are easily accessible in the anthology of writings on Kafka entitled *The Kafka Problem*[9] which provides a fair sample of the state of Kafka criticism shortly after the end of the Second World War. Many of the articles are slight. In some cases, one wonders whether the essayist ever read Kafka in the original German, but they appear under some famous names and a number of them contain interesting observations. Albert Camus sees in Kafka a protagonist of the existentialist philosophy of the absurd which has affinities with his own writings.[10] W. H. Auden also insists on the metaphysical character of Kafka's work.[11] The titles of other contributions indicate their approach: we find "Kafka and Kierkegaard," [12] "*The Trial* and the Theology of Crisis," [13] "Faith and Vocation," [14] "The Tragedy of Faithlessness," [15] "The Economy of Chaos." [16] Other symposia on Kafka were published in the *Quarterly Review of Literature*[17] and in *Focus*[18] and proceeded on similar lines.

Herbert Tauber's study of Kafka's work[19] is also metaphysical in outlook. It has all the advantages and disadvantages of a Ph.D. thesis (for the University of Zürich). Dr. Tauber discusses in turn Kafka's individual works and seeks to offer explanations of their meaning, but he shows next to no awareness of Kafka's art. Erich Heller, indeed, in his essay "The World of Franz Kafka," shows an understanding of the imaginative

---

[8] Edwin Muir (translator), *Introductory Note to Franz Kafka, The Castle* (London, 1930) and *Introductory Note to Franz Kafka, The Great Wall of China* (London, 1933).

[9] Angel Flores (editor), *The Kafka Problem* (New York, 1946). (Many of the essays contained in this volume were published elsewhere at an earlier date.)

[10] Albert Camus, "Kafka: Hope and Absurdity," *ibid.*, pp. 251-61.

[11] W. H. Auden, "Kafka's Quest," *ibid.*, pp. 47-52.

[12] Jean Wahl, "Kierkegaard and Kafka," *ibid.*, pp. 262-75.

[13] John Kelly, "*The Trial* and the Theology of Crisis," *ibid.*, pp. 151-71.

[14] D. S. Savage, "Faith and Vocation," *ibid.*, pp. 319-36.

[15] Hans Joachim Schoeps, "The Tragedy of Faithlessness," *ibid.*, pp. 287-95.

[16] T. Weiss, "The Economy of Chaos," *ibid.*, pp. 363-75.

[17] Cf. *Quarterly Review of Literature*, II, 3 (New Haven, Conn., 1945).

[18] *Focus I*, edited by B. Rajan and Andrew Pearse (London, 1945).

[19] Herbert Tauber, *Franz Kafka, eine Deutung seines Werkes* (Zürich, 1941). (Trans. G. Humphreys Roberts and Roger Senhouse, London, 1948.)

character of Kafka's work.[20] But he is, in the main, concerned with interpreting Kafka in terms of a specific view of the "history of the human mind." While Professor Heller has much of interest to say on the nature of Kafka's spiritual struggles and offers not a few striking remarks on the originality of Kafka's writing, his over-simplified view of the history of ideas often spoils his argument.

Kafka has had quite a vogue in France where, on the whole, he has been viewed as a thinker rather than as an artist; Camus was only the most notable writer to write about him. Essays on Kafka appeared in many of the leading literary magazines, such as *L'Arche, Cahiers du Sud, Critique;*[21] a few monographs were also published. Michel Carouges in his *Franz Kafka* (Paris, 1948) is, despite an informative opening chapter on Kafka's art, mainly interested in the content of his work, for he sets out to expound aspects of his work that touch upon society, sex, family relations, and religion. Likewise, Robert Rochefort's *Kafka ou l'irréducible espoir* (Paris, 1947) aims at writing a kind of spiritual history and inner biography of Kafka. He claims that Kafka had voluntarily taken upon himself the rôle of a modern Job; the evidence upon which he bases his argument is extremely flimsy. André Nemeth, whose *Kafka ou le mystère juif* (Paris, 1947) was translated from the Hungarian by Victor Hintz, sees in Kafka the prototype of a Jewish writer and thinker. Mr. Nemeth briefly analyzes the novels and longer stories with great skill, and occasionally elucidates obscure passages, but his main concern is to elaborate Kafka's philosophy of religion. Kafka, for him, is a man who has rebelled against the powers that be, since they wish to separate him from God. Even R. Dauvin, in his scholarly article on *The Trial*,[22] is predominantly interested in the ideas of the novel.

In Germany Kafka was virtually unknown until after the Second World War, owing to the political and racial hatred fostered by the Nazi regime. With the end of German intellectual isolation Kafka was again published in Germany and critics and scholars took an increasing interest in him. The prevalent first reaction was, perhaps inevitably,

[20] Erich Heller, *op. cit.*, pp. 157-81.

[21] *Cf.* for instance: Maurice Blanchot, *"La Lecture de Kafka," L'Arche*, II (November 1945). René Micha, *"Le Fantastique Kafkaien sur le plan d'art," ibid.*, XVI (Paris, June 1946). Pierre Klossowski, *"Introduction au journal intime de Franz Kafka," Cahiers du Sud*, XXII, No. 270, (Paris, 1945). François Léger, *"De Job à Kafka," ibid.* Jean Starobinski, *"Kafka et Dostoievski," ibid.*, XXXII, No. 304. A. Girard, *"Kafka et le problème du journal intime," Critique*, I, 1 (Paris, 1945). George Bataille, *"Kafka devant la critique communiste," ibid.*, VI, No. 41 (Paris, 1950). Pierre Klossowski, *"Kafka Nihiliste," ibid.*, VII, 30, (Paris, 1948). Maurice Blanchot, *"Kafka et l'exigence de l'Oeuvre," ibid.*, VIII, 58 (Paris, 1952). Joseph Gabel, *"Kafka romancier de l'accusation," ibid.*, IX, 78 (Paris, 1953).

[22] R. Dauvin " Le procès' de Kafka," *Etudes Germaniques,* I, 1 (Lyon-Paris, 1949).

quasi-metaphysical, following an only too well established trend of German writing on literature. Max Bense's *Theorie Kafkas* (Cologne, 1951), for instance, is rather an account of the author's own "metaphysics" of literature than of Kafka's creative work. For Professor Bense, Kafka illustrates the development of metaphysics, and he seeks to show affinities with Heidegger (pp. 67 etc.). Important periodicals such as *Die Neue Rundschau*,[23] *Merkur*,[24] and *Hochland*[25] also evaluate Kafka the thinker rather than the creative artist. Günther Anders's rather clever though highly controversial book *Franz Kafka, Pro und Contra* (Munich, 1951) [Translated and adapted by A. Steer and A. K. Thorlby as *Franz Kafka*, London and New York 1960] affords a good example of this tendency. For Mr. Anders, Kafka was a nihilistic writer, therefore a precursor of "Nazi philosophy," whose thought was to be condemned outright. This book so greatly angered Max Brod that he publicly accused Anders of a complete misinterpretation, in an article which he significantly entitled *"Die Ermordung einer Puppe namens Franz Kafka."*[26] Polemics, too, is the keynote of Hermann Pongs' comments[27] on Kafka, whom he considers as the prototype of modern ambivalence, of which he strongly disapproves. He, therefore, attacks the thesis of Walter Muschg,[28] who had called Kafka the only consecrated poet of the age. Josef Mühlberger, however, sees in Kafka a religious figure.[29]

Mr. Anders verges upon a sociological interpretation of Kafka's work. In this approach he has some forerunners in Rudolf Fuchs,[30] Edwin Berry Burgum,[31] Egon Vietta,[32] and Max Lerner,[33] who similarly sought to discern affinities between Kafka's work and his social background. The

[23] Günther Anders, *"Franz Kafka: Pro und Contra,"* *Die Neue Rundschau* (Stockholm, 1947). Hans Joachim Schoeps, *"Theologische Motive in der Dichtung Franz Kafkas,"* *ibid.*, LXII (Frankfurt/Main, 1951). K. H. Volkmann-Schluck, *"Bewusstsein und Dasein in Kafkas 'Der Prozess,' "* *ibid.* Theodor W. Adorno, *"Aufzeichnungen zu Kafka,"* *ibid.*, *ed. cit.*, LXIV, 1953.

[24] Gerhard F. Hering, *"Franz Kafkas Tagebücher,"* *Merkur*, II (Baden-Baden, 1948). Rainer Grünter, *"Beitrag zur Kafka-Deutung,"* *ibid.*, *ed. cit.*, IV, 1950.

[25] Eugen Gürster, *"Das Weltbild Franz Kafkas,"* *Hochland*, XLIV (München-Kempten, 1952).

[26] Max Brod, *"Die Ermordung einer Puppe namens Franz Kafka, Replik"* (reprinted in *Franz Kafka, eine Biographie*, *ed. cit.*, pp. 340-58) *Neue Schweizer Rundschau*, Neue Folge, XIX (Zürich, 1951-52). *Cf.* also Günther Anders, *"Kafka Pro und Contra,"* *NSR*, *ed. cit.*, XX, and Max Brod, *"Duplik,"* *ibid.*

[27] Hermann Pongs, *Im Umbruch der Zeit* (Göttingen, 1952), pp. 67-87.

[28] Walter Muschg, *Tragische Literaturgeschichte* (Bern, 1948), p. 103.

[29] *Cf.* Josef Mühlberger, *Hugo von Hofmannsthal. F. Kafka. Zwei Vorträge* (Esslingen, 1953).

[30] Rudolf Fuchs, "Social awareness," *The Kafka Problem*, *ed. cit.*, pp. 247-50.

[31] Edwin Berry Burgum, "The Bankruptcy of Faith," *ibid.*, pp. 298-318.

[32] Egon Vietta, "The Fundamental Revolution," *ibid.*, pp. 337-47.

[33] Max Lerner, "The Human Voyage," *ibid.*, pp. 38-46.

latter approach is also predominant in Pavel Eisner's *Franz Kafka and Prague*.[34] Mr. Eisner maintains that Kafka's work is above all valuable as a social document, for it records the world of Jewish intellectuals in pre-1938 Prague, a world which is now dead. However, he considerably overstates his case. Quite a few critics have stressed the Jewish roots of Kafka's themes and mode of presentation, but not infrequently do they infer more than the evidence warrants.[35]

Given the close interrelation between Kafka's life and work it was inevitable that he would attract those who base their study of literature on the methods of psychology, especially of psychoanalysis. The most startling exponent of this approach in recent years has been Charles Neider, though his book *The Frozen Sea*[36] is hardly less extreme than Helmut Kaiser's *Franz Kafkas Inferno* published in Vienna as early as 1931. Mr. Neider rather uncharitably indicts other Kafka critics whom he dubs "the Cabalists" because their comments obscure Kafka's "real" intention. He then puts forward the astounding claim that he has discovered *the* secret key to Kafka's work, a key so carefully concealed by that most tantalizingly secretive of all writers, that no explicit reference is to be found in any of his writings, even in his diaries or letters. According to Mr. Neider, it was Kafka's aim to elaborate Freudian psychoanalytical theory in his work. For him, Kafka's writing is full of sexual symbols, which he finds everywhere in the opening scene of *The Trial*. He comments:

> The pleats, pockets, buttons and belt of the first warder are all sexual symbols. Others are nightshirt, underwear, thirtieth birthday (use of trinity), dipping bread-and-butter into honey pot, pincushion, grouping objects around the candle, uniforms, the inspector and the two warders (three), the three young men, the inspector's "hard round hat" which he places carefully on his head "as if he were trying it on for the first time," K.'s hat, et cetera. (p. 154)

If Mr. Neider's method were applied to his own work, the following passage might suggest that his study, too, could be explained in terms of a secret key:

[34] Pavel Eisner, *Franz Kafka and Prague* (New York, 1950). *Cf.* also Rudolf Vasata, "Kafka—A Bohemian Writer?" *The Central European Observer*, XXIII (London, 1946).

[35] *Cf.*, for instance, Hans Joachim Schoeps, *op. cit.*, William C. Rubinstein: "Franz Kafka's 'A report to an academy'" in *Modern Language Quarterly*, XIII (Seattle, Wash., 1952). Robert Kauf, "Once again Kafka's 'A report to an academy'" in *MLQ*, ed. cit., XV, 1954. P. P. van Caspe, *"Josefine und Jeremias. Versuch einer Deutung,"* *Neophilologus*, XXXVIII (Gröningen, 1953). André Nemeth, *Kafka ou le mystère juif* (Paris, 1947).

[36] Charles Neider, *The Frozen Sea* 'New York, 1948).

To accept unquestioningly an artist's pronouncements about his work is the height of gullibility. The history of literary hoaxes is proof of this— not to speak of an artist's sincere delusions concerning himself. (p. 183)

The bias of Paul Goodman's *Kafka's Prayer* (New York, 1947) is also mainly psychoanalytical. Like Neider, Mr. Goodman treats Kafka's writings as if they were a code that could be deciphered with a Freudian key. To this, he adds a dose of a pseudo-theological interpretation and claims that Kafka, though not a master-theologian (p. 52) was at least a very remarkable one and certainly a greater theologian than Kierkegaard (p. 36)! Written in what is often obscure and turgid English and based, as the author admits in the preface, on a poor knowledge of German, this book cannot be taken very seriously. Other instances of the psychoanalytical approach are Erich Fromm's study of symbolical language and Joachim Seypel's account of the animal images in Kafka, while Frederick T. Hoffman discusses Freud's influence on Kafka.[37]

There have been, of course, studies of Kafka which do not belong to any specific school of thought, but which seek to give an objective account. Hannah Arendt's essay[38] is gratifyingly sensitive and balanced. Austin Warren supplies a sensible evaluation of the stature of Kafka,[39] while Edmund Wilson is, as is to be expected, brilliant and impressive when he "debunks" the Kafka fashion and seeks to reduce our view of Kafka's achievement to saner proportions.[40] He provides a refreshing antidote; though in order to achieve his aim he underrates Kafka more than is perhaps just.

The present author's *Franz Kafka, eine Betrachtung seines Werkes*[41]

---

[37] Erich Fromm, "Symbolic Language in Myth, Fairy Tale, Ritual, and Novel." ch. 5: "Kafka's *The Trial*," *The Forgotten Language* (London, 1952), pp. 213-24. Joachim H. Seypel, "The Animal and Totemism in Frank Kafka," *Literature and Psychology*, IV (New York, 1954). Frederick J. Hofman, "Kafka and Mann," *Freudianism and the Literary Mind* (Baton Rouge, La., 1945).

[38] Hannah Arendt, "Franz Kafka," *Sechs Essays* (Heidelberg, 1948). *(Cf.* also "Franz Kafka, A Revaluation," *Partisan Review*, XI, New York, 1944.)

[39] Austin Warren, "Cosmos Kafka," *The Kafka Problem, ed. cit.*, pp. 60-74. (*Cf.* also *Rage for Order*, Chicago, 1948.) General accounts of much lesser importance are found in: William Hubben, *Four Prophets of Our Destiny* (New York, 1952). Francis Russell, *Three Studies in Twentieth Century Obscurity* (Aldington, Ashford, Kent, 1954). Nathan A. Scott, *Rehearsals of Discomposure* (London, 1952). Eliseo Vivas, "Kafka's Distorted Mask," *The Kenyon Review*, X (Gambier, Ohio, 1948). F. Waismann, "A philosopher looks at Kafka," *Essays in Criticism*, III (Oxford, 1953). There are, however, some very stimulating remarks in J. Isaacs, *The Assessment of Twentieth Century Literature* (London, 1951).

[40] Edmund Wilson, "A Dissenting Opinion on Kafka," *Classics and Commercials* (New York, 1950), pp. 383-92.

[41] H. S. Reiss, *Franz Kafka, eine Betrachtung seines Werkes* (Heidelberg, 1952). (*Cf.* review, *German Life and Letters*, N.S. V, 4, 1953.)

was intended as a critical study of Kafka's work and of his achievement
as a creative writer. Its aim was to give a concise account of both Kafka's
thought and art. In retrospect, however, it would appear that the value
of the book might have been enhanced if a closer integration of both
content and form of Kafka's work had been attempted.

Serious Kafka scholarship is slowly coming into its own. Studies based
on the method of comparative literature have been especially valuable.
Maurice Gravier in a closely reasoned analysis seeks to indicate the affinities between Kafka and Strindberg.[42] Kafka, who was greatly influenced
by Strindberg is, like him, a stranger who has lost contact with his environment. More attractive still is the concise essay by Idris Parry[43] in
which he stresses the close parallel which both Gogol's and Kafka's imaginative representation of obsession reveal. Rudolf Kassner's essay on
Swift, Gogol, and Kafka offers interesting perspectives.[44] Max Brod
points out the affinity of *The Castle* to Bozena Nemcová's *The Grand-
mother*.[45] Slighter studies compare Kafka to Dostoevsky,[46] to Dickens,[47]
to Lessing and Vigny,[48] to Pascal,[49] who are seen as religious satirists, to
Rex Warner,[50] and even to Charlie Chaplin.[51] An attempt by Erich A.
Albrecht to trace the literary origins of *Ein Landarzt* to tales about country doctors in Balzac, Flaubert, Turgenev, and Carossa is not entirely
convincing.[52] Peter Demetz provides a lucid account of Kafka's reception
in England,[53] whilst Ilse Meidinger-Geise tells of Kafka's influence on
recent German writers.[54]

[42] Maurice Gravier, "Kafka et Strindberg," *Études Germaniques*, VIII (Lyon-Paris,
1953).

[43] Idris Parry, "Kafka and Gogol," *German Life and Letters*, N.S. VI, 2, 1953.

[44] Rudolf Kassner, *"Stil und Gesicht. Swift, Gogol, Kafka,"* *Merkur*, VIII (Stuttgart,
1954).

[45] Max Brod, *Franz Kafka, eine Biographie*, ed. cit., pp. 334-9.

[46] René Poggioli, "Kafka and Dostoyevsky," *The Kafka Problem*, ed. cit., pp. 97-107.
Jean Starobinski, *op. cit.*

[47] R. Vasata, "Kafka and Dickens," *ibid.*, ed. cit., pp. 134-9.

[48] Vernon Hall, Jun., "Kafka, Lessing, and Vigny," *Comparative Literature*, I
{Eugene, Ore., 1949).

[49] Karl Heinrich Höfele, *"Kafkas Selbstporträt und das Menschenbild Pascals,"*
Zeitschrift für Religions- und Geistesgeschichte, V (Cologne, Leiden, 1933).

[50] B. Rajan, "Kafka—A Comparison with Rex Warner," *Focus I*, ed. cit., pp. 7-11.
George Woodcock, "Kafka and Rex Warner," *ibid.*, pp. 59-65 (also in *The Kafka
Problem*, ed. cit., pp. 108-16).

[51] Parker Tyler, "Kafka and Chaplin's America," *Sewanee Review*, LXIII (Sewanee,
1950).

[52] Erich A. Albrecht, *"Die Entstehungsgeschichte von Kafkas 'Der Landarzt,'"* MDU,
XLVI, 1954.

[53] Peter Demetz, "Kafka in England," *German Life and Letters*, N.S. IV, 1, 1950.

[54] Ilse Meidinger-Geise, *"Franz Kafka und die junge Literatur,"* *Welt und Wort*, VII
{Tübingen, 1952).

Some interesting conclusions have resulted from the study of individual works. F. D. Luke supplies a penetrating psychological analysis of *Die Verwandlung*.[55] Mr. Luke's essay has the great merit of treating the story as an aesthetic whole. He sees it as a *Familienkatastrophe* taking place on two levels, the primitive or infantile level and the moral adult one where aesthetic and moral judgments are relevant. He also points out the dramatic effect of its tripartite division. Other writings of Kafka: *Der Bau*,[56] *Blumfeld, ein älterer Junggeselle*,[57] *Das Ehepaar*,[58] *Gib's Auf!* [59] *In der Strafkolonie*,[60] *Josefine oder das Mäusevolk*,[61] *Ein Bericht für eine Akademie*,[62] *Ein Hungerkünstler*,[63] *Eine kleine Frau*,[64] *Auf der Galerie, Eine kaiserliche Botschaft, Vor dem Gesetz*,[65] *Briefe an Milena*,[66] and his aphorisms,[67] have attracted specific attention. Heinz Politzer has written a penetrating study of Kafka's *Brief an den Vater*. This letter, Professor Politzer suggests, enables us to grasp how Kafka used the biographical data of his life to comment upon his writings, and used his writings to comment upon his life. It shows Kafka "infatuated by words and images, their cadence and their ambivalence." [68]

[55] F. D. Luke, *"Kafka's 'Die Verwandlung,'"* *The Modern Language Review*, XLVI (Cambridge, 1951). Paul Landsberg's *"The Metamorphosis"* in *The Kafka Problem, ed. cit.*, pp. 117-21, does not reach quite the same high level.

[56] Lienhard Bergel, "The Burrow," *ibid., ed. cit.*, pp. 199-206.

[57] Lienhard Bergel, "Blumfeld, an Elderly Bachelor," *ibid., ed. cit.*, pp. 127-31.

[58] Werner Kraft, *"Franz Kafkas Erzählung Das Ehepaar,"* *Die Wandlung*, IV, 2 (Heidelberg, 1949). (The same author's *"Über Franz Kafkas 'Elf Söhne,'"* *Die Schildgenossen*, XII, Augsburg, V, has not been available for review.)

[59] Heinz Politzer: "Give it Up!" *The Kafka Problem, ed. cit.*, pp. 117-21. (*Cf.* also E.L., *"Franz Kafka: Gib's Auf!"* *Trivium*, IX, 2, Zürich, 1952.)

[60] Austin Warren, *"The Penal Colony,"* *ibid.*, pp. 140-2.

[61] P. P. J. van Caspel, *"Josefine und Jeremias. Versuch einer Deutung," ed. cit.* P. P. J. van Caspel, *"Totemismus bei Kafka,"* *Neophilologus*, XXXVIII (Gröningen, 1954).

[62] William C. Rubinstein, *"Franz Kafka's 'A Report to an Academy,'" ed. cit.*, Robert Kauf, *op. cit.*

[63] William C. Rubinstein, "Franz Kafka, 'A Hungry Artist,'" *MDU*, XLIV, 1952. R. W. Stallman, "The Hungry Artist," *Accent* (Urbana, Ill., 1948), has not been available for review.

[64] Johannes Pfeiffer, *"Franz Kafka, 'Eine kleine Frau,'"* *Wege zur Erzählkunst* (Hamburg, 1953), pp. 108-16.

[65] Werner Zimmermann, *"Franz Kafka: 'Auf der Galerie.' 'Eine kaiserliche Botschaft.' 'Von dem Gesetz,'"* *Deutsche Prosadichtungen der Gegenwart* (Düsseldorf, 1954), pp. 159-74.

[66] H. S. Reiss, "Kafka's Letters to Milena," *German Life and Letters*, N.S. VII, 1, 1953.

[67] Felix Weltsch, *"Kafkas Aphorismen,"* *Neue Deutsche Hefte*, I (Gütersloh, 1954).

[68] Heinz Politzer, "Franz Kafka's Letter to his Father," *The Germanic Review*, XXVIII, 3 (New York, 1953), p. 175.

Fritz Schaufelberger in an essay on Kafka's prose fragments[69] suggests that their fragmentary character is the keynote of his work. The present author analyses *Der Schlag ans Hoftor* and *Die Prüfung*[70] on the basis of their structure and language and discovers a continuous oscillation between moods of hope and despair as characteristic of Kafka's mode of writing. In another article he assesses the function of humor in Kafka's work by studying it in its specific context.[71]

Clemens Heselhaus in *Kafkas Erzählformen*[72] considers the genre to which Kafka's writings belong. He classes it as *Anti-Märchen*, basing his terminology on André Jolles' *Einfache Formen* (Halle, 1931). He calls the *Anti-Märchen* a form of narrative which, in contradistinction to the *Märchen*, reveals the hero's failure to attain the goal of his quest—a view not unlike that held by W. H. Auden.[73] While, then, Kafka's work represents an accusation against the world itself, this accusation is counterbalanced by the important rôle the parable plays in Kafka's work. Professor Heselhaus' formulations, however, tend to over-subtlety, and to mar his undoubted insight into Kafka's work. The same defect also spoils the often very relevant argument of Wilhelm Emrich, who argues that it may even be necessary to modify aesthetic theory in order to do justice to Kafka.[74] In another essay Professor Emrich[75] maintains that Kafka's world appears so strange and enigmatic because he seeks to depict it from an Archimedean point-of-view, outside space and time. Man's imprisonment in the world is revealed, but Kafka's vision of truth and freedom radiates through the distortions which everyday life entails. Eugene Reed also discusses the moral implications of some of Kafka's writings,[76] but, like Professor Emrich, he avoids a too exclusive "metaphysical" interpretation by an awareness of the formal aspects of Kafka's work. This applies equally to the approach of Fritz Martini who, in a chapter of *Das Wagnis der Sprache*, a study of modern German prose, bases his

---

[69] Fritz Schaufelberger, *"Franz Kafkas Prosafragmente,"* Trivium, VII, 1 (Zürich, 1949).

[70] H. S. Reiss, *"Zwei Erzählungen Franz Kafkas, eine Betrachtung,"* ibid., VIII, 3, 1950.

[71] H. S. Reiss, "Franz Kafka's Conception of Humour," The Modern Language Review, XLIV, 4 (Cambridge, 1949).

[72] Clemens Heselhaus, *"Kafkas Erzählformen,"* Deutsche Vierteljahresschrift für Literaturwissenschaft und Geistesgeschichte, XXVI, 3 (Tübingen, 1952).

[73] Cf. W. H. Auden, op. cit.

[74] Wilhelm Emrich, *"Zur Aesthetik der modernen Dichtung,"* Akzente, I (Munich, 1954).

[75] Wilhelm Emrich, "Franz Kafka," Deutsche Literatur im XX. Jahrhundert (Heidelberg, 1954).

[76] Eugene A. Reed, "Moral Polarity in Kafka's Der Prozess and Das Schloss," MDU, XLVI, 1954.

interpretation on a characteristic section from *The Castle*.[77] Professor Martini notes the prosaic character of Kafka's language, the absence from his work of the poetically beautiful or of the fullness of ordinary life, but he also stresses his power as an observer and his capacity to view himself as if he were another. It is part of this thesis that Kafka is yet another instance of a modern writer who seeks to shape his experience of life in the form of his creative prose.

Friedrich Beissner in a booklet, *Der Erzähler Franz Kafka*,[78] draws attention to the function of the narrator in Kafka's writings. He maintains that Kafka's narrative points to a new phase in the development of the European novel, for it allows the narrator to identify himself with the hero, but also with the reader, and even makes of the reader a part of the story.[79] Kafka's appeal, in his view, depends to a large extent on this technique.

Pride of place among recent Kafka studies belongs to Herman Uyttersprot's *Zur Struktur von Kafkas 'Der Prozess.'* [80] In this detailed study he has raised some fundamental problems of Kafka scholarship which have previously been ignored. He advances the interesting hypothesis that Max Brod's arrangement of that novel is in many important respects mistaken. His argument is thorough and lucid, and is firmly based on internal evidence, particularly on the time factor. In his view, it was Kafka's aim to compose a carefully planned work and to tell the story of the gradual entanglement of the hero in his trial. Professor Uyttersprot has discovered that the events of the novel cannot be fitted into the time interval between Kafka's thirtieth and thirty-first birthday within the present framework. In order to make this possible he was constrained to rearrange the chapters. Consequently he was also able to include the fragments which Brod classes as paralipomena, thus giving weight to his argument. The more the novel advances the more, in accordance with this rearrangement of the chapters, does Joseph K. get involved with his case, and the less does he occupy himself with his work. Finally, his death reveals the reverse of the situation depicted in the opening scene, where he is only beginning to be case-conscious. In a further article[81] Professor

[77] Fritz Martini, *"Franz Kafka: 'Das Schloss,' "* *Das Wagnis der Sprache* (Stuttgart, 1954).

[78] Friedrich Beissner, *op. cit.*

[79] *Cf.*, for instance, my article "Franz Kafka," *German Life and Letters*, N.S. I, 3, 1948, p. 192.

[80] Herman Uyttersprot, *Zur Struktur von Kafkas 'Der Prozess,' "* ed. cit.

[81] Herman Uyttersprot, *"Zur Struktur von Kafkas Romanen,"* ed. cit. These two studies of Professor Uyttersprot's are more fully discussed in the forthcoming second edition of my book *Franz Kafka, eine Betrachtung seines Werkes.* (*Cf.* also my review article "Eine Neuordnung der Werke Kafkas," *Akzente*, II, Munich, 1955.)

Uyttersprot extends his hypothesis to other works of Kafka and argues that they all possess a definite pattern: a sudden opening, a turning-point, usually caused by a letter or document, and the dénouement which is always the death of the hero. In this article he specifically casts doubts upon Max Brod's interpretation of *America* and suggests, basing his view on a diary entry, that this novel was to end in the death of its hero. Professor Uyttersprot's analysis is always fascinating, thorough, and perceptive, revealing a profound understanding of Kafka. If one has some reservations about his hypotheses—he stakes his claims no higher and wisely refrains from making dogmatic statements—it is firstly because he gives perhaps too little credence to Max Brod's statements. Although it is quite possible that Brod's memory may have failed him, one should hesitate before refusing to accept his word on such important statements that Kafka said that "The Oklahoma Nature Theater" was the last chapter of *America*. Yet even so it is proper to be sceptical about Brod's pronouncements on matters of detail. Secondly, the fact that Kafka did not finish his novels suggests that he may not have had finally decided on their structure; of course, the manuscripts may, when they become generally available, yield more definite evidence. Reluctance to commit oneself to any one hypothesis may prove to be the wisest course, and two or more interpretations of the structure of a Kafka novel may be possible, none of which need run counter to the author's intention since any one of them might have been realized in his final arrangement. It is also possible that Professor Uyttersprot's arrangement of *The Trial* reveals the original conception of the novel, while Brod's reveals a later one which was never completely carried out. And again, Kafka may have composed the individual chapters without paying attention to their chronological sequence, though this is less likely. Professor Uyttersprot has thus opened a fruitful line of Kafka study, and the alternate readings of *The Trial* might well have to be accepted as variants of which every reader should take note.

Space prevents discussion of every instance of recent Kafka criticism. Indeed, there may well be contributions which have escaped the reviewer's notice.[82] It remains only to acknowledge such useful guides to *Kafka-Forschung* as Heinz Politzer's "Probleme und Problematik der Kafka-Forschung,"[83] Paul Kurt Ackermann's "A History of Critical

---

[82] I had to restrict myself to studies in English, French, and German which were published before the end of 1954. I have, for instance, been unable to read: Hugo Siebenschein, Emil Utitz, Edwin Muir, Peter Demetz, *Franz Kafka a Praha* (Prague, 1947), Jan Molitor, *Asmodai in Praag*, ('s Graveland, 1950). Herman Uyttersprot, "Kleine Kafkaiana," *Langues Vivantes*, XLIV (Brussels, n.d.). G. Boden, *Franz Kafka, Aspects de son oeuvre* (Algiers, 1947), has not been available for review.

[83] Heinz Politzer, *"Problematik und Probleme der Kafka-Forschung,"* ed. cit.

Writing on Kafka," [84] Angel Flores' "bibliography" of writings by and on Kafka,[85] and Klaus W. Jonas' "Franz Kafka, an American Bibliography." [86] There is, however, no need to be dismayed by the spate of Kafka literature. It is in the nature of critical investigations that views or hypotheses are put forward which may or may not stand the test of time. A new phase of Kafka criticism has now been reached, and the period of the *terribles simplificateurs* has probably been left behind. Kafka may no longer be "in fashion," and this is no great loss. But Kafka need not therefore become the sole property of *Germanisten*.[87] On the contrary, some of the less-ambitious critical studies should deepen and refine out understanding of Kafka without producing a decline of his reading public.

Owing to unavoidable delay in the publication of this survey it has been possible to append a note on Kafka scholarship in 1955. Attention was focused on individual aspects of his work. E. W. Tedlock, in his valuable comparative study of Kafka's *America* and Dickens' *David Copperfield,* argues that Kafka felt for *David Copperfield* one of those affinities of the sensibility and the imagination that are stimulating and subtly enriching. In his view, Kafka was influenced by the moral ambiguity and the technique of the grotesque in Dickens' work.[88] A comparative study of a different kind is undertaken by Heinz Politzer in whose view affinities between Kafka, Rilke, and Werfel exist which are a result of their Prague origins.[89] Peter Demetz also probes into Kafka's social background when he discusses similarities between Kafka, Freud and Husserl in the light of their Jewish family history.[90] The present author examines the work of Thomas Mann, Kafka, and Musil with a view to exploring stylistic and structural trends in modern German fic-

[84] Paul Kurt Ackermann, "A History of Critical Writing on Franz Kafka," *German Quarterly*, XXIII, 2 (Appleton, Wis., 1950).

[85] Angel Flores, "Bibliography," *The Kafka Problem, ed. cit.,* pp. 447-63. (A version bringing it up to date is in progress.)

[86] Klaus W. Jonas, "Franz Kafka, an American Bibliography," *Bulletin of Bibliography and Dramatic Index,* XX (Boston, Mass., 1950-1953).

[87] Perhaps Gottfried von Einem's operatic version of *The Trial* will start a new fashion in musical criticism. (*Cf.* Willi Reich, "Current Chronicle, Austria," *Musical Quarterly*, XL, New York, 1954, for an account of this opera.)

[88] E. W. Tedlock, "Kafka's Imitation of David Copperfield," *Comparative Literature,* VII (Eugene, Ore., 1955).

[89] Heinz Politzer, "Prague and the Origins of Rainer Maria Rilke, Franz Kafka, and Franz Werfel," *Modern Language Quarterly*, XVI (Seattle, Wash., 1955).

[90] Peter Demetz, *"Kafka, Freud, Husserl. Probleme einer Generation,"* Zeitschrift für Religions- und Geistesgeschichte, VII (Cologne-Leiden, 1955).

tion.[91] Other comparisons reveal a more metaphysical approach. In this vein, Neville Braybrooke compares Kafka to Saint Teresa[92] while Robert Ulshöfer compares *Die Verwandlung* to Thomas Mann's *Tod in Venedig*, Brochert's *Kurzgeschichten* and Goethe's *Hermann und Dorothea*.[93]

Several individual tales such as *Der Nachbar*,[94] *Ein Landarzt*,[95] *Auf der Galerie*,[96] *Der Kübelreiter*[97] are subjected to a more detailed analysis. Meno Spann ventures into quite a different field: he seeks to establish the date of composition of *Forschungen eines Hundes, Ein Hungerkünstler* and *Der Bau*.[98] Augusta Walker examines the scope of allegory using *Der Bau* as an example of her theory.[99]

[*Since Dr. Reiss's survey was completed, the following studies in book form have appeared, in addition to those subjoined to the footnotes:*]

Goth, Maja, *Franz Kafka et les lettres françaises: 1928-1955* (Paris, 1956).

Gray, Ronald, *Kafka's Castle* (Cambridge, 1956).

Emrich, Wilhelm, *Franz Kafka* (Bonn, 1958).

Flores, Angel and Homer Swander (eds.), *Franz Kafka Today* (Madison, Wis., 1958).

Hemmerle, Rudolf, *Franz Kafka, Eine Bibliographie* (Munich, 1958).

Wagenbach, Klaus, *Franz Kafka, eine Biographie seiner Jugend* (Berne, 1958).

[91] H. S. Reiss, "*Zum Stil und zur Komposition in der deutschen Prosaerzählung der Gegenwart*," *Studium Generale*, VIII (Berlin-Göttingen-Heidelberg, 1955).

[92] Neville Braybrooke, "Celestial Castles. An Approach to Saint Teresa and Franz Kafka," *Dublin Review*, CCXXIV (London, 1955).

[93] Robert Ulshöfer, "*Die Wirklichkeitsauffassung in der modernen Prosadichtung. Dargestellt an Manns 'Tod in Venedig,' Kafkas 'Verwandlung,' und Borcherts 'Kurzgeschichten,' verglichen mit Goethes 'Hermann und Dorothea,'*" *Der Deutsche Unterricht*, VII (Stuttgart, 1955).

[94] Seigfried Hajek, "*Die moderne Kurzgeschichte im Unterricht. Franz Kafka, 'Der Nachbar,'*" *ibid.*

[95] Helmut Motekat, "*Interpretation als Erschliessung dichterischer Wirklichkeit (Mit einer Interpretation von Franz Kafkas Erzählung 'Ein Landarzt'),*" *Interpretationen moderner Prosa* (Frankfurt, 1955), pp. 7-27.

[96] Hermann Glaser, "*Franz Kafka: 'Auf der Galerie,'*" *ibid.*, pp. 40-8.

[97] Ludwig Halers, "*Franz Kafka: 'Der Kübelreiter,'*" *ibid.*, pp. 49-54.

[98] Meno Spann, "*Die beiden Zettel Kafkas,*" *MDU*, XLVI, 1955. (*Cf.* H. S. Reiss, "A Comment on '*Die beiden Zettel Kafkas,'*" *MDU*, XLVIII, 3, 1956).

[99] Augusta Walker, "Allegory: A Light Conceit," *Partisan Review*, XXII (New York, 1955).

Brod, Max, *Verzweiflung und Erlösung im Werk Franz Kafkas* (Frankfurt, 1959).

Walser, Martin, *Beschreibung einer Form* [Versuch über Franz Kafka] (Munich, 1961).

Chronology of Important Dates

1883	Franz Kafka born on July 3 in Prague.
1889-93	Primary school, "am Fleischmarkt," Prague.
1893-1901	High school (*Gymnasium*) in Prague.
1901-06	*Deutsche Universität,* Prague. Read Chemistry, then Law.
1902	First meeting with Max Brod.
1904-05	*Description of a Struggle* written, extracts published 1909.
1906	Working in uncle's advocate's office, Prague. *Wedding Preparations* written.
1907-08	Working at the "Assicurazioni Generali."
1908	Enters "Workers' Accident-Insurance Office" as assistant. Closer friendship with Max Brod.
1909	First publications: "Conversation with a Beggar," and "Conversation with a Drunkard."
1912	Meets Fräulein F.B. Writes "The Sentence" ("The Judgment") (published 1913), "The Stoker" (first chapter of *America*), "The Metamorphosis," (published 1915.)
1913	*Reflections* published (five pieces published 1910).
1914	Engaged to "F.B." in Berlin. Writes "In the Penal Settlement" (published 1919). Begins *The Trial.*
1915	Leaves his parents and lives alone. Continues *The Trial.*
1916	Engagement with "F.B." broken off. Some stories in *A Country Doctor* written (also in 1917).
1917	Renews engagement to "F.B." but breaks it off. Tuberculosis is diagnosed.
1918	Some work on *The Great Wall of China.*
1919	*A Country Doctor* and *In the Penal Settlement* published. "Letter to his Father" written.
1920-23	Letters to Milena written. Kafka frequently on sick-leave and in sanatoria, less often in Prague.

1920   Manuscript of *The Trial* in the care of Max Brod.

1923   Manuscript of *The Castle* in the care of Max Brod. Kafka lives with
            Dora Dymant in Berlin, later in Prague.

1924   In hospitals in or near Vienna. *A Hunger-Artist* published. Kafka
            died on June 3, 1924 and was buried in Prague.

1925   *The Trial* published.

1926   *The Castle* published.

1927   *America* published.

1931   Previously unprinted stories published.

Notes on the Editor and Authors

RONALD GRAY, editor of the anthology, is a Fellow of Emmanuel College, Cambridge. He is the author of *Goethe the Alchemist, Kafka's Castle,* and *Brecht.*

EDWIN MUIR, poet and critic, made Kafka's work widely known through the translations by himself and his wife, Willa Muir.

R. O. C. WINKLER studied at Cambridge University and was a contributor to *Scrutiny.* He now lives in London.

JOHANNES PFEIFFER lives in Hamburg and has written a wide variety of critical studies of German literature and philosophy.

CAROLINE GORDON is Resident Writer at the University of California at Davis. Her novels include *Aleck Maury, None Shall Look Back, The Strange Children,* and *The Malefactors.* Her short stories have been collected in a volume, *The Forest of the South.* Her critical works include *How to Read a Novel,* and, with Allen Tate, a critical anthology of the short story, *The House of Fiction.*

IDRIS PARRY is a Welshman and teaches at the University College of North Wales, Bangor. He has published articles on German literature and has had plays performed by the British Broadcasting Corporation.

EDMUND WILSON's best known works include *Axel's Castle, To The Finland Station, The Wound and the Bow, Memoirs of Hecate County.*

ERICH HELLER taught at Cambridge and Swansea before becoming Professor of German at Northwestern University. He has published a collection of essays on German literature and thought, *The Disinherited Mind,* and *The Ironic German,* a study of Thomas Mann.

AUSTIN WARREN is Professor of English at the University of Michigan. His books include a study of Alexander Pope, *The Elder Henry James, Richard Crashaw, Rage for Order,* and *New England Saints.* With René Wellek he wrote *Theory of Literature.*

ELISEO VIVAS has been Venezuelan Consul in Philadelphia and has taught philosophy and English at several universities. He is now Professor of Moral and Intellectual Philosophy at Northwestern University. His books include *The Moral Life and the Ethical Life, Creation and Discovery,* and *D. H. Lawrence, the Failure and the Triumph of Art.*

ALBERT CAMUS, French novelist, dramatist and philosopher, cofounder of the Resistance newspaper *Combat,* was strongly influenced by Kafka in his novel *The Stranger.* Other well-known works include the novel, *The Plague,* the collection of essays, *The Myth of Sisyphus,* and the play, *Caligula.*

MARTIN BUBER, best known for his theological work, *I and Thou,* one of the most influential works in contemporary religious thought, published stories by Kafka in his Zionist journal *Der Jude* and may have influenced him through his concern with Chassidism.

H. S. REISS is Professor of German at McGill University. He has published numerous essays and bibliographical articles on Kafka and a full-length study, *Franz Kafka, eine Betrachtung seines Werkes.*

TWENTIETH CENTURY VIEWS

British Authors

TWENTIETH CENTURY VIEWS

European Authors